Going Global?

U.S. GOVERNMENT POLICY and the DEFENSE AEROSPACE INDUSTRY

Mark A. Lorell · Julia Lowell · Richard M. Moore
Victoria Greenfield · Katia Vlachos

Prepared for the United States Air Force
Approved for public release; distribution unlimited

RAND
Project AIR FORCE

The research reported here was sponsored by the United States Air Force under Contract F49642-01-C-0003. Further information may be obtained from the Strategic Planning Division, Directorate of Plans, Hq USAF.

Library of Congress Cataloging-in-Publication Data

Lorell, Mark A., 1947–
    Going global: U.S. government policy and the defense aerospace industry /
Mark A. Lorell, Julia Lowell, Richard M. Moore.
      p. cm.
    "MR-1537."
    Includes bibliographical references.
    ISBN 0-8330-3193-7
    1. Aerospace industries. 2. International division of labor. 3. International trade.
I. Lowell, Julia, 1961– II. Moore, Richard M.

HD9711.5.A2 L674 2002
338.4'76291—dc21

2002075151

Cover line drawing courtesy of
Lockheed Martin, JSF Communications.

RAND is a nonprofit institution that helps improve policy and decisionmaking through research and analysis. RAND® is a registered trademark. RAND's publications do not necessarily reflect the opinions or policies of its research sponsors.

Cover design by Maritta Tapanainen

Published 2002 by RAND
1700 Main Street, P.O. Box 2138, Santa Monica, CA 90407-2138
1200 South Hayes Street, Arlington, VA 22202-5050
201 North Craig Street, Suite 202, Pittsburgh, PA 15213-1516
RAND URL: http://www.rand.org/
To order RAND documents or to obtain additional information,
contact Distribution Services: Telephone: (310) 451-7002;
Fax: (310) 451-6915; Email: order@rand.org

This report presents an overview of Phase I research conducted for the RAND Project AIR FORCE research effort entitled "Gaining from Globalization: Enhancing Air Force Management of an Increasingly Globalized Aerospace Industrial Base." The goal of this research is to develop evidence, information, and analysis so that the Air Force can provide assessments to the Office of the Secretary of Defense and Congress on the effects of industry changes, new procurements, and proposed laws and regulations that affect the industrial base. In addition, it is intended to assist the Air Force in developing new strategies and policies that will help the Air Force exploit potential opportunities and mitigate potential problems that may arise from structural changes and increasing globalization of the industrial base.

This report provides an introductory survey of issues and trends related to the emergence of a variety of new forms of cross-border business relationships and activities that are increasingly characteristic of the U.S. defense aerospace industrial base. Examining a broad spectrum of case studies of innovative cross-border relationships, it establishes a framework for analysis and presents initial findings. Economic data are also analyzed to identify trends in the globalization of the U.S. aerospace industry. A survey of the complex U.S. regulatory environment that influences cross-border business relationships in the defense industry is also presented. The report identifies gaps in the findings and suggests follow-on research approaches to fill those gaps during Phase II of the project. Most of the data and other information on which this analysis is based were collected from a wide variety of open published sources, supplemented with interviews with U.S. and foreign government and industry officials. The data collection cutoff point for this document was September 2001.

This research is sponsored by the Office of the Assistant Secretary of the Air Force (Acquisition). It is conducted in the Resource Management Program of RAND's Project AIR FORCE.

PROJECT AIR FORCE

Project AIR FORCE, a division of RAND, is the Air Force federally funded research and development center (FFRDC) for studies and analysis. It provides the Air Force with independent analyses of policy alternatives affecting the development, employment, combat readiness, and support of current and future aerospace forces. Research is performed in four programs: Aerospace Force Development; Manpower, Personnel, and Training; Resource Management; and Strategy and Doctrine.

CONTENTS

FIGURES

TABLES

In fiscal year 2001, the U.S. Air Force tasked RAND with providing an analysis to help it respond to the potential new opportunities—and problems—arising from an increasingly globalized and consolidated aerospace industrial base. Between 1990 and 1998, a horizontal and vertical integration took place across all segments of the U.S. aerospace industry. The number of credible U.S. prime contractors for integrating fighters and bombers fell from seven to two; the number of U.S. missile manufacturers from fourteen to four; and the number of space launch vehicle producers from six to two. By the end of the 1990s, the European defense aerospace industry had also begun to experience a dramatic cross-border consolidation and restructuring. This growing consolidation of defense prime integrators and subsystem suppliers has resulted in increased numbers of strategic and product-specific alliances, international teaming and joint ventures, and cross-border mergers and acquisitions (M&As) among defense firms, together with heightened interest in foreign exports and foreign lower-tier suppliers.

Because the globalization of the aerospace defense industry is a relatively recent phenomenon, its effects are not yet well understood. The Air Force therefore asked RAND to help assess the benefits and risks associated with these new cross-border business agreements and procurements, as well as proposed laws and regulations affecting the defense industrial base. The resulting project has been shaped in large part by three major Air Force objectives relevant to the issue of globalization:

- The need to equip aerospace forces with affordable yet highly capable weapon systems, both today and in the future (the economic and technological dimension);

- The need to prepare the United States, its allies, and other friends to fight future wars as coalitions (the political-military dimension); and

- The need to protect U.S. national security (the national security dimension, mainly related to technology security and industrial base viability).

RAND's objective for our overall program of research on this project is to help determine how and to what extent globalization can be managed to best promote the achievement of both economic and political-military objectives while minimizing potential risks from the perspective of the U.S. Air Force. The findings will be reported in two parts: the current report and a follow-up study to be completed in FY 2002.

This report focuses on four key questions:

- How far has the globalization of the U.S. defense aerospace industry already progressed?

- What are the potential economic, political-military, and national security implications of U.S. defense aerospace industry globalization?

- What laws, regulations, and policies constrain, guide, and inform Air Force management of the globalization process and industry structuring of cross-border relationships?

- Which partnerships now being formed by U.S. and foreign companies are most likely to promote the three fundamental Air Force interests tied to greater globalization?

CHAPTER SUMMARIES

Indicators of Aerospace Industry Globalization

In broad terms, the most visible manifestation of globalization lies in the growing number and value of cross-border purchases and sales of goods, services, and financial assets. Our assessment of statistical data suggests that the U.S. aerospace industry is an active but heavily export-oriented participant in the global economy. The United States is by far the world's leading arms exporter, accounting for about half of all shipments. There is less evidence of aerospace imports, however, and data suggest that military aerospace producers are less internationally active than are nonmilitary producers. The growth and geographic pattern of investment by U.S. defense firms have been somewhat slower and have an even stronger bias toward the United Kingdom than that exhibited by firms in other industries.

To better understand recent globalization trends, we developed a typology of cross-border business relationships and activities prevalent in the defense aerospace industry. The joint or cooperative activities on which we focus herein include cross-border shipments of finished platforms, systems, or major subsystems; licensed coproduction; Foreign Military Sales (FMS) coproduction; "partnership" coproduction; and codevelopment. The last three of these activities generally involve a relatively greater level of collaboration among participating firms. All these international activities can be supported by several types of cross-border business relationships, the most common forms of which are prime/subcontractor, marketing agreement, team, joint venture, and parent/subsidiary. Broadly speaking, prime/subcontractor relationships represent traditional types of arrangements, while the others represent the new, more highly integrated face of defense aerospace industry globalization.

A review of the recent historical record suggests that U.S. defense-related industries, including military aerospace producers, are not yet as fully integrated as their counterparts in nondefense industries. Nevertheless, deeper industry-led cross-border relationships such as teams and joint ventures are growing in importance relative to simpler export and cross-border licensed production arrangements.

Implications of U.S. Defense Aerospace Industry Globalization

We examined the potential implications of U.S. defense aerospace industry globalization in light of the Air Force's economic-technical, political-military, and national security objectives. In each case, we found both benefits and risks to be inherent in increased globalization.

The many potential economic and technical benefits of globalization include lower costs, higher productivity, better quality, and increased innovation. Exports help lower the costs of new equipment through economies of scale and help reduce the costs of legacy equipment by keeping open production lines for replacement parts and components. Imports provide access to state-of-the-art foreign technologies and industrial capabilities while exposing U.S. industry to international competition, which can help spur innovation and efficiency. At the same time, globalization can also present economic challenges. Both unemployment and unprofitable and underused plants and equipment could potentially present a national security risk for the United States to the extent that they indicate a longer-term loss of industrial capability. Moreover, if international marketing agreements, teams, joint ventures, or subsidiaries serve to leverage rather than dilute U.S. domestic firms' market power, a loss of competition could result.

The net effects of globalization are similarly ambiguous with respect to the Air Force's political-military objectives. Globalization can help achieve technical interoperability through common platforms for U.S. and allied weapon systems and equipment as well as compatibility in areas such as command, control, communications, intelligence, surveillance, and reconnaissance (C^3ISR) systems and munitions. Such technical advances would likely help narrow the technology gap between the United States and European members of the North Atlantic Treaty Organization (NATO). Mergers, acquisitions, and other forms of collaborative business relationships between U.S. and NATO European defense firms also have the potential to encourage some degree of system-level interoperability because, for purely economic reasons, these types of arrangements tend to feature the sharing of design concepts, technology standards, and inputs.

On the other hand, increased collaboration among U.S., European, and non-European foreign firms—combined with the consolidation of the European defense aerospace industry—may make European and other foreign alternatives to U.S.-designed platforms and systems more capable and hence more competitive. This is likely to encourage NATO Europe and other important allies to adopt home-grown alternatives, thereby reducing the interoperability of their forces with those of the United States. Moreover, it can be argued that closer integration of the U.S. and foreign defense industrial bases is unlikely to affect interoperability in either direction if U.S. allies do not increase their procurement budgets significantly.

In terms of national security, globalization also poses significant risks as well as rewards. With respect to rewards, globalization provides the Air Force with more "bang for the buck" as global competition forces costs down and quality up. It also strengthens overall U.S. military capabilities both by providing greater access to foreign technologies and by improving the financial health of U.S. defense firms. However, the risks are potentially significant. Globalization's most potent threat lies in its potential to equip hostile nations and groups with advanced weapons and technologies designed by the United States and paid for by the U.S. government. Technology transfers become harder to control with globalization because they are a desired feature of many cross-border business relationships. Other risks stemming from globalization include worldwide weapon proliferation; the loss of certain domestic defense capabilities and technologies, coupled with an associated dependence on foreign sources of supply; and foreign control over U.S. industry.

The Regulatory Framework for Aerospace Industry Globalization

Air Force management of the globalization process is informed by an extremely complex network of laws, regulations, executive orders, policies, directives, and procedures. This regulatory environment greatly affects the types of cross-border relationships established by industry. The primary instrument for controlling unclassified defense-related trade and technology transfers currently lies in the International Traffic in Arms Regulations (ITAR), which govern all military Security Assistance and International Armaments Cooperation programs. Contained within the ITAR is the U.S. Munitions List (USML), which includes all goods, services, and technologies designated as defense-related. All exports of USML items or technologies must be licensed by the Office of Defense Trade Controls (DTC), a division of the State Department's Bureau of Political and

Military Affairs. The Export Administration Act of 1979 (EAA 1979) controls the transfer of technologies that have both commercial and military (dual-use) applications. There are two key policy tools for regulating foreign ownership, control, and influence (FOCI) of the U.S. industrial base. The Committee on Foreign Investment in the United States (CFIUS) oversees proposed foreign mergers with and acquisitions of U.S. businesses. The National Industrial Security Program (NISP) governs U.S. classified information released during any phase of a U.S. government contract, license, certificate, or grant.

These laws, regulations, and policies affect the ability of the Air Force to achieve its objectives relating to globalization. With regard to competition, laws and regulations require and encourage acquisition personnel to allow international sources to compete, and more general policies promoting competition have the potential to encourage greater competition from abroad. However, foreign industry has thus far not been viewed as an essential part of competition-based strategies, although this view may be changing: The shrinking number of U.S.-owned and -located defense contractors has raised the specter of collusion and thereby triggered support for competition-enhancing linkages between U.S. and foreign firms.

Current laws and regulations provide varying degrees of support for the Air Force's political-military and national security objectives. In order to prepare for coalition operations, the Department of Defense (DoD) has stated its strong support for International Armaments Cooperation programs and promotes Security Assistance programs to encourage allies and other friendly states to procure U.S.-designed equipment. At the same time, regulations and policies place major limitations on exports by virtue of concerns about defense-related trade and technology transfers and FOCI over key sectors of the U.S. industrial base.

Our reading of the literature indicates that both the Office of the Secretary of Defense (OSD) and the Air Force now believe that certain aspects of the U.S. export control regime have become ineffective and even counterproductive. Many perceive the ITAR as an impediment both to the leveling up of NATO and other allied forces and to greater interoperability of such forces with those of the United States. EAA 1979 is believed to encumber international defense cooperation and to impede efficient DoD use of U.S. commercial industry by restricting firms' ability to participate in international exchanges of technology.

In response to such concerns, DoD has undertaken a wide-ranging reform effort. A key component of these reforms is the Defense Trade Security Initiative (DTSI), which is a joint effort by DoD and the Department of State to reform the ITAR and related export practices. The full implementation of DTSI could eliminate the need for authorized U.S. companies to acquire individual licenses for unclassified equipment exports or technology transfers when part of a major program or project involves a NATO government, Japan, Australia, or Sweden.

Other reforms are also being discussed. Bilateral negotiations are under way with the UK, Australia, and other close allies to establish congruence and reciprocity in several major areas, including export control processes and industrial security policies and procedures. Various congressional amendments have also been proposed to EAA 1979, including the removal of controls on items widely available from foreign suppliers and the establishment of an interagency dispute resolution process for license applications. At this point, it is not yet clear how far such reforms have proceeded.

The New Cross-Border Business Relationships: Case Studies

A key objective of this report is to help identify the types of cross-border business relationships that are now emerging; to assess which are most likely to achieve the Air Force's economic and political-military objectives while minimizing potential risks; and to examine to what extent these relationships are positively or negatively affected by the regulatory environment. To increase our understanding, we conducted a survey of 38 cross-border business relationships and programs.[1]

An initial review of the cases reveals that the types of programs that show the most promise for promoting the potential military-political

---

[1]Some programs are counted twice as they evolve from one type of business relationship to another.

and economic benefits of globalization possess some or all of the following characteristics:

- They are voluntarily structured and often initiated by defense firms rather than by governments on the basis of internal business calculations of market conditions and best business practices.

- They are painstakingly structured to satisfy the existing U.S. arms export and technology security regulatory regime and CFIUS.

- They often focus on promoting existing products or modifications thereof, or on specific product market sectors.

- They frequently focus on subsystems, munitions, or discrete components or areas rather than on large, complex programs for the development of entire weapon system platforms.

- They are designed to gain and expand active reciprocal market access through new programs.

- They are often motivated by a desire to add to a company's product portfolio a highly competitive product in a market sector dominated by another firm or firms.

- They are characterized by mutual perception of balanced and complementary bilateral market access opportunities and technology transfer.

- The most aggressive and innovative among these relationships depend on continued reform of the U.S. export control regime in order to achieve their full potential.

For further research, we suggest an examination of case studies for in-depth analysis to better illustrate the issues and problems involved with greater globalization as well as the menus of policy options the Air Force has to manage them. Two proposed case studies are shown in Table S.1.

Proposed follow-up research into these case studies will focus on two central questions. First, what forms of the new industry-initiated cross-border business relationships and cross-border activities are most likely to promote key Air Force objectives regarding globalization? Second and most important, what key "lessons learned" can

Table S.1

Case Studies of Cross-Border Strategic Market Sector Collaboration

Program	Business Structure	Activity	Competition[a]	Globalization Issues
Surveillance radar, command and control	U.S. French market sector joint venture	Codevelopment, coproduction	Variable	Tech transfer, tech security, work share, NATO RSI,[c] competition
NATO alliance ground surveillance	To be decided	Codevelopment, coproduction	Euro Hawk, ASTOR, SOSTAR, Eagle+, NATAR[b]	NATO RSI, tech transfer, tech security, interoperability

[a]The "Competition" column indicates separate programs that are clearly in competition. See the main text for a detailed discussion of specific programs.

[b]ASTOR = Airborne Standoff Radar; SOSTAR = Standoff Surveillance and Target Acquisition Radar; NATAR = NATO Transatlantic Advanced Radar.

[c]RSI = rationalization, standardization, and interoperability.

these cases provide to guide the Air Force on how and to what extent it can play a more proactive role in effectively managing globalization?

CONCLUSIONS

The Response of U.S. Industry to Globalization

- **Numerous innovative cross-border strategic market sector agreements initiated by U.S. and foreign companies are emerging.** Leading U.S. aerospace prime contractors and subcontractors are aggressively seeking creative new forms of cross-border linkages in efforts to gain or maintain foreign market access. The most innovative of these linkages appear to be long-term strategic teaming or joint venture agreements aimed at entire market sectors rather than the more traditional approach focusing on specific projects or systems.

- **U.S. aerospace firms are not significantly increasing their acquisition of wholly owned subsidiaries of foreign defense aerospace firms.** There are few indications that U.S. defense aerospace firms have dramatically increased their interest in acquiring wholly owned foreign subsidiaries, although there seems to be some increase in U.S. M&A activity overseas in the defense industry as a whole. As noted above, the preferred industry-initiated cross-border business relationships appear to take the form of teams and joint ventures.

- **Teaming and joint ventures with non-UK and non-Europe-based firms are increasing.** Over the past several years, there has been an apparent increase in M&As, teaming, and joint ventures with non-UK-headquartered European companies as well as with non-European companies. This represents a shift from traditional U.S. practice, in which most direct investments and U.S.-initiated cross-border investments involved UK firms.

Implications of European Consolidation and Increased Aerospace Globalization

- **U.S. industry collaboration with one country's firm increasingly means collaboration with many countries' firms.** The consolidation that is taking place both with the European defense aerospace industry and with that of other important foreign industrial bases has made it increasingly problematic for U.S. government policymakers and industry leaders to think in terms of bilateral collaborative relationships between the United States and specific European or other foreign countries. As a result, the traditional U.S. government and U.S. industry approach of negotiating bilateral, country-specific agreements may have to be modified or adjusted.

- **Consolidated European and other foreign firms mean potentially more equal partners as well as stronger competitors.** The consolidation of the European defense aerospace industry is producing pan-European companies of roughly the same size and sales turnover as the leading U.S. firms in many product sectors. These new, consolidated pan-European firms are eager to offer European solutions for European and third-country weapon system requirements that are fully competitive with U.S. products. Similar consolidation trends are visible in other countries.

- **European and other foreign firms seek U.S. market access but resent barriers.** With an overall smaller market and smaller R&D funding base, the newly emerging pan-European firms and other foreign companies strongly desire greater access both to the U.S. market and to U.S. technology. However, European and other foreign firms are insisting with increasing aggressiveness on more equal business relationships with U.S. firms as well as on less restrictive U.S. policies regarding access to the U.S. market, technology transfer, and third-party sales of technology and products.

- **European and other foreign firms view the acquisition of U.S. firms as the most effective means of penetrating the U.S. market.** The most successful recent penetrations of the U.S. market by European firms have been through acquisition of existing U.S. firms rather than through joint ventures or programs. To date, however, newly acquired foreign subsidiaries primarily service DoD and are often restricted with regard to technology flow back to Europe. Thus, such market penetration does not necessarily promote equipment standardization or interoperability or help close the capability gap with Europe.

- **Non-European foreign firms are forming strategic relationships with European and U.S. firms, potentially enhancing competition but complicating standardization and interoperability objectives.** The defense industries of some other important non-NATO allies have been aggressively seeking U.S. and European market access through the forging of new business relationships based on strategic alliances. Israeli industry has been particularly active in this area. In many cases, these alliances have clearly increased competition in key niche product sectors within both the U.S. and European markets in a manner that would appear to be beneficial to the Air Force. In some cases, however, these relationships seem to have undermined U.S. attempts to promote equipment standardization if not interoperability.

- **The findings above suggest that European and other foreign industry consolidation present U.S. government and industry with unprecedented opportunities as well as risks.** If new, mutually beneficial cross-border collaborative business relationships take hold, the consolidation of European and other foreign industries greatly increases the prospects for allied procurement of standardized or interoperable systems while potentially reducing system costs. On the other hand, the persistence of frictions over technology transfer and security issues as well as foreign direct investment, combined with the increased capabilities and competitiveness of European and other multinational defense industries, means that the Europeans and other allies may be tempted to move increasingly toward indigenous solutions and more widespread global competition with U.S. firms.

Directions for Future Research

The findings of this initial study point to the need for greater understanding of the opportunities and problems associated with an increasingly globalized and consolidated aerospace industrial base. Three issues in particular stand out for future research.

First, to what extent are greater competition and allied equipment standardization possible given the need for the United States to safeguard its defense technology in the interests of national security?

Second, what is the effect of the regulatory reforms undertaken beginning in the late 1990s in enhancing globalization while also protecting U.S. national security objectives such as technology security and maintaining critical national capabilities?

Third, to what extent and in what specific ways will the changes taking place in Europe affect the prospects for global reform and greater transatlantic collaboration? In addition, how will political and military factors in Europe affect the prospects for the expansion of the U.S. defense industry into overseas markets?

Further analysis of these broad questions in the follow-up study, together with additional in-depth case study analysis, will help fill the gaps in our understanding and provide guidance to the Air Force in developing new strategies and policies regarding the globalization of the industrial base.

ACKNOWLEDGMENTS

The authors greatly appreciate the support and feedback provided by our Air Force project sponsor, Lieutenant General Stephen B. Plummer, Principal Deputy, Office of the Assistant Secretary of the Air Force for Acquisition (SAF/AQ), and our Office of Primary Responsibility, Colonel Paul Coutee, Chief of the Engineering and Technical Management Division and Deputy Assistant Secretary of the Air Force for Science, Technology, and Engineering (SAF/AQRE). Our Project Monitor, Lieutenant Colonel Erica Robertson, SAF/AQRE, provided crucial commentary on our draft along with other important support.

The authors would also like to thank the numerous U.S. and Foreign government and industry officials who provided the information and insights used in this report. In addition, we are especially grateful for the many constructive comments and criticisms provided by the formal technical reviewers of our draft report: the Honorable Jacques Gansler, former Under Secretary of Defense for Acquisition, Technology, and Logistics and current Director of the Center for Public Policy and Private Enterprise at the University of Maryland; and RAND Senior Economist Lloyd Dixon. Alan Vick, Associate Director of RAND Project AIR FORCE, offered several useful suggestions that were incorporated into the report. Kristin Leuschner, RAND Communications Analyst, also made important contributions to the draft.

Finally, we would like to express our gratitude to Natalie Crawford, RAND Vice President and Director of RAND Project AIR FORCE, and C. Robert Roll, Director of the Project AIR FORCE Resource Management Program, for their unflagging support and encouragement of this research. Of course, all errors in fact and interpretation are the sole responsibility of the authors.

ACRONYMS

AAAV	Advanced Amphibious Assault Vehicle
AADC	Allison Advanced Development Company
ACCS	Air Command and Control System
ACSI	Air Command Systems International
AECA	Arms Export Control Act
AESA	Active electronically scanned array
AEW	Airborne early warning
AFFARS	Air Force Federal Acquisition Regulation Supplement
AFI	Air Force Instruction
AFMCFARS	Air Force Materiel Command FAR Supplement
AFPD	Air Force Policy Directive
AGM	Air-to-Ground missile
AGS	Alliance Ground Surveillance
AIA	Aerospace Industries Association
AIAA	American Institute of Aeronautics and Astronautics
AMRAAM	Advanced Medium-Range Air-to-Air Missile

ASARS	Advanced Synthetic Aperture Radar System
ASD(C^{3}I)	Assistant Secretary of Defense for Command, Control, Communications, and Intelligence
ASRAAM	Advanced Short-Range Air-to-Air Missile
ASRV	Armored Scout and Reconnaissance Vehicle
ASTOR	Airborne Standoff Radar
ATBM	Anti-Theater Ballistic Missile
ATFLIR	Advanced Tactical Forward-Looking Infrared
ATP	Advanced Targeting Pod
AWACS	Airborne Warning and Control System
BEA	Bureau of Economic Analysis (U.S. Department of Commerce)
BGT	Bodenseewerk Geraetetechnik [GmbH]
BVR	Beyond visual range
BVRAAM	Beyond Visual Range Air-to-Air Missile
BXA	Bureau of Export Administration (U.S. Department of Commerce)
CAIV	Cost as an independent variable
CALCM	Conventional Air-Launched Cruise Missile
CASA	Construcciones Aeronauticas SA
CCL	Commerce Control List
CEA	Council of Economic Advisers
CFIUS	Committee on Foreign Investment in the United States
CFR	Code of Federal Regulations

CNAD	Conference of National Armaments Directors
COTS	Commercial off the shelf
C^2ISR	Command, control, intelligence, surveillance, and reconnaissance
C^3ISR	Command, control, communications, intelligence, surveillance, and reconnaissance
DASA	Deutsche Aerospace SA
DBP	Defense Budget Project
DCI	Defense Capabilities Initiative
DCS	Direct Commercial Sales
DFARS	Defense Federal Acquisition Regulation Supplement
DISAM	Defense Institute of Security Assistance Management
DoD	Department of Defense
DoDD	Department of Defense Directive
DoDI	Department of Defense Instruction
DoS	Department of State
DSB	Defense Science Board
DSCA	Defense Security Cooperation Agency
DSS	Defense Security Service
DTC	[office of] Defense Trade Controls
DTRA	Defense Threat Reduction Agency
DTSA	Defense Technology Security Agency
DTSI	Defense Trade Security Initiative

DUSD(IA)	Deputy Under Secretary of Defense for Industrial Affairs
DUSD(IC)	Deputy Under Secretary of Defense for International Cooperation
DUSD(P)	Deputy Under Secretary of Defense for Policy
EAA 1979	Export Administration Act of 1979
EADS	European Aeronautic Defence and Space Company
EAR	Export Administration Regulations
ECCM	Electronic counter-countermeasures
ELOP	Electro-Optics [Industries Ltd.]
EMAC	European Military Aircraft Company
EO	Electro-optics
EU	European Union
EW	Electronic warfare
FACO	Final assembly and checkout
FAR	Federal Acquisition Regulations
FLIR	Forward-looking infrared
FMF	Foreign Military Financing
FMS	Foreign Military Sales
FOCI	Foreign ownership, control, or influence
FPA	Focal plane array
FSCS	Future Scout and Cavalry System
GAO	[U.S.] General Accounting Office
GDP	Gross domestic product

GEC	General Electric Company
GMTI	Ground moving target indication
GPS	Global Positioning System
HARM	High-Speed Anti-Radiation Missile
IAC	International Armaments Cooperation
IAI	Israel Aircraft Industries
IBP	Industrial Base Planning
ICP	International Cooperative Program
ICR&D	International cooperative research and development
ICRD&A	International cooperative research, development, and acquisition
ICRDT&E	International cooperative research, development, test, and evaluation
ICRDTE&A	International cooperative research, development, test, evaluation, and acquisition
IEEPA	International Emergency Economic Powers Act
IHPTET	Integrated High-Performance Turbine Engine Technology
IISS	International Institute for Strategic Studies
INS	Inertial navigation system
IR&D	Independent research and development
ITA	International Trade Administration
ITAR	International Traffic in Arms Regulations
JASSM	Joint Air-to-Surface Standoff Missile
JAST	Joint Advanced Strike Technology

JDAM	Joint Direct Attack Munition
JPATS	Joint Primary Aircraft Training System
JSF	Joint Strike Fighter
JSOW	Joint Standoff Weapon
JSTARS	Joint Surveillance Target Attack Radar System
LANTIRN	Low-Altitude Navigation and Targeting Infrared for Night
LGB	Laser-guided bomb
LMAES	Lockheed Martin Aerospace Electronics Systems
LOA	Letter of Offer and Acceptance
LOC1	Level of Operational Capability 1
LOI	Letter of Intent
M&A	Merger and acquisition
MAIS	Major Automated Information System
MBDA	Matra BAe Dynamics
MBT	Main Battle Tank
MDA	Milestone Decision Authority
MDAP	Major Defense Acquisition Program
MEADS	Medium Extended Air Defense System
MoD	Ministry of Defence [UK]
MoU	Memorandum of Understanding
MP RTIP	Multi-Platform Radar Technology Insertion Program
NAICS	North American Industrial Classification System
NATAR	NATO Transatlantic Advanced Radar

NATO	North Atlantic Treaty Organization
NDI	Nondevelopmental item
NGO	Nongovernmental organization
NID	National Interest Determination
NISP	National Industrial Security Program
NISPOM	National Industrial Security Program Operating Manual
OSD	Office of the Secretary of Defense
PGSUS	Precision Guided Systems United States
R&D	Research and development
RAF	Royal Air Force
RDT&E	Research, development, test, and evaluation
RDTE&A	Research, development, test, evaluation, and acquisition
RSI	Rationalization, standardization, and interoperability
RTIP	Radar Technology Insertion Program
SAF/AQ	Assistant Secretary of the Air Force for Acquisition
SAF/AQC	Deputy Assistant Secretary of the Air Force for Contracting
SAF/AQRE	System Engineering Division with SAF/AQ
SAF/IA	Deputy Under Secretary of the Air Force for International Affairs
SAIC	Science Applications International Corporation
SAMM	Security Assistance Management Manual
SAR	Synthetic aperture radar

SDB	Small Diameter Bomb
SDD	System development and demonstration [phase]
SIC	Standard Industrial Classification
SIPRI	Stockholm International Peace Research Institute
SLAM-ER	Standoff Land Attack Missile—Extended Response
SOSTAR	Standoff Surveillance and Target Acquisition Radar
SSA	Special security agreement
STOVL	Short takeoff and vertical landing
SVG	Silicon Valley Group
THAAD	Theater High-Altitude Area Defense
TI	Texas Instruments
TMD	Theater Missile Defense
TRACER	Tactical Reconnaissance Armored Combat Equipment Requirement
UAE	United Arab Emirates
UAV	Unpiloted aerial vehicle
UFH	Ultralightweight Field Howitzer
USC	United States Code
USD(A&T)	Under Secretary of Defense for Acquisition and Technology
USD(AT&L)	Under Secretary of Defense for Acquisition, Technology, and Logistics
USML	U.S. Munitions List
WCMD	Wind-Corrected Munitions Dispenser

WTO	World Trade Organization
XR	Extended Range

Chapter One

INTRODUCTION

In the early 1990s, the U.S. aerospace industry entered a period of profound change and uncertainty characterized by extensive consolidation as well as by some divestiture or "demerger" activities. Beginning in the late 1990s, European industry also consolidated dramatically to the point at which leading European companies are now on roughly the same financial and technological plane as leading U.S. companies. The resulting U.S. and European "megafirms" have increasingly begun to initiate cross-border business relationships that encompass more than just trade. Most of these relationships are between U.S. and European firms, but some involve companies headquartered in other parts of the world. Thus, the consolidation of the U.S. aerospace industry appears to be evolving in the direction of greater globalization, with both the structure and the characteristics of the more globalized industry remaining uncertain.

The U.S. Air Force needs to understand the changes that are taking place both in the United States and overseas in order to develop strategies for proactively shaping those changes as well as responding to them. In 2001, the Air Force tasked RAND to examine and report on the rapidly consolidating and globalizing aerospace industrial base. One objective of this research is to develop evidence, information, and analysis that the Air Force can use to provide assessments both to the Office of the Secretary of Defense (OSD) and to Congress of the effects of new cross-border business arrangements as well as other industry changes, new procurements, and proposed laws and regulations affecting the industrial base. The research is also intended to assist the Air Force in developing strategies and policies that will help it exploit potential opportunities and mitigate potential problems that may result from structural changes to the industrial base.

RAND's first step was to conduct an exhaustive survey of OSD, Air Force, and other U.S. government–published analyses and evaluations, as well as the open literature, with respect to the structure and performance of—and the future prospects for—a highly consolidated and increasingly globalized U.S. aerospace industry. This evaluation led to the following findings:

- Many authoritative observers, including leading U.S. aerospace executives, view increased globalization—including foreign outsourcing and other types of international alliances and collaboration—as a key strategy for maintaining a healthy U.S. industrial base following a decade of mega-mergers.

- They further believe that globalization will promote increased competition, innovation, and fair prices in an increasingly concentrated aerospace industry.

- They also believe that further globalization is inevitable.

- Nevertheless, relatively few in-depth analytical studies have been undertaken on the implications of globalization compared to other aspects of the aerospace industry.

Together, these findings led us to focus our research on the implications of a globalizing U.S. aerospace industry. This report presents the findings from our initial FY 2001 research activities and discusses gaps in our understanding that would benefit from further research.[1]

OVERVIEW

Consolidation and Globalization

According to most expert observers, the central aspects of the changes that have taken place in the U.S. aerospace defense industrial base over the past decade, as well as those that have more re-

---

[1]The information cutoff date for this document is September 2001.

cently shaped the European aerospace defense industrial base, include the following:

- "Merger mania," or horizontal and vertical consolidation and integration on the prime-contractor level and, to a lesser degree, on the second and lower-tier subsystem supplier levels.

- Increased globalization through strategic as well as product-specific alliances, international teaming and joint ventures, cross-border mergers and acquisitions (M&As), and a heightened interest in foreign exports and foreign lower-tier suppliers.

- Increased dependence on already highly globalized commercial markets and products.

A fundamental cause of the consolidation and restructuring of the aerospace industry in the United States, in Europe, and elsewhere has been a dramatic decline both in overall defense authorizations and, particularly, in military aircraft procurement budgets since the end of the Cold War.[2] Between 1985 and 1997 the Department of Defense (DoD) aircraft procurement budget declined by nearly 75 percent. During the same period, DoD missile procurement and space procurement went down by 82 and 56 percent, respectively.[3] Military aircraft production in the United States fell from a high of about 450 a year in 1986 to fewer than 100 per year from 1993 through 2000.[4] In Europe, procurement expenditures for "heavy equipment" declined by 18 percent from the late 1980s to the early 1990s. Initial cuts were largest in Germany, one of the most important European weapon-procuring nations. By the mid-1990s, other

---

[2]See, for example, the American Institute of Aeronautics and Astronautics (AIAA) (2001), Chapter 1. Note, however, that extensive consolidation also took place in many other sectors of the U.S. economy during this period. Although the 1990s "procurement holiday" appears to be ending in the wake of the events of September 11, most analysts believe that the current industry structure on the U.S. prime-contractor level will remain stable for some time, while consolidation on the second and lower tiers will continue.

[3]Procurement budget authority in 1997 dollars. Data are from the Defense Contract Management Command (1997).

[4]See, for example, Meth et al. (2001), which presents data from an unpublished study conducted by the Office of the Director, Industrial Capabilities and Assessments, Deputy Under Secretary of Defense for Industrial Affairs, Office of the Under Secretary of Defense for Acquisition, Technology, and Logistics.

key European players such as France began slashing procurement budgets as well.[5] According to one industry executive, North Atlantic Treaty Organization (NATO) European defense budgets declined overall by 21 percent from 1995 through 2000, while NATO European expenditures on research and development (R&D) went down by an even greater percentage (Kresa, 2001).

The natural response of aerospace contractors to a rapidly shrinking market was to consolidate horizontally and vertically through M&As; to lay off workers; to sell excess assets; and, in some cases, to exit the industry. As a result, during the 1990s the number of credible U.S. combat aircraft prime contractors as integrators for fighters and bombers declined from seven to two. Similarly, from 1990 to 1998, the number of U.S. missile manufacturers fell from fourteen to four, while space launch vehicle producers declined from six to two. By 2001, only one credible U.S. developer of air-to-air missiles remained active. In most major avionics subsystem and propulsion areas, one or two firms now dominate the U.S. market; in some instances, these firms have been acquired by one of the remaining dominant aerospace prime contractors. The naval and land weapon sectors of the defense industry experienced similar declines in numbers of firms. Overall, the number of defense companies that accounted for two-thirds of all defense sales shrank by 60 percent between 1990 and 1998.

By the beginning of the new millennium, similar consolidation trends had begun to reach fruition in NATO Europe. The leading European aerospace firms consolidated into three large, closely linked megafirms: the European Aeronautic Defence and Space Company (EADS), BAE Systems, and the Thales Group. EADS— which is composed of Aerospatiale Matra, DaimlerChrysler Aerospace (formerly Deutsche Aerospace SA [DASA]), and Construcciones Aeronauticas SA (CASA)—also owns a 46.5 percent share in Dassault Aviation and is forming a 50-50 joint venture with Alenia Aeronautica called the European Military Aircraft Company (EMAC). Following its recent acquisition of major divisions of Lockheed Martin, BAE Systems—formed after British Aerospace ac-

---

[5]See Brzoska et al. (1999). The dates chosen for comparison represent the "peaks and valleys" of procurement and R&D spending and thus represent the extreme points in the period of change.

quired General Electric Company's (GEC's) Marconi Electronic Systems in 1999—has become the world's largest defense contractor by revenues. BAE Systems has also linked up with Dassault to study next-generation fighter technologies in a 50-50 joint venture called European Aerosystems. The third European giant is the Thales Group, the former Thomson-CSF of France. Thales has acquired numerous other European companies, including a major British defense contractor, Racal Electronics PLC. As shown in Table 1.1, these three newly structured European firms are on roughly the same scale as the new, consolidated U.S. primes.

With government political backing, these three megafirms have the potential to dominate the European military aerospace market and thus to reduce U.S. industry's historically significant share of that market. This was dramatically demonstrated by the recent unexpected victory of a BAE Systems/Saab marketing joint venture for the JAS 39 Gripen fighter in Hungary and the Czech Republic, in competition with the Lockheed Martin F-16. The new European megafirms will also pose even more vigorous competition in third-country markets, where the battle for sales among U.S. and European firms is already fierce. Further, BAE Systems, Rolls-Royce, Smiths Industries, and other European firms (mostly British) have been highly successful in penetrating the U.S. market through new acquisitions, the most important of which are Lockheed Sanders and Allison Engines. At the same time, their larger size and growing technological and system integration capabilities make these megafirms more attractive potential partners for collaboration with U.S. firms.

DoD's Position on Defense Industry Consolidation

In the early 1990s, DoD strongly encouraged greater defense industry consolidation.[6] European government officials adopted a similar approach throughout the decade. The reasons were simple and straightforward. As noted above, procurement budgets (and, to a lesser extent, R&D budgets) had diminished dramatically since their high point in the mid-1980s and were continuing to go down. Consolidation and commercialization were seen as potential ways to

---

[6]DoD was especially supportive of consolidation at the plant level, rather than simply at the corporate accounting level, because of the greater potential for cost savings.

Table 1.1

Global Ranking of Aerospace and Defense Companies, 1999

Rank/Company	Country	1999 Defense Revenues ($ billion)
1: BAE Systems	UK	19.0[a]
2: Lockheed Martin	United States	17.8
3: Boeing	United States	16.3
4: Raytheon	United States	14.5
5: EADS	France/Germany/Spain	6.1
6: Northrop Grumman	United States	6.0
7: Thales Group	France	3.6

SOURCE: Barrie and Mackenzie (2000).

[a]Takes into account BAE Systems' purchase of Lockheed Martin Aerospace Electronics Systems.

retain essential industrial base capabilities in an efficient and cost-effective manner as the market significantly declined.

Yet at the same time, some DoD and other expert observers expressed concern about the excessive concentration of the U.S. aerospace industry.[7] According to the U.S. General Accounting Office (GAO), as early as 1994 the Defense Science Board (DSB) reported to DoD that

> Reducing the number of firms capable of developing a suitable design for a new weapon system may lead to higher prices, poorer products, smaller advances in technology, and a reduction in the number, variety, or quality of the proposals that companies submit to DOD (GAO, 1997, p. 22).

In like manner, DoD's 1996 annual report noted that

> Consolidation carries the risk that DOD will no longer benefit from the competition that encourages defense suppliers to reduce costs, improve quality, and stimulate innovation (GAO, 1997, p. 21).

---

[7]At least some senior DoD officials subscribed to the view that in the defense sector, two firms are often enough to ensure fierce competition owing to the "lumpy" nature of DoD demand. A formal version of this argument was first made by Peck and Scherer (1962).

A 1997 DSB task force also examined the possible anticompetitive potential of increased vertical integration in the industry, noting that "vertical integration enables several potential behaviors that may negatively affect defense product cost, quality and performance" (DSB, 1997, p. v). Concluding that "vertical integration poses future concern to DoD," the task force recommended that DoD "revise its policy and practices to increase the focus on retaining competition and innovation in its acquisition and technology programs" (DSB, 1997, p. xii).

The July 1997 announcement by Lockheed Martin and Northrop Grumman of their intention to merge deepened these concerns and led the senior levels of DoD to cooperate with the Justice Department in quashing the merger plans. The reasons given were the same as those expressed in DoD documents cited above—namely, that reduced competition among a much smaller number of vertically and horizontally integrated prime contractors and second-tier contractors could result in declining technological innovation and increased cost to the government.

Although the pace of consolidation slowed somewhat after the government blocked the proposed Lockheed Martin/Northrop Grumman merger, concerns persisted about the reduced levels of competition in the industry and its potential effects on innovation and price. Added to these concerns was a continuing perception of other weaknesses in the industry that might negatively affect competition, quality, price, and innovation. Chief among these were worries about allegedly insufficient levels of research, development, test, and evaluation (RDT&E) funding; the change in industry emphasis toward short-term, project-specific goals; and a decline in independent research and development (IR&D) expenditures (American Institute of Aeronautics and Astronautics, 2001, p. 2). A 1999 National Research Council report expressed great concern that industry-funded R&D for aircraft and missiles had declined by nearly 50 percent between 1988 and 1997 (National Research Council, 1999).

Uneasiness over declining competitiveness and innovation also emerged from perceptions that, over the long term, there would be insufficient numbers of fixed-wing combat aircraft and related technology projects to support more than one or two full design, RDT&E,

and manufacturing engineering teams. This was particularly the case in the area of fighter aircraft, where it was widely believed that the Joint Strike Fighter (JSF) would be the last manned fighter development and procurement project for decades. Following the downselect to one prime contractor in the fall of 2001, some observers envisioned the losing contractor effectively withdrawing from the fighter market sector, leaving only one viable fighter developer/integrator in the United States with a de facto monopoly on the market.[8] Indeed, in the FY 2002 National Defense Authorization Act, Congress mandated that DoD direct a major study of the potential negative effects of such a monopoly on innovation and cost in future fighter aircraft development.

The Globalization Strategy

One possible solution to the problem of an increasingly concentrated U.S. aerospace industry lies in greater government encouragement of the existing trend toward globalization.[9] In the early 1990s, for example, many observers believed that heavier government emphasis on U.S. aerospace exports could expand the market, support more domestic competitors, and help maintain U.S. industry capabilities. Given the rapid consolidation and restructuring of European industry, however, it had become evident by the beginning of the new millennium that the exporting of finished major weapon systems to Europe would become increasingly untenable. In fact, it was apparent that competition from the new European megafirms for third-country markets could become increasingly intense (Zakheim, 2000).

Therefore, rather than merely promoting exports, a more complex approach to globalization calls for increased participation of foreign

---

[8]For a variety of other concerns and proposed solutions, see DSB (2000).

[9]A second mechanism that has been widely advanced as a way to promote greater competition and innovation in a U.S. defense aerospace industry that has downsized dramatically and become increasingly concentrated involves promoting greater integration of the civil and military industrial bases, or civil-military integration. Such an approach envisions reforms in the DoD acquisition process that would (1) encourage more commercial firms to compete for DoD business, and (2) promote far greater use of commercial designs, subsystems, components, parts, technologies, and processes in weapon systems. For a discussion and analysis of the broad literature on this subject, see Lorell et al. (2000).

contractors in the U.S. defense market on all levels, as well as more cross-border teaming, joint ventures, mergers, strategic alliances, foreign direct investment in the United States, and weapon system development collaboration. Many economists and other expert observers have pointed out that expanded participation of foreign contractors in the U.S. market would increase competition, thereby providing economic benefits to the U.S. government.[10] Generally, however, closer international linkages among aerospace firms could also bring noneconomic benefits, foremost among which would be the potential for greater equipment rationalization, standardization, and interoperability (RSI) among the United States, NATO Europe, and other key allies.[11] At the same time, globalization also poses challenges, in particular how to preserve national capabilities and prevent the proliferation of advanced U.S.-developed military technologies.

Regardless of the costs and benefits of globalization as perceived by the U.S. government, given the contraction of the domestic market over the last decade and the strongly favorable attitudes of U.S. industry leaders, increased globalization seems inevitable. A recent major survey of aerospace and defense CEOs by a leading business consulting firm, for example, concluded that U.S. defense business leaders now view globalization as "an imperative" (Deloitte & Touche and Deloitte Consulting, 1998, p. 6). According to the report:

> Globalization of the aerospace and defense industry is rapidly increasing as manufacturers move beyond national markets to exploit new opportunities in uncharted markets abroad. Indeed, economic necessity is beginning to wear away the industry's insulation, forcing companies to compete as well as cooperate across frontiers . . . This marks a dramatic turnaround from the

---

[10]See, for example, Kovacic (1999).

[11]RSI is a NATO-related acronym that was coined in the late 1970s. Rationalization refers to the avoidance of unnecessary duplication and to the rational allocation of funding and work tasks among NATO alliance members for weapon system R&D and manufacture. Equipment standardization refers to allied procurement of weapon systems that are identical or nearly identical. Equipment interoperability signifies allied procurement of weapon systems that may not be identical but can use the same consumables, such as fuels, lubricants, and ammunition, and can communicate through common frequencies, data formats, and the like. The U.S. government has promoted RSI in NATO for at least two decades, if not since the inception of the alliance.

views of executives who participated in the *1993 Vision in Manufacturing* study. In 1993, globalization was not a top initiative, executives did not have clear global strategies and capabilities were low. Today, the survey finds that leading executives have changed their perspective and are actively taking steps to "go global" (Deloitte & Touche and Deloitte Consulting, 1998, p. 7).

Yet although numerous studies have examined and assessed the domestic aspects of U.S. aerospace industry consolidation over the past ten years, increased globalization—and the effects on U.S. industry of the more recent European consolidation—have not been subjected to equally intensive analysis. Indeed, few assessments of appropriate government responses to globalization issues are available.[12]   One important reason may be the relative lack of reliable data on—and analysis of—the nature and current degree of aerospace industry globalization. Yet devising policies that enhance industry competition, improve preparedness for coalition operations, and maintain the national security requires a better understanding of how, why, and with whom U.S. aerospace companies are establishing international business relationships.

RESEARCH GOALS AND ORGANIZATION OF THIS REPORT

The central purpose of this report is to examine issues related to aerospace industry globalization; to outline initial findings; and to propose a future research agenda that will help the Air Force develop a more effective policy and strategy for exploiting the claimed benefits of globalization while minimizing its associated risks. During FY 2001, the project thus pursued four major research goals:

- The collection and analysis of a wide range of government, industry, and private databases related to aerospace industry globalization, and the development of a typology of cross-border

---

[12]This is not to suggest that globalization issues are rarely addressed. Indeed, many government and privately supported studies of the subject have been undertaken. Recent government studies related to globalization include DSB (1996 and 1999). AIAA (2001) also includes an important discussion of globalization issues. Nonetheless, most of these studies rely on anecdotal evidence and the insights of industry and government "wise men" rather than on in-depth and systematic analysis of data.

business relationships and activities prevalent in the defense aerospace industry.

- The examination and analysis, based on OSD, Air Force, and other U.S. government analyses as well as the open literature, of both the opportunities and challenges the Air Force faces as a result of the ongoing globalization of the aerospace industrial base.

- A detailed examination of OSD, Air Force, and other U.S. government regulations, policies, and procedures with respect to purchases of foreign military equipment and services; foreign direct investments in the United States, including international M&As; and other forms of international industry alliances and collaboration.

- A survey of more than 30 case studies providing recent examples of cross-border business relationships, focusing mainly on the U.S. and European aerospace industries and stressing new and innovative types of approaches.

Analysis of aerospace and defense industry trade and investment data suggests that U.S. industry is closely tied to the global economy through exports but, compared to some other high-technology and manufacturing industries, does not heavily exploit imports or foreign technology. Most major U.S. weapon system platforms appear to have only small foreign content by value (DoD, 2001). This conclusion tentatively suggests that U.S. industry is not fully exploiting the potential economic and technological benefits of cross-border outsourcing. However, the data also show an increasing trend toward deeper industry-led cross-border relationships. These business relationships, although heavily oriented toward UK firms, could strengthen U.S. ties to all of the European NATO allies and offset any tendency toward competing transatlantic fortresses.

We identified three overarching objectives motivating Air Force interest in and concern about globalization: (1) the need to equip aerospace forces with affordable yet exceptionally capable weapons systems, both today and in the future; (2) the need to prepare the United States, its NATO partners, and other key allies to participate in future coalition operations, in part through the procurement of interoperable or standardized equipment; and (3) the need to protect U.S. national security, including technology security and domestic industrial capabilities. Although we found at least some discussion of the implications of globalization for each of these objectives, there appears to be very little analysis of how globalization may affect trade-offs among them.

We also found that while competition is seen as key to equipping U.S. warfighters with superior yet affordable weapon systems, the potential role of foreign contractors in making U.S. defense markets more competitive is not given prominence. Further, while there is considerable emphasis on international cooperative development, procurement, and support of weapon systems in the context of coalition operations with NATO and other friendly nations, national security–related constraints on technology transfer and foreign direct investment in the United States may be preventing improved transatlantic collaboration. This appears to be the case despite major policy reform efforts such as the Defense Trade Security Initiative (DTSI) and the Defense Capabilities Initiative (DCI).

We conclude that industry-initiated cross-border business relationships may well be the most promising approaches toward achieving the economic benefits and equipment interoperability sought by DoD if they are organized as marketing agreements, teams, or joint ventures that are motivated by business and market factors rather than by government-mandated programs, and if they focus on subsystems, smaller programs, or narrow market sectors rather than on large traditional platform programs. We also conclude that further research is necessary to answer many crucial questions that remain, including the following:

- How do the current domestic and foreign regulatory environments affect the structuring of industry-initiated cross-border relationships, and how are DoD and foreign reform efforts changing the environment?

- What types of industry business relationships and structures are most effective in promoting both U.S. economic and political-military objectives?

- How are legitimate security of supply, technology transfer, and other technology security issues being handled, particularly in the new multipolar, multinational business environment?

To answer these questions, we propose the need for follow-on research using a detailed case study analysis.

Chapter Two of this report establishes a framework for analysis consisting of quantitative and qualitative indicators of globalization. On the basis of aggregate data on cross-border trade and investment as well as arms transfers, it assesses developments in U.S. aerospace globalization by comparing that industry to other major high-technology and manufacturing sectors in the United States.

Chapter Three draws on the open literature as well as on economic theory to review the economic, political-military, and national security opportunities and challenges posed by greater globalization of the U.S. aerospace industry. While it discusses issues surrounding globalization of the low-value parts and components supplier base, it focuses on the implications of globalization for the design, development, manufacture, and integration of high-value systems and subsystems.

Chapter Four reviews some of the more important existing legislation, regulations, and policy approaches that influence how the U.S. defense aerospace industry interacts globally. It also discusses how the Air Force implements DoD as well as its own unique policies and regulations related to industry globalization and international collaborative procurement, and it then offers an initial assessment of the effectiveness and influence of these policies. It concludes by reviewing some of the major globalization reform initiatives recently launched by NATO and by the U.S. government, concentrating on NATO's DCI and on DTSI as jointly put forward by DoD and the Department of State (DoS).

Finally, Chapter Five surveys recent cross-border business relationships, organized under the categories of market agreements, teams, joint ventures, and parent/subsidiary arrangements. The focus is on cross-border business relationships initiated by the aerospace defense industry. The purpose of this survey is to gain initial insights into whether or not the new forms of cross-border business relationships are bringing the hoped-for benefits of increased globalization and, if so, which types of business relationships appear to be most effective. Chapter Six summarizes our findings, identifies gaps in our research results, and suggests future research to provide the Air

Force with a more comprehensive understanding of, and potential policy options for, effectively managing industry-initiated globalization.

THE U.S. DEFENSE AEROSPACE INDUSTRY: HOW GLOBALIZED IS IT?

INTRODUCTION

To analyze the implications of a globalizing U.S. defense aerospace industry for the Air Force, we must first address two questions:

- What do we mean by "globalization"?

- How globalized is the U.S. defense aerospace industry?

In the ongoing debate over how to define globalization, some observers make a clear distinction between the process of becoming a "global" industry and that of becoming merely an "international" one. For example, Frankenstein (1996) argues that a truly global company has design, manufacturing, and marketing capabilities in multiple locations around the world, while an international company buys components and markets products abroad but locates its primary design and manufacturing capabilities in its home country. According to this view, increases in cross-border trade flows might indicate the "internationalization" of an industry, but there must be deeper business relationships between domestic and foreign firms before it can be described as "globalized."

We take a broader view of globalization in this report, encompassing both "global" and "international" companies in our definition of what it means for the defense aerospace industry to be globalized. We believe a broad view is appropriate because even if trade were the only form of international activity in which defense aerospace firms participated, it would still give rise to significant policy issues. Nevertheless, we recognize that the effectiveness of particular government policies in managing globalization will depend on the nature of that globalization. For example, policies designed to restrict the foreign outsourcing of widgets are unlikely to deal effectively with issues raised by U.S.-foreign collaboration on major weapon system development programs. Therefore, a key objective of this chapter is to review the available evidence not only on the magnitude but also on the character of U.S. defense aerospace industry globalization.

When defined broadly, the most visible manifestation of globalization can probably be found in the growing cross-border purchase and sale, by number and by value, of goods, services, and financial assets. We know from widely available aggregate data on international trade and investment that according to these measures, the U.S. economy at the start of the 21st century is more globalized than ever before (Council of Economic Advisers [CEA], 2000). Unfortunately, the changes in the nature of international business relationships and activities that have almost certainly accompanied this increase in cross-border trade and investment are hard to track, primarily because there are so few data sources that capture them. There are no widely accepted definitions for many of the terms used to describe them.

Nevertheless, recent studies of defense companies by Bitzinger (1999) and GAO (2000c) indicate that global linkages among defense firms are becoming deeper and more complex. Our own case study evidence—which uses a typology of cross-border relationships and activities common to the defense aerospace industry—suggests that aerospace firms, too, are responding to the imperatives of globalization by creating innovative cross-border business structures.[1] What these new structures may imply in terms of Air Force objectives for the defense industrial base, however, is not yet well understood.

Finally, the increasingly multinational character of the U.S. industrial workforce is also an important feature of globalization, although it is not always recognized as such because of a severe lack of data. One

_____
[1]See Chapter Five for a discussion of these cases.

source of information is the National Science Foundation's biennial Survey of Doctorate Recipients (National Science Foundation, 2001). This survey indicates that of roughly 630,000 U.S.-trained doctoral scientists and engineers in the United States in 1999, just over 10 percent were non–U.S. citizens.[2] In the field of aerospace/aeronautical engineering, however, non–U.S. citizens constituted 13.7 percent of doctorate holders, while the proportion of non–U.S. citizens who held doctorates in information sciences was 27.3 percent.[3] Unfortunately, these data provide no insight into the number of foreign-born scientists and engineers working in the United States who did not receive degrees from U.S. universities, and they cannot tell us how many are employed in the military aerospace industrial base. We therefore do not pursue them further in this report. Nevertheless, the fact that the military aerospace industrial base, like the United States as a whole, relies to a significant extent on noncitizens to fill highly skilled technical positions may have important implications for U.S. national security.

DEFENSE AEROSPACE GLOBALIZATION: DATA SOURCES AND TERMINOLOGY

Defense Aerospace Trade

There is little statistical data specific to the production and consumption of or trade in defense aerospace systems and subsystems—or at least little at useful levels of disaggregation.[4] Nevertheless, several sources do provide data that shed light on the extent of trade-related globalization of the defense aerospace industry. Each source has its own strengths and weaknesses, but the perspectives they provide fall into three major categories:

---

[2]The survey covers all persons under the age of 76 who hold a doctorate in science or engineering from a U.S. institution, where "science" includes the social sciences and psychology as well as the physical, information, and mathematical sciences.

[3]For comparison purposes, the U.S. Bureau of the Census estimates that the proportion of non–U.S. citizens in the total U.S. population was 6.5 percent in March 2000 (U.S. Department of Commerce, Bureau of the Census, 2000).

[4]As far as we know, no comprehensive DoD databases relevant to these issues exist.

- Production, consumption, and international trade in aerospace products, both civil and military (e.g., the U.S. Department of Commerce's International Trade Administration [ITA] and the Aerospace Industries Association [AIA]);[5]

- The production and international transfer of conventional armaments, including both aerospace and nonaerospace equipment (e.g., DoS, the International Institute for Strategic Studies [IISS], and the Stockholm International Peace Research Institute [SIPRI]);[6]

- Government expenditures on and procurement of products and services related to national defense (e.g., AIA, DoS, IISS, NATO).

The data on aerospace products have the advantage of being specific to aerospace while also distinguishing between finished (or "complete") products and production inputs.[7] This is important because a growing number of cross-border transactions involve the outsourcing of production inputs to unrelated foreign suppliers as well as shipments between the internationally located business units of the same firm (Hummels et al., 2001; Fernald and Greenfield, 2001). This vertical specialization of trade—or "intra-industry" trade—raises complex national security issues when applied to defense industries, but unfortunately breakouts for civil and military aerospace products are not always available. Shipment data, for example, distinguish between complete civil and military aircraft but not between civil and military engines or aircraft parts.

Another major problem with most aerospace data is that they capture only inputs formally classified within the "aerospace" categories of the U.S. Standard Industrial Classification (SIC) system or the

---

[5]ITA and AIA provide data to each other; both also get data from the Bureau of the Census, U.S. Department of Commerce.

[6]The Bureau of Verification and Compliance within DoS now issues *World Military Expenditures and Arms Transfers*. The U.S. Arms Control and Disarmament Agency, which has merged with DoS, issued previous editions.

[7]Finished aerospace products include fixed-wing aircraft, helicopters, and space vehicles, while inputs range from commodity goods such as tubes, pipes, and hoses to more specialized equipment such as launching gear and gas turbine engines for aircraft. These data cover only merchandise goods, which is unfortunate because trade in engineering and other technical services is likely to be an important feature of aerospace industry globalization.

North American Industrial Classification System (NAICS).[8] Commodity inputs such as many types of fasteners and hoses are not included. Even more problematic from a policy perspective is the fact that certain high-cost, high-technology inputs to the aerospace industry also cannot be analyzed using published ITA data. Radar, navigation, and guidance systems, for example, all fall within the non-aerospace-specific category "search and navigation equipment" and thus are not analyzed here.

The data on conventional arms production and transfers have the advantage of being specific to defense, and although they are not specific to aerospace, they are dominated by it.[9] The three sources we analyze differ slightly in their coverage. SIPRI collects data on major conventional weapon systems that are voluntarily transferred from one country to the armed forces, paramilitary forces, or intelligence agencies of another country.[10] Weapon systems covered include complete aircraft, armored vehicles, artillery, radar systems, missiles, and ships. DoS and IISS add small arms, ammunition and other ordnance, uniforms, some dual-use equipment, and some military services to this definition but do not include the value of arms obtained by subnational groups.[11] IISS's figures for the United States derive from DoS, but its export figures are often higher because of generally higher estimates of U.S. direct commercial sales (IISS, 2000, p. 288). No data on trade in inputs to weapon system production are publicly available.

The data on aerospace production and consumption, defense expenditures, and government procurement provide a context for the trade and transfer data. Specifically, they allow us to establish the

---

[8]The NAICS formally replaced the SIC system in 1997.

[9]According to SIPRI (2000), for example, eight of the world's top ten arms-producing companies ranked by 1998 sales were involved in the production of aircraft or missiles or both.

[10]As described in a report by SIPRI (2001), "This includes weapons delivered illegally—without proper authorization by the government of the supplier or recipient country—but excludes captured weapons and weapons obtained through defectors." SIPRI data are obtained from open sources rather than directly from governments.

[11]See DoS (April 2000, p. 205) for a fuller description of the items these two sources define as conventional arms.

significance of foreign suppliers and markets relative to U.S. suppliers and markets for U.S. defense aerospace firms.

The sources for data on aerospace products use standard definitions of merchandise exports and imports: Exports are shipments to and imports are shipments from firms or units of firms located across a national border, including both complete products and intermediate inputs. The nationalities of particular buyers and sellers are irrelevant; for example, U.S. exports consist of all shipments from the United States to destinations outside the United States, and U.S. imports are all shipments to the United States from sources outside the United States. The sources for conventional armament data generally refer to "transfers" and "deliveries" rather than to "trade" and "shipments" because they include aid and gifts as well as commercial sales (SIPRI, 2001). The terms "export" and "import" are sometimes used with respect to arms transfers, but these data do not capture all cross-border sales related to the weapon industry. Rather, they capture the narrower set of finished-product transactions that involve suppliers and recipients of different nationalities.

A distinguishing feature of international trade in defense aerospace is that so much of it is governed by "offset" agreements—that is, by conditions negotiated by foreign governments with U.S. companies seeking to export major systems to their countries (Presidential Commission on Offsets in International Trade, 2001).[12] Common types of defense offset transactions, which are almost always designed to benefit national firms in the recipient country, include the following:

- Subcontracts related to the manufacture and assembly of system parts and components;

- Licensed coproduction of the system;

- Counterpurchases of unrelated goods;

- Related or unrelated technology transfers and training;

- Related or unrelated credit transfers; and

---

[12]Much less is known about the nature and extent of commercial, as opposed to defense, offsets because there is no government requirement for reporting them.

- Related or unrelated investment.

According to data collected by the Commerce Department's Bureau of Export Administration (BXA), between 1980 and 1998 the value of defense offset agreements ranged from 34 to 98 percent of total defense export sales.[13] According to the Presidential Commission on Offsets in International Trade (2001), 89 percent of defense offsets (measured by value) from 1993 to 1998 were associated with aerospace exports. Offset agreements complicate the analysis of defense aerospace industry globalization because they induce U.S. firms to engage in cross-border transactions in which they might not otherwise elect to participate. In particular, U.S. investment in foreign aerospace firms is likely to be larger than it would be were offsets not so prevalent. It is likely that U.S. aerospace exports benefit considerably from offset arrangements.

Defense Aerospace Investment

Statistical data relevant to the international investment activities and business relationships of U.S. defense aerospace firms are even scarcer than data on their cross-border trade. In this report, we make use of publicly available data from four sources:

- Economy-wide data on cross-border investment activity involving U.S. firms (e.g., the U.S. Department of Commerce's Bureau of Economic Analysis [BEA]);

- Data on domestic and international M&As involving U.S. firms (Mergerstat);

- Data on foreign acquisitions of U.S. defense firms (Ciardello, 2001); and

- Data on U.S. industry involvement in defense acquisition programs worldwide (Bitzinger, 1999).

---

[13]The "value" of defense offset transactions is measured as the amount of offset credit awarded to U.S. exporters by the nations receiving the offsets. It generally does not represent an actual cost to the exporter. See Presidential Commission on Offsets in International Trade (2001, pp. 6–8).

The first data source provides official U.S. government estimates of foreign direct investment in the United States and U.S. direct investment abroad, spanning all industries and sectors, including nonmanufacturing sectors such as agriculture and services. These data provide useful benchmark statistics to which the investment activities of defense aerospace firms may be compared, but the published industry breakdowns are too broad to offer any further insights.

The second source consists of privately collected data on domestic and international M&As involving U.S. firms. M&As, defined below, represent a subset of investment activities that have particular significance for the Air Force because they involve changes in ownership and thus control. Once again, the publicly available data from these sources are not specific either to defense or to aerospace, but they provide a useful benchmark.[14]

Ciardello (2001) reports the number of foreign acquisitions, mergers, and takeovers reviewed by the Committee on Foreign Investment in the United States (CFIUS) under the Exon-Florio Amendment to the Defense Production Act of 1950. Exon-Florio requires that restrictions be imposed on foreign acquisitions, mergers, or takeovers that have the potential to threaten U.S. national security. Notification of proposed transactions to CFIUS is provided voluntarily by the parties concerned.[15] Threats to national security are broadly defined to include threats to U.S. technology leadership as well as threats to the U.S. domestic industry's capability and capacity to meet national defense requirements (see Chapter Four), but Ciardello focuses on cases that are defense-related.

Finally, the Defense Budget Project's (DBP's) Globalization Database, described in Bitzinger (1999), provides a perspective on defense-related cross-border investment that comes close to our own. Covering the period 1961 to 1995, the DBP database contains two types of information: a classification and listing of cross-border defense acquisition programs and activities, and a classification and

---

[14]Mergerstat does offer limited data on aerospace-related M&A activity for a fee.

[15]CFIUS member agencies may also refer proposed transactions to the committee that they perceive as posing a possible threat to national security (U.S. Department of the Treasury, undated).

listing of the types of cross-border business relationships that have been formed to carry out those programs and activities.[16] Breakouts by system type—including aircraft and guided missiles—are provided. The database also distinguishes industry-initiated relationships from government-initiated arrangements in which firms of different nationalities share R&D and/or production responsibilities, usually in proportion to the financial contributions of their respective governments.

The U.S. Department of Commerce's BEA as well as Mergerstat and Ciardello (2001) all use definitions that derive from U.S. government sources.[17] According to U.S. official usage, for example, the term direct investment—which implies a degree of operational involvement in a firm's operation—requires an ownership stake of at least 10 percent of the voting securities of an incorporated business enterprise or an equivalent interest in an unincorporated business enterprise.[18] This quantitative criterion applies both to foreign direct investment in the United States and to U.S. direct investment abroad. By definition, a foreign affiliate is a foreign business in which there is U.S. direct investment; a U.S. affiliate is a U.S. business in which there is foreign direct investment. A majority-owned foreign affiliate has combined ownership by all U.S. parents of over 50 percent; the same percentage criterion applies to the U.S. affiliates of foreign parents.

Both internationally and domestically, one company's establishment of a controlling interest in another company is called an "acquisition"; the company acquired is often called a "subsidiary." In most cases, U.S. firms' foreign subsidiaries are also technically their foreign affiliates and vice versa. In cases where 10 percent ownership does not confer a controlling interest, however, an affiliate is not also a subsidiary, and where less than 10 percent does, a

---

[16]Unfortunately, the DBP database does not always distinguish between these two types of information. Although the DBP database includes the cross-border activities of and relationships among a global spectrum of defense firms, we are interested only in those that involve U.S. firms.

[17]U.S. usage of investment vocabulary is not uniformly consistent with that of other countries. For an overview of key U.S. terms, see BEA (2000a, p. 58).

[18]In the United States, anything below the 10 percent threshold constitutes portfolio investment. In some other countries, however, foreigners must own 25 percent of the voting stock before their investment is termed "direct."

subsidiary is not also an affiliate. In the case where a single company purchases 100 percent of another company's voting stock, the company that has been taken over is called a "wholly owned subsidiary" of the purchasing company. A merger is a special type of acquisition in which two companies become one by exchanging shares.[19] Measures of cross-border direct investment are usually larger than measures of cross-border M&As because the former include the continuing flow of equity, debt, and reinvested earnings between parents and their already established foreign affiliates.

While the term direct investment implies some degree of managerial control or operational involvement, it does not speak to the nature or intent of the business relationship that generated the investment. A 10 percent stake may allow a firm to create or participate in a variety of enterprises for a variety of reasons, ranging from a joint venture that targets a specific product to a wholly owned foreign subsidiary that targets an entire market segment. Further, there are many activities or programs, including simple cross-border trade, that could in theory be conducted within a particular business relationship.

Of special interest, therefore, is our fourth data source, the DBP Globalization Database, which lists international cooperative activities and business relationships formed specifically for the purpose of developing and/or producing major weapon systems and components. Unfortunately, this database does not contain financial or cost information on the programs it lists, and it does not always distinguish the *activities* of firms—such as selling the rights to one firm to assemble or manufacture a weapon system that a different firm has developed—from their *relationships*, such as that between a prime and its subcontractors or between the parent companies in a joint venture. As a result, the DBP database cannot be used either to compare the relative importance (by value) of alternative business arrangements and activities or to determine which types of business relationships have most often been associated with which types of activities. Nevertheless, as far as we know it is the only source that provides quantitative evidence of the increasingly "global" as op-

---

[19]Mergers between companies located across national borders often result in the creation of a wholly owned subsidiary in the home country of one of the original companies.

posed to "international" character of the U.S. defense aerospace industry.

A Typology of Defense Aerospace Activities and Relationships

To better understand recent globalization trends in the defense aerospace industry and the role played by legislation, policy, and guidance in shaping those trends, we have developed a typology that distinguishes between the joint or cooperative activities of firms located across national borders and the business relationships they establish in order to facilitate those activities. For our purposes, the most relevant activities carried out by U.S. defense aerospace firms are those shown in Table 2.1, which borrows terminology from the *International Armaments Cooperation Handbook* (Deputy Under Secretary of Defense for International and Commercial Programs, 1996).[20] In brief, these are

- Cross-border shipments of platforms, systems, or major subsystems;

- Licensed coproduction;

- "Partnership" coproduction;[21]

- Foreign Military Sales (FMS) coproduction; and

- Codevelopment.

With respect to the export of finished equipment, an important issue is the extent to which system or subsystem subcontracts or other

---

[20]All of these activities can also include adapting, modifying, or upgrading existing complete or semifinished products.

[21]We use the term *partnership coproduction* as opposed to *cooperative production* in order to distinguish the former from other forms of cooperative production. Both terms are defined in Chapter 19 of the *International Armaments Cooperation Handbook* (Deputy Under Secretary of Defense for International and Commercial Programs, 1996, p. x).

Table 2.1

n Types of Activities Carried Out by U.S. Aerospace Firms Involved in Cross-Border Business Rela

Activity	Description[a]
ale or purchase of complete or hed products (e.g., platforms, or major subsystems)[b]	Often involves offsets arrangements with foreign companies.
coproduction	The commercial sale or transfer of rights to overseas FACO as well as varying d component manufacturing of an aircraft or major subsystem originally design developed by one or more U.S. companies. May or may not be intended for be and allied inventories.
roduction	The sale or transfer of rights to overseas FACO as well as varying degrees of cor manufacturing of a U.S.-designed and -developed aircraft or major subsystem terms of a formal FMS agreement. Generally applies to aircraft or subsystems U.S. inventory.
ip coproduction	Manufacture and assembly by at least one U.S. and one foreign company of pa a system or major subsystem originally collaboratively developed by those cor under a formal armaments cooperation program. (See "codevelopment.")
pment	Joint design and development by at least one U.S. and one foreign company of of a system or subsystem under a formal armaments cooperation program inv international agreement between the United States and an allied country. Usu followed by partnership coproduction.

ions derived from Deputy Under Secretary of Defense for International and Commercial Programs, *Internationa ts Cooperation Handbook*, Chapter 10, June 1996.

much narrower definition than that for the term *trade*, which includes all cross-border movements of goods, inc ty items such as fasteners and other small parts.

offset agreements are involved.[22] A key issue with respect to all of the activities is whether the equipment in question is intended for both U.S. and allied inventories, thereby furthering equipment standardization and interoperability objectives.

All three forms of coproduction involve the transfer of rights to final assembly and checkout (FACO) of U.S.-developed equipment to a foreign country. They are termed *coproduction* rather than *production* in order to emphasize their collaborative nature: Even for straightforward licensing arrangements, it has rarely if ever been the case that the developer of a system as complicated as a fighter jet has sold its FACO rights to a foreign company and simply walked away. Licensed coproduction differs from FMS coproduction in two key respects. First, licensed coproduction may or may not involve a system or subsystem that is in the inventories of the U.S. armed services, while FMS coproduction always involves articles used by the U.S. armed services. This distinction is important because it relates to the crucial question of equipment standardization and interoperability with U.S. allies. Second, licensed coproduction involves a direct commercial sale from the developer; FMS coproduction arrangements are negotiated under the terms of an FMS Letter of Offer and Acceptance (LOA) issued by the U.S. government. Thus, with FMS coproduction the U.S. government formally handles the details for procuring the equipment as an agent of the foreign government, thereby further promoting interaction and interoperability with an ally. Partnership coproduction is a special type of coproduction that represents the production phase of an international cooperative research, development, and acquisition (ICRD&A) agreement. The first phase of an ICRD&A agreement is commonly referred to as codevelopment. In partnership coproduction arrangements, FACO is generally carried out in both of the participating countries. Partnership coproduction thus implies a qualitatively more profound level of collaboration, since both R&D and production are shared among two or more allies.

These international collaborative activities can be supported by several different types of cross-border business relationships. As shown

---

[22]In cases where the offset required for the sale of a U.S.-developed system involves transfer of rights to overseas FACO, the activity is classified as coproduction and not as a cross-border shipment.

in Table 2.2, the most common relationships among defense aerospace companies fall into the following categories:

- Prime/subcontractor;
- Marketing agreement;
- Team;
- Joint venture; and
- Parent/subsidiary.

All of the relationships are also more or less common among domestic firms within a purely national context.

Prime/subcontractor arrangements are traditional business relationships found throughout many industries. Under these arrangements, the system designer/integrator (the prime contractor) hires other firms to manufacture—and, increasingly, to design and develop—particular subsystems and components. Primes possess final decisionmaking authority for the overall design, development, integration, and (usually) final assembly of the aircraft and are responsible for marketing the finished aircraft. Primes may choose to work with foreign subcontractors for a number of reasons, but market access considerations are often just as or more important to them than cost considerations. Much of the international trade in defense aerospace subsystems, parts, and components takes place between subcontractors and primes located across national borders.

In the international arena, marketing agreements represent a set of arrangements whereby a firm in one country acquires the right to market and distribute a system or subsystem developed by a firm in another country. International marketing agreements are often set up to allow foreign firms to access national markets in which legal and/or political conditions heavily favor domestic firms. These types of agreements often involve significant modification of the original system, either by the original developer or by the foreign marketer of the system, and tend to be carried out through licensed coproduction. They are often industry-initiated.

Teams are created when companies agree to work together to pursue a particular project or an entire market segment. An important char-

Table 2.2

nmon Types of Cross-Border Business Relationships Within the Defense Aerospace Industry

Description	R
One company (the prime) hires another company (the subcontractor) to perform a specific ta The subcontractor is legally required to meet objectives specified under the terms of the contr May be government- or industry-initiated.	
Two or more companies agree to distribute an existing product, i.e., one that has already been developed by one of the partners. Marketing agreements may include modification of the item licensed coproduction of the item by the nondeveloping partner. Industry-initiated.	
Two or more companies agree to work together as approximately equal partners to pursue a specific project or a larger market segment. Our focus is on teams formed to cooperatively dev and/or manufacture products under collaborative production or FMS coproduction arrangem May be government- or industry-initiated.	
Two or more companies form a separate legal entity in order to pursue a particular program o larger market segment. Our focus is on joint ventures formed to cooperatively develop and/ov manufacture products. Industry-initiated.	
One company (the subsidiary) is wholly owned or effectively controlled by another company l parent) physically located in another country. A subsidiary may be formed either as a new establishment or as a result of a purchase of an existing establishment. Our focus is on the for acquisition of established U.S. defense firms or divisions of firms and vice versa. Industry-init	

acteristic of teams—as opposed to, say, parent/subsidiary relation-ships—is that international teams are not formally subject to CFIUS review (see Chapter Four).[23] Teams formed to target entire market segments are sometimes called "strategic alliances." Decision-making authority within teams is shared; who decides what and how depends on rules established by the team members or, if the team was initiated by governments, sometimes by the participating governments. We are most interested in teams that are formed for purposes of codevelopment and partnership coproduction or for FMS coproduction.

Finally, international subsidiaries and joint ventures are each created when a parent company in one country either acquires an existing foreign firm or establishes a new affiliate in a foreign country—or, in other words, engages in direct investment abroad. For many but not all legal purposes, both subsidiaries and joint ventures are indepen-dent entities from the parent companies that control them. In the past, international joint ventures were generally formed in order to target specific weapon system programs; more recently they also ap-pear to serve as "test runs" for the potential merger of their parent companies. Foreign subsidiaries are established or acquired for a number of reasons, including access to foreign technology, access to a foreign market, and economies of scope and scale. Although joint ventures and parent/subsidiary relationships are both industry-initi-ated, a key difference between them is the nature of management control. While subsidiaries are controlled by a single parent, joint ventures must answer to two. Because corporate parents can have conflicting—or just different—goals and priorities, joint ventures frequently do not have a long life-span.

---

[23]It is sometimes difficult to distinguish between teams and more formal prime/subcontractor relationships. On the JSF program, for example, Northrop Grumman and BAE Systems are formally subcontractors but are often described as part of a Lockheed-led team.

U.S. TRADE IN AEROSPACE AND ARMS: STATISTICAL EVIDENCE

Trade in Aerospace Products: A Statistical Snapshot

In absolute terms, according to AIA (2000), U.S. exports of aerospace products in 1999 totaled just over $62 billion, while imports stood at less than half that amount, at $25 billion. The export orientation of U.S. aerospace producers is evident when exports and imports are measured in relation to total U.S. production and apparent consumption of aerospace products: Between 1997 and 1999, U.S. aerospace exports on average accounted for roughly 44 percent of total U.S. aerospace product shipments, while U.S. aerospace imports accounted for roughly 22 percent of all U.S. aerospace consumption (ITA, 2000).[24] As shown in Figure 2.1, compared with several other high-technology and manufacturing industries over the same period, the difference between import and export shares places the aerospace industry squarely at the export-dependent end of the spectrum.

More detailed data, however, reveal some divergence within the industry. ITA (2000) divides the U.S. aerospace industry into six segments:

- Complete aircraft, accounting for about 47 percent of all U.S. aerospace shipments by value in 1999;

- Aircraft engines and their parts, accounting for about 18 percent of shipments;

- Aircraft parts and equipment, accounting for about 20 percent of shipments;

- Guided missiles and finished space vehicles, accounting for about 11 percent of shipments;

- Space propulsion units and parts, accounting for about 3 percent of shipments; and

---

[24]Following the ITA, export dependence ratios are calculated by dividing exports by total shipments (production), while import penetration ratios are derived by dividing imports by "apparent consumption"—that is, by the sum of total shipments and total imports less total exports.

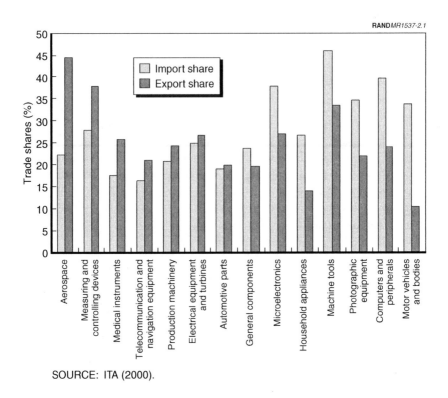

SOURCE: ITA (2000).

Figure 2.1—Trade Shares of U.S. Consumption and Shipments for Selected Manufacturing Industries (1997–1999 averages)

- Space vehicle equipment, accounting for about 2 percent of shipments.

As shown in Figure 2.2, between 1997 and 1999 the average difference between export and import shares was widest for complete aircraft, where the export share of product shipments was about 54 percent and the import share of consumption about 18 percent. The export and import shares for aircraft parts and equipment, space vehicle equipment, and guided missiles and space vehicles also diverged significantly, with the export shares all much higher. The ex-

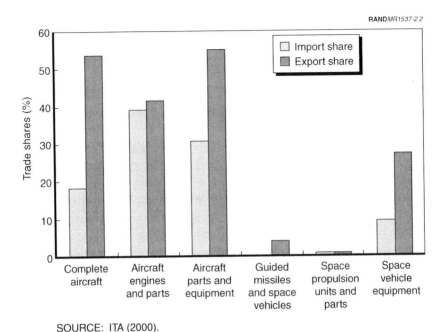

RAND*MR1537-2.2*

SOURCE: ITA (2000).

**Figure 2.2—Trade Shares of U.S. Consumption and Shipments for Six
Aerospace Industry Subcategories (1997–1999 averages)**

port and import shares for engines and engine parts and for space propulsion units and parts, however, were nearly the same.[25]

Unfortunately, ITA does not distinguish between military and nonmilitary categories of products for the six aerospace industry segments described above. However, by combining ITA and AIA data we can compare the export and import shares for complete military and civil aircraft (Figure 2.3).[26] The differences between export and import shares—and between military and civil aircraft trade—are striking. For military aircraft, the average export share of shipments from 1997 to 1999 was about 24 percent. The import

---

[25]Note that there is very little trade in space propulsion units and parts.

[26]As a result of differences in coverage, these numbers are not strictly comparable to those presented above.

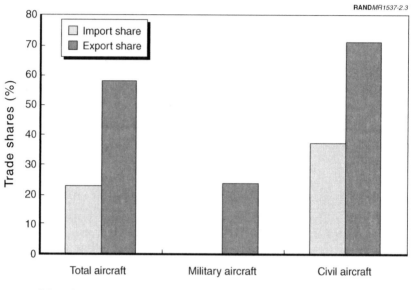

SOURCE: ITA (2000); AIA (2000).

**Figure 2.3—Trade Shares of U.S. Military and Civil Aircraft Consumption
and Shipments (1997–1999 averages)**

share of consumption over the same period was less than 1
percent—invisible in the figure. For civil aircraft, the export share of
shipments over the period was about 71 percent, while the import
share of consumption was about 37 percent.

These numbers support two conclusions: first, that the United States
imports almost no finished military aircraft; and second, that exports
play a smaller role for producers of military aircraft than they do for
producers of nonmilitary aircraft.

Finally, ITA provides some country-specific data on U.S. aerospace
trade.[27] These data are limited, however, because they are available
only for the industry in aggregate; no breakdowns by military or
nonmilitary end use or by manufacturing stage are available. As

_____

[27]The country-specific data provided by AIA come from ITA.

shown in Table 2.3, the top export market for U.S. aerospace products in 1998 was the United Kingdom, followed by Japan, Saudi Arabia, France, and Germany. With respect to imports, the top supplier to the U.S. market in 1998 was France; the UK, Canada, Japan, and Germany round out the top five.[28]

Trade in Conventional Arms: A Statistical Snapshot

The three primary sources of data on the global arms market (that is, conventional arms production and transfers) all agree that the United States is the world's leading exporter and producer of conventional arms (Table 2.4). Between 1995 and 1999, U.S. producers accounted for roughly half of all world exports and about the same share of world production. The top four exporting countries—the United States, the UK, France, and Russia—accounted for between 75 and 85 percent of the global market, depending on the data source and time period chosen. Delivery data for 1997–1999 from IISS, for example, identify the world's top three exporters as the United States, UK, and France, together accounting for about 80 percent of all conventional arms exports over that period (IISS, 2000). The top exporters were also the top producers overall: SIPRI finds, for example, that the world's three largest arms-producing countries in

Table 2.3

U.S. Trade Patterns in Aerospace, 1998

	Exports			Imports	
	Value ($M)	Share (%)		Value ($M)	Share (%)
United Kingdom	7248	12	France	5539	25
Japan	5922	10	United Kingdom	4635	21
Saudi Arabia	4946	8	Canada	4445	20
France	4100	7	Japan	1878	8
Germany	4048	7	Germany	1841	8
Top five	26,264	44	Top five	18,338	82

SOURCES: ITA (2000); AIA (2000).

---

[28]France's position as the top exporter of aerospace products to the United States is probably due to shipments of commercial transports. Airbus Industries' primary assembly plant is located in Toulouse.

Table 2.4

Leading Exporters of Conventional Arms According to Three Data Sources
(percentage of world exports)

	DoS	IISS		SIPRI	
	1995–1997	1995–1997	1997–1999	1995–1997	1997–1999
United States	55	49	48	45	50
UK	13	19	18	8	7
France	8	11	14	9	13
Russia	7	6	5	15	11
United States, UK, France	76	79	80	62	70
United States, France, Russia	70	66	67	69	74
Top four	83	85	85	77	81

SOURCES: DoS (April 2000); IISS (2000); SIPRI (2000).
NOTE: Percentages are based on period average export values.

1996, excluding China, were the United States, the UK, and France (SIPRI, 2000). These three countries together accounted for slightly more than 65 percent of global production, while the United States, Russia, and France accounted for about 60 percent.[29]

As shown in Table 2.5, arms exports are highly concentrated geographically in comparison to other manufacturing exports, such as office and telecommunications equipment and automotive products. According to the World Trade Organization (WTO) (2000), the cumulative concentration ratio in 1999 for the top three countries exporting automotive products was about 44 percent. This was less than the United States' individual share of global arms exports at any time between 1995 and 1999, whether estimated by DoS, IISS, or SIPRI.

At the same time, Table 2.5 indicates that the geographic concentration of conventional arms imports is considerably lower than that for exports and also lower than that for other manufactured products. For example, SIPRI's top three arms importers—based on period average data for 1995–1999—were Taiwan, South Korea, and Saudi Arabia. Together, these three countries accounted for 20 percent of

---

[29]Calculations are based on SIPRI (2000, Table 10.7).

Table 2.5

Leading Exporters and Importers of Selected Manufactures, 1999

All Manufactures		Office Machines and Telecommunications Equipment		Automotive Products		Conventional Arms[a]	
Percentage of World Exports							
United States	14	United States	16	Germany	17	United States	51
Germany	11	Japan	12	Japan	15	Russia	15
Japan	9	Singapore[a]	8	United States	12	France	8
Top three	34	Top three	36	Top three	44	Top three	74
Percentage of World Imports							
United States	19	United States	22	United States	28	Taiwan	8
Germany	8	UK	7	Germany	8	South Korea	6
UK	6	Germany	6	Canada	8	Saudi Arabia	6
Top three	33	Top three	35	Top three	44	Top three	20

SOURCES: WTO (2000), Tables IV.30, IV.56, and IV.64; SIPRI (2000), Table 7A.1

[a]Period average data for 1995–1999.

[b]Data for Singapore include reexports.

total world imports of major conventional weapons, compared to 1999 percentages of 33, 35, and 44 percent, respectively, for the top three importers of all manufactures, office machines and telecommunications equipment, and automotive products.[30] Using the broader DoS definition of the arms trade results in a slightly different top three consisting of Taiwan, Japan, and Saudi Arabia—which together accounted for about 36 percent of average global receipts from 1995 to 1997. This estimate of the arms import concentration ratio is more in line with import ratios for other manufacturing in-

---

[30]These figures must be interpreted with care. For example, Canada's large import share of the world automotive market primarily represents imports of automotive production inputs rather than consumer purchases of finished automobiles.

dustries but is still significantly lower than any of the estimated geographic concentration ratios for arms exports.

For the United States, the combined share for the top three export destinations identified by SIPRI—which also happen to be Taiwan, South Korea, and Saudi Arabia—averaged roughly 38 percent between 1995 and 1999. If treated as a single entity, the European Union accounted for 22 percent of all U.S. deliveries over this period—a surprisingly low figure given America's historical focus on promoting transatlantic NATO equipment standardization and interoperability through collaborative programs and exports. The broader DoS estimates place Saudi Arabia, Taiwan, and Japan as the top three destinations for U.S. arms exports from 1995 to 1997. According to DoS, these three countries accounted for approximately 37 percent of U.S. deliveries to foreign countries (DoS, April 2000).

In contrast to its critical role as a major exporter of conventional arms, the United States plays a relatively modest role as an importer. From 1995 to 1997, the United States accounted for no more than 3 percent of the world's imports on average (DoS, Bureau of Verification and Compliance, 2000). Yet over the same period, the United States accounted for about 34 percent of the world's total defense expenditures. Unfortunately, the U.S. share of global weapon procurement—a more accurate measure of the demand for conventional arms—is unclear because reliable worldwide data on weapon procurement are unavailable.[31] Between 1997 and 1999, however, the U.S. share of NATO's total defense expenditures and its share of budgeted equipment procurement were both roughly equal to 60 percent, while the United States accounted for no more than about 14 percent of NATO's total arms imports (IISS, 2000; NATO, 2000b; DoS, April 2000).[32]

Those weapon systems that are bought by the United States appear to come mostly from European NATO allies and non-NATO Western Europe. SIPRI does not provide geographic breakdowns for U.S. receipts of arms from abroad, but according to DoS, European NATO

---

[31]Data on defense expenditures are an inexact proxy for procurements because they cover a broad range of nonprocurement activities.

[32]SIPRI (2000) puts the U.S. share of NATO imports at about 12 percent for the period 1995–1997 but drops it to 7.3 percent on average from 1997 to 1999.

allies plus non-NATO Western Europe accounted for roughly three-quarters of all U.S. imports from 1997 to 1999. The UK alone accounted for almost 30 percent of total U.S. arms receipts. Exports to the United States amounted to about 7 percent of European and NATO countries' total arms exports over the 1997–1999 period; in the case of the UK, the United States accounted for 10 percent of total transfers. Nevertheless, one European government agency estimates that between 1995 and 1999, the value of U.S. defense exports to Europe was more than eight times greater than the value of European exports to the United States.[33]

INTERNATIONAL INVESTMENT INVOLVING U.S. FIRMS: STATISTICAL EVIDENCE

Broad Trends in International Investment Activity

A number of data sources help place cross-border investment involving aerospace firms in the broader context of the global economy and defense-related industries. According to BEA (July 2001), in 1999 the U.S. affiliates of foreign companies accounted for a record 6.4 percent of total private-industry gross domestic product (GDP), continuing a four-year upward trend.[34] Direct investment inflows—which include equity, debt, and reinvested earnings flows to existing affiliates as well as investments in new acquisitions—were strong, increasing by 25 percent between 1999 and 2000.[35] Foreign companies and their U.S. affiliates increased their outlays for new and existing U.S. businesses by 17 percent over the same period. This unprecedented level of foreign spending to establish or acquire U.S. businesses is consistent with a worldwide increase in M&A activity in which U.S. firms were both the leading purchasers and the leading sellers (BEA, June 2001; KPMG, 2001).[36]

---

[33]This estimate was provided to the authors from a British Ministry of Defence official.

[34]See BEA (August 2001, p. 141) for details on the calculation methodology for private-industry GDP.

[35]Estimated on a current cost basis. See BEA (July 2001, p. 7) for definitions.

[36]A KPMG finance survey suggests that for the decade of the 1990s, the United States accounted for about 22 percent of the value of all cross-border purchases of companies and 30 percent of the value of all cross-border sales (KPMG, 2001).

By country of ultimate beneficial owner, BEA (June 2001) reports that European investors accounted for 75 percent of total outlays to acquire or establish U.S. businesses in 1998–2000. British investors led the pack, spending more than three times as much as investors from the country with the next-largest outlays, the Netherlands.[37] In fact, British investors accounted for fully one-third of new direct investment outlays over the period.

Strong financial ties between the United States and the UK are also evidenced in the data on U.S. direct investment abroad, where the UK is the destination of choice for many U.S. firms seeking foreign affiliates. The UK was a focal point for new U.S. investment in 1998, accounting for about 18 percent of the number, 35 percent of the asset value, and 32 percent of the sales of all newly acquired or established majority-owned foreign affiliates in 1998. According to BEA (2000b, pp. 33–34), the UK is favored by U.S. investors "because of its language and its cultural similarities with the United States, its relatively low level of market regulation . . . and its duty-free access to customers in other member countries of the European Union." Overall, total U.S. net financial outflows to all foreign affiliates were at a near record in 2000, reflecting numerous large acquisitions abroad. Net equity capital outflows (as opposed to intercompany debt or reinvested earnings) represented roughly one-third of the total (BEA, July 2001).

Mergerstat data point to an economy-wide increase in the M&A activities of all U.S. firms in terms of both numbers and value while also providing some information on the activities of aerospace firms. Figure 2.4 shows the rise in U.S. overall domestic and cross-border M&A activity over the past decade. According to Mergerstat, the U.S. aerospace industry accounted for less than one-quarter of a percent of the value of all U.S. domestic and cross-border M&As during the

---

[37]According to BEA (June 2001, p. 28), the "ultimate beneficial owner is that person, proceeding up a U.S. affiliate's ownership chain, that is not owned more than 50 percent by another person."

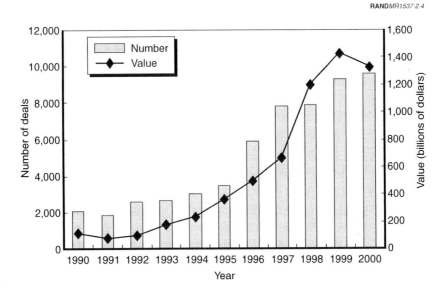

SOURCE: Downloaded with permission from Mergerstat.

NOTE: Value is the base equity price offered.

Figure 2.4—U.S. Domestic and Cross-Border Mergers and Acquisitions, 1990–2000

1990s, placing it 37th among all U.S. industries.[38] This is somewhat less than aerospace's share of domestic economic activity, which in recent years has accounted for approximately 0.7 to 0.9 percent of U.S. GDP.[39]

Mergerstat data also indicate that the aerospace industry was somewhat less active in domestic and cross-border M&As relative to other

---

[38]The aerospace data also cover firms whose primary products are combat vehicles. In 2000, the top three industries for M&As by value were computer software and services, entertainment and leisure, and banking and finance. Mergerstat tracks almost all M&A transactions that occur; however, some transactions between privately held companies may be missed.

[39]Calculated from 1997–1999 value-added data in the *Annual Survey of Manufacturers* (U.S. Department of Commerce, Bureau of the Census, 2001) and the *Economic Report of the President* (CEA, 2000).

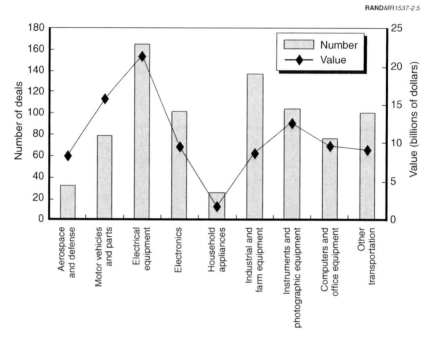

SOURCE: Downloaded with permission from Mergerstat.
NOTE: Value is the base equity price offered.

Figure 2.5—Domestic and Cross-Border Mergers and Acquisitions, Selected U.S. Manufacturing Industries (1995–1999 averages)

U.S. manufacturing industries. As shown in Figure 2.5, aerospace ranked second to last in terms of both the average number and the average total value of manufacturing M&As between 1995 and 1999. At the top of the list were electrical equipment manufacturers, followed by car companies and measuring instruments and photographic equipment manufacturers.[40]

---

[40]Unfortunately, we were not able to find data on the relative number of firms or total value of these industries. We believe it is telling, however, that the number of M&As in the category "Industrial and Farm Equipment," for example, was much higher than that for "Aerospace and Defense."

International Investment in Defense-Related Industries

In a recent DoD study, Ciardello (2001) provides information on a subset of defense-related, though not necessarily aerospace-related, foreign direct investment in the United States. The Ciardello data distinguish between total and specifically "defense-related" cases from 1996 to 2000. Of 322 CFIUS cases filed and reviewed by DoD over the past five years, the data identify 235, or nearly three-quarters, as defense-related. As shown in Figure 2.6, the number of cases reviewed has increased—though not dramatically—in recent years. This probably points to an increase in the total number of defense-related foreign acquisitions.

Figure 2.7 shows the distribution of defense-related CFIUS cases from 1996 through 2000 for the top three countries of origin. Over this five-year period, the UK, France, and the Netherlands accounted for almost two-thirds of the cases. At about 46 percent of the total, Figure 2.7 shows the distribution of defense-related CFIUS cases from 1996 through 2000 for the top three countries of origin. Over this five-year period, the UK, France, and the Netherlands accounted for almost two-thirds of the cases. At about 46 percent of the total, the UK accounted for the largest number of cases, followed by France at roughly 12 percent and the Netherlands at approximately 6 percent.

Ciardello (2001) also presents data on measures designed to eliminate possible security violations resulting from transactions that put U.S. firms under foreign ownership, control, or influence (FOCI). These measures, which are described in more detail in Chapter Four, mitigate foreign influence and control for companies performing U.S. classified work. As shown in Figure 2.8, the UK accounts for the largest single country share of FOCI mitigation measures, about 48 percent. This is consistent with the UK's dominant share of defense-related CFIUS activity as well as with its role as the single largest foreign direct investor in the U.S. economy.

Finally, the DBP's Globalization Database, described in Bitzinger (1999), distinguishes between licensed production—which is assumed to involve minimal collaboration—and more collaborative

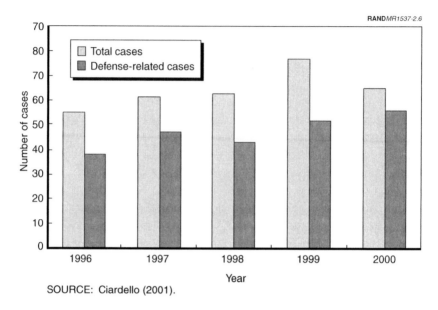

SOURCE: Ciardello (2001).

Figure 2.6—Total and Defense-Related CFIUS Reviews, 1996–2000

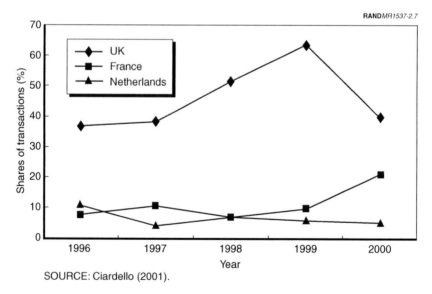

SOURCE: Ciardello (2001).

**Figure 2.7—Shares of Defense-Related CFIUS Transactions for Top Three
Countries, 1996–2000**

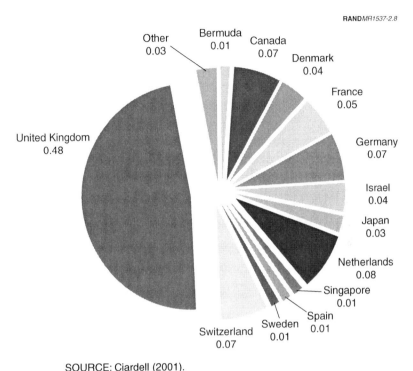

SOURCE: Ciardell (2001).

Figure 2.8—Country Shares of 75 FOCI Negation Measures

activities such as marketing agreements, coproduction, and codevelopment.[41] Within the last category, the data further distinguish between relationships initiated by governments (where company work shares are often allocated according to governmental shares of the program budget) and those initiated by industry (where cost minimization strategies are presumably more likely to be followed). Programs covered include RDT&E and production programs for large weapon systems such as aircraft, missiles, and armored vehicles, as

---

[41]Coproduction activities are defined as the "joint production of a common weapon system" (Bitzinger, 1999, p. 311). The DBP data do not distinguish between FMS coproduction and partnership coproduction programs, but both are assumed to require more complex cross-border business relationships than simple licensed production activities.

well as for major components such as radar systems and jet engines (Bitzinger, 1999, p. 331).

Figure 2.9, which uses DBP data, shows the declining numbers of traditional licensed-production arrangements relative to U.S. participation in international aircraft and missile codevelopment and coproduction programs (as defined by Bitzinger). To convey a better sense of long-term trends, program startups are organized into five-year cohorts. We see that prior to about 1981, licensed production was the dominant form of international collaboration in armament ICRD&A programs. Beginning in the early 1980s, however, licensed production began to decline in importance relative to codevelopment, partnership coproduction, and FMS coproduction.[42] By 1991–1995, licensed production program startups constituted less than half the total.

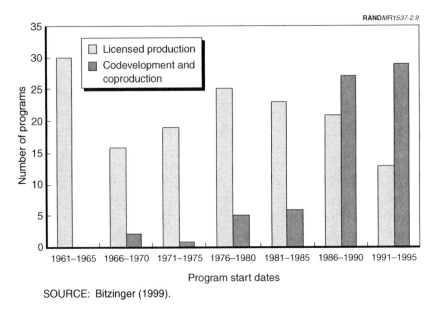

SOURCE: Bitzinger (1999).

Figure 2.9—Cross-Border Collaborative Activities of U.S. Firms in Military Aircraft and Missiles

---

[42]These figures represent startups only; some programs may not have been completed.

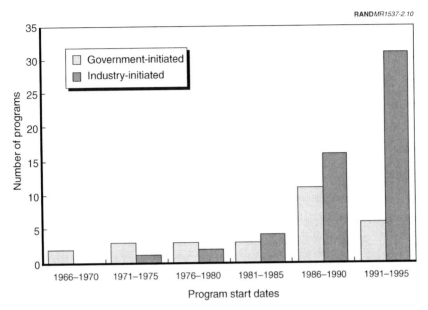

SOURCE: Bitzinger (1999).

Figure 2.10—Government-Initiated Versus Industry-Initiated U.S. Participation in Cross-Border Aircraft and Missile Programs

The DBP data also provide an important insight into the increasingly market-driven character of the relationships being formed by U.S. aerospace and other defense firms. As shown in Figure 2.10, the number of program starts involving industry-initiated collaboration among U.S. and foreign firms to market, produce, and/or develop aircraft and missile systems rose from fewer than five during the 1971–1975 period to more than 30 from 1991 to 1995. This suggests that aerospace companies, rather than national governments, are increasingly responsible for determining the nature of their own cross-border business relationships. Bitzinger (1999, p. 316), describes the trend in this way: "As a result of defense firms themselves taking the lead, international arms production increasingly has involved ever more complex, integrated, and permanent cross-border industrial partnerships."

SUMMARY OF STATISTICAL EVIDENCE

Although there is relatively little statistical data specific to defense aerospace systems and subsystems, aggregate data on the production, consumption, and trade of aerospace products—as well as on the production and international transfers of conventional armaments—reveal certain patterns that help inform our analysis of defense aerospace industry globalization. For aerospace products, our major findings are as follows:

- The U.S. aerospace industry has a strong export orientation relative to other U.S. manufacturing industries.

- Nonmilitary producers are more internationally active than are military producers.

- With the exception of aircraft engines and space propulsion units, levels of import penetration in the U.S. aerospace industry are low.

- The United States imports almost no finished military aircraft.

- In 1998, the top two destinations for U.S. combined civil and military aerospace products were the UK and Japan; the leading suppliers to U.S. industry were France and the UK.

For conventional armaments, we found the following:

- The United States leads the world in both the export and the production of conventional arms.

- Exports and production of conventional arms are highly concentrated geographically relative to other manufacturing industries.

- Global imports are fairly diffuse geographically.

- The United States leads the world in defense expenditures but receives relatively few conventional arms transfers from abroad.

- U.S. purchases of foreign armaments come overwhelmingly from Europe, primarily from the UK.

With respect to financial flows, aggregate data on foreign direct investment in the United States as well as U.S. direct investment abroad indicate the following:

- U.S. firms are both the leading purchasers of foreign firms and the leading targets of foreign acquirers.

- Europeans, led by the British, are the most active foreign investors in U.S. businesses, while the UK is the most popular destination for new U.S. investment abroad.

- The number and value of U.S. domestic and cross-border mergers rose dramatically during the 1990s.

Data on selected foreign direct investments in U.S. defense companies and on international collaborative activities suggest that

- There has been a slight increase in CFIUS reviews of foreign defense acquisitions in recent years.

- Two-thirds of the cases reviewed by CFIUS involved British, French, or Dutch firms, with British firms alone accounting for almost half the cases.

- Traditional licensed production arrangements are declining in importance relative to U.S. participation in codevelopment and coproduction programs (as defined by Bitzinger, 1999).

- Aerospace companies, rather than national governments, are increasingly responsible for determining the nature of their own cross-border relationships.

Our analysis of the statistical data confirms two frequently stated observations about the U.S. defense aerospace industry: Its products are highly competitive on world markets, and it is not very reliant on foreign suppliers. Although the data on cross-border investment in defense cannot automatically be extrapolated to aerospace firms, they are also consistent with the observation that U.S. defense firms are partnering with foreign firms in a variety of ways for a variety of activities. British firms are frequently their partners of choice.

What these statistical snapshots cannot tell us is how patterns of trade and investment in defense aerospace have changed over time; how they have been affected by changes in the U.S. regulatory environment or in DoD policy; or what sorts of opportunities and challenges these changes pose to the Air Force. For example, the statistical data do not reveal to what extent offset agreements—such as counterpurchases of goods, technology transfers, credit transfers, and various forms of investment—have been imposed on would-be exporters. Nor do they record the capabilities or degree of sophistication of defense aerospace exports and imports. With the exception of Bitzinger (1999), the data do not provide any information about the companies that develop and produce air-based weapon systems—for example, who their suppliers and partners are or to what extent they rely on foreign inputs, foreign technology, or foreign markets. Finally, the data do not provide sufficient information to assess whether and how much current patterns might change in the absence of existing U.S. government legislation, regulations, and statutes.

In the section that follows, we present a brief historical overview of some of the major trends in U.S. defense aerospace system trade and cross-border business relationships. With this short descriptive survey, we hope to deepen our understanding of the changes that are taking place both in the United States and overseas, thereby helping identify key issues the Air Force must address with respect to shaping and managing those changes.

DEFENSE AEROSPACE GLOBALIZATION: HISTORICAL TRENDS

Trends in U.S. Defense Aerospace Exports

As revealed by the statistical snapshot above, the United States is the world's undisputed leader in arms exports, laying claim to more than half of the global market. Yet the characteristics and requirements of the arms export market have changed significantly over the decades since the end of World War II. These changes in arms export markets have greatly contributed to the evolution of the more complex business relationships we observe today.

For approximately the first two decades following World War II, U.S. contractors typically exported finished defense goods—including complete military aircraft—even to industrially sophisticated Western European markets. In the 1950s, for example, the Republic F-84 and the North American F-86 were widely exported as complete aircraft to countries with historically robust military aircraft industries, such as France.[43]

By the late 1960s, however, many European countries as well as Japan increasingly insisted on coproducing U.S.-designed military aircraft under license rather than importing finished products. One of the most important early programs involved the coproduction of the Lockheed F-104G (a specially modified variant of the F-104A) by a consortium of European countries that included Germany, Italy, Belgium, and the Netherlands.[44] Initially, Lockheed provided complete aircraft. Next, knockdown kits of parts of aircraft for FACO overseas were provided along with extensive technical manufacturing process and engineering assistance. Over time, however, the European partners began to build more and more of the F-104G and its subcomponents indigenously while simultaneously undertaking FACO. Some European coproducers, such as the Germans, even began to modify and develop their own manufacturing processes for various parts of the U.S.-designed aircraft.[45]

By the 1970s, Western European countries with a long history of indigenous aircraft development were no longer interested in importing finished U.S. military aircraft or in coproducing them. Instead, France, Germany, the UK, and Italy moved toward the development and production of indigenous or collaboratively developed European combat aircraft, including the French Mirage III/5/2000 series, the British/French Jaguar, the British/German/Italian Tornado, and the French/German Alpha Jet.[46] Although "second-tier" European NATO countries such as Belgium and the Netherlands continued to coproduce U.S. aircraft (e.g., the Northrop F-5 and the Lockheed/General Dynamics F-16), it had become clear that with the possible exception of highly specialized, low-production platforms, the leading European countries were unlikely ever again to buy or

---

[43]Many of these exports were elements of U.S. military assistance programs to European allies still recovering from the ravages of World War II.

[44]The F-104 was also coproduced in Canada and Japan.

[45]From an interview with a German government defense procurement official.

[46]Sweden maintained its long tradition of developing its own indigenous fighter designs throughout the jet era but imported some U.S. components and subsystems.

coproduce a wholly U.S.-developed fighter or other first-line combat aircraft.[47]

In the 1960s and 1970s, U.S. companies did continue to export finished combat aircraft to developing countries such as Turkey; these deals often involved specially designed, lower-capability export combat aircraft such as the Northrop F-5. By the 1980s and 1990s, however, even developing countries began to demand and receive first-line U.S. combat aircraft. They also began insisting on offsets, including coproduction and technology transfer. With European manufacturers competing with increasing vigor for every third-country sale of combat aircraft, competitive pressure on U.S. manufacturers grew more intense. In order to sell its F-16 to Turkey in the 1980s, for example, General Dynamics (now Lockheed Martin) agreed to coproduce and to establish a manufacturing facility outside Ankara that duplicated on a smaller scale its vast production facilities in Fort Worth, Texas. General Dynamics also agreed to seek out and train Turkish firms to manufacture even some of the most sophisticated components of the fire control radar and other electronics.[48]

Table 2.6 shows some typical examples of the more complex business activities involved in recent export sales. The Greek Air Force's third purchase lot of F-16s, concluded in the spring of 1999, includes offsets in the form of related subcontracts and involves an upgraded long-range variant with conformal fuel tanks (F-16 Block 50+) that is not in the U.S. Air Force inventory. The sale was a commercial deal rather than part of a government-sponsored FMS program. The Israeli Air Force, which already operates the largest fleet of F-16s outside the U.S. Air Force, decided to purchase more of a specially modified Block 50+ variant in July 1999. The Israeli variant incorporates major airframe modifications not seen on U.S. Air Force F-16s, including conformal fuel tanks and, on some two-seat models, a

---

[47]European purchases of specialized U.S.-developed aircraft include the French Navy's purchase of the Grumman E-2C airborne early warning (AEW) aircraft and both French and British purchases of the Boeing E-3 Airborne Warning and Control System (AWACS).

[48]Turkey later gained the right to produce F-16s for a third-country sale to Egypt. As of this writing, 13 foreign countries are involved in offset agreements that include coproduction of the F-16 or supplier relationships on the program.

Table 2.6

Examples of Recent U.S. Military Aerospace System Exports

System	Purchaser	Conditions of Sale or Prospective Sale
F-16	Korea, Greece, Israel	Offsets, modifications
E-3 AWACS	France, UK	Offsets of 130 percent
F-16C/D Block 60+	United Arab Emirates	Major modification R&D
F-X program	South Korea	Baseline 70 percent industrial offset; other technology transfer and assistance

special humped dorsal spine stretching from the cockpit to the vertical stabilizer. This special spine is used for the installation of Israeli electronic warfare (EW) systems and other avionics. According to one report, an upgraded radar jointly developed by U.S. and Israeli industry will also be installed. Up to one-quarter of the manufacturing work will be conducted in Israel (Dworkin, 1999).[49] These modifications are intended to transform the Israeli two-seat variant of the F-16 into a long-range interdictor, or a "poor man's" F-15E. The aircraft will thus be used for different types of missions than are typical for standard U.S. Air Force F-16s. Lockheed subsequently sold the same dorsal hump airframe modification to Singapore, but with different avionics.

The United Arab Emirates (UAE) F-16 deal finally approved in the summer of 2000, which called for 60 dramatically upgraded Block 60+ fighters, is particularly revealing. The UAE F-16 will include mostly new avionics, the most important of which will be an active electronically scanned array (AESA) fire control radar developed by Northrop Grumman Electronic Systems. The new radar and avionics will make the UAE F-16 more capable in some respects than any F-16 in the U.S. Air Force inventory. This program is also of interest because its final approval was delayed more than one year as a result of a dispute over the transfer of sensitive software source code to the purchaser.

---

[49]Although the Israeli F-16I is a specially modified variant not used in the U.S. Air Force inventory, it is still considered an FMS coproduction arrangement because U.S. military assistance funds will be used to purchase the aircraft.

Finally, the competition for the Korean F-X future fighter, which was nearing its climax in late 2001, illustrates the intensity of competition between U.S and European contractors for the few large fighter-aircraft export deals that remain. It also illustrates how these competitions lead to extraordinary offers of offsets and technology transfer to the buyer. The finalists in this competition in late 2001 were Boeing St. Louis with its F-15K; the British/German/Italian/Spanish Eurofighter consortium with its Typhoon; Dassault Aviation with its Rafale; and Russia's Rosvorgenia with its Sukhoi Su-37. A baseline requirement established by the Korean government was at least a 70 percent direct industrial offset arrangement. In addition, Korean President Kim Dae Jung stated in March 2001 that Korea intended to begin the development of a new-generation indigenous fighter by 2005, implying that the winner of the F-X competition should offer technology and design and engineering assistance in achieving this goal.

Not surprisingly, all four competitors claimed that their offset packages would exceed the 70 percent baseline, with each insisting that it would transfer the most technology and know-how if chosen. In addition, each argued that its proposal would do the most to support Korea's efforts to develop a new-generation indigenous fighter by 2015. Dassault, for example, offered a direct partnership with Korean Aerospace Industries in manufacturing a significant percentage of the Rafale for the French armed forces and other foreign buyers as well as for the Korean Air Force. The French also argued that their technology transfer package was aimed specifically at aiding the development of a Korean indigenous fighter in 15 years. Boeing went one step further and "guaranteed the development of an indigenous fighter by 2015" if its F-15K was chosen (Kim, 2001).

The severe competitive pressures associated with programs such as the F-X—where foreign governments are able to demand generous direct offsets and significant technology transfer from firms and consortia that believe they must win to remain economically viable—has resulted in heavy lobbying by U.S. primes and industry associations to further liberalize U.S. export regulations and procedures. In the case of the Boeing F-15, which lost a hard-fought battle with the Lockheed F-16 for the Israeli fighter program in July 1999, a loss in the Korean program could mean the permanent shutdown of the F-15 production line, and with it the disappearance of a significant percentage of the work performed at its St. Louis facilities.[50] With so much at stake, it is not surprising that competing prime contractors are now routinely offering extremely generous offset and technology transfer incentives—and that U.S. firms bitterly complain about the export and technology transfer restrictions under which they must operate in this area compared to their European competitors.[51]

Trends in U.S. Defense Aerospace Imports

Several points can be made with respect to the post–World War II history of U.S. imports of finished combat aircraft, which stands in stark contrast to U.S. export history:

- Imports are rare.

- They are usually UK-developed.

- They usually involve significant modification by U.S. contractors.

- They are largely coproduced in the United States.

With the possible exception of the British Aerospace (now BAE Systems) AV-8A Harrier, the United States has never deployed a first-line jet fighter/attack aircraft developed in a foreign country. In the early 1950s, the U.S. Air Force did procure a version of the English Electric Canberra twin-engine jet bomber. Called the B-57 in U.S. Air Force service, the Canberra was built under license by Martin Aircraft. However, most of the versions built in the United States were significantly modified to meet U.S. requirements.

The only combat aircraft in U.S. service to be built largely overseas was the AV-8A Harrier. As a result of U.S. Marine Corps requirements, however, this aircraft was also modified. The follow-on AV-8B Harrier II is a radically modified Harrier developed primarily by

---

[50]The pressure on Boeing to win the F-X competition became even greater following the October 26, 2001, announcement that Lockheed Martin had been selected over Boeing to lead the development of the JSF.

[51]On the other hand, European producers claim that U.S. firms (in this case Boeing) have a significant advantage because of the close security relationship between the United States and Korea, as well as the fact that purchase of the F-15K would provide the Korean Air Force with greater standardization and interoperability with U.S. forces.

McDonnell Douglas (now Boeing) and coproduced with BAE Systems for both the UK and the United States. Indeed, the AV-8B Harrier II is virtually an all-new aircraft in design and materials. Similarly, the T-45 Goshawk, the U.S. Navy's advanced jet trainer version of the BAE Hawk Royal Air Force trainer/light attack aircraft, includes numerous modifications to meet U.S. Navy requirements. Coproduced by BAE Systems and Boeing St. Louis (the prime contractor), it entered service in the early 1990s.

The Joint Primary Aircraft Training System (JPATS), which later became the Raytheon Beech T-6 Texan II, was intended to be a lightly modified off-the-shelf nondevelopmental item (NDI) from a foreign contractor teamed with a U.S. firm for coproduction in the United States. The goal was to reduce procurement costs and eliminate development costs. The Swiss Pilatus PC-9 won the original competition, but Navy and Air Force requirements as well as developmental problems evolved in such a way that they ultimately led to major modifications of the original aircraft.[52] The resulting Raytheon Beech T-6A Texan II is practically an all-new aircraft that is manufactured at the Raytheon Beech Wichita plant. This program, too, would appear to illustrate that when the United States imports a foreign platform—which it rarely does—it often modifies that platform so significantly that anticipated benefits from the elimination of development costs are substantially reduced. Table 2.7 shows several examples of recent foreign-developed military aircraft and other aerospace system imports to the United States.

In areas other than complete combat aircraft, there have been several instances in which the United States has imported off-the-shelf foreign items. Often, U.S. firms have later developed long-term strategic relationships with the foreign partner to upgrade and further market such items. Prime examples include the original Popeye/HAVE NAP air-to-ground missile developed by the Israeli

---

[52]Each of the seven competing foreign developers was teamed with a U.S. contractor; for example, Pilatus was teamed with Beech/Raytheon.

Table 2.7

Examples of Recent U.S. Military Aerospace System Imports

U.S. System and Contractor	Country of Origin	Original System and Contractor
AV-8A Harrier	UK	Modified BAE Harrier combat aircraft
AV-8B Harrier, coproduced by Boeing (formerly McDonnell Douglas)	UK	Radically modified BAE Harrier combat aircraft
T-45 Goshawk, coproduced by Boeing	UK	Modified BAE Hawk trainer/light attack aircraft
T-6A Texan II (JPATS), produced by Raytheon Beech	Switzerland	Greatly modified Pilatus PC-9 combat trainer
Popeye/HAVE NAP[a]	Israel	Air-to-ground missile developed by the Rafael Armament Authority
Pioneer unpiloted aerial vehicle (UAV)	Israel	Surveillance aircraft developed by Israel Aircraft Industries (IAI)

[a]See Chapter Five for more on the Popeye.

Rafael Armament Authority and the Pioneer unpiloted aerial vehicle (UAV) developed by Israel Aircraft Industries (IAI). In both cases, the foreign firm eventually formed joint ventures with U.S. companies to facilitate the marketing and support of the item for the U.S. government. In 1991, IAI joined with the U.S. AAI Corporation, located in Hunt Valley, Maryland, to form a jointly owned corporation called Pioneer UAV, Inc., to act as the prime contractor to the U.S. government. The Pioneer was procured by the U.S. Navy, Marines, and Army and was extensively employed in the Gulf War. AAI later developed at least two improved upgraded variants of the Pioneer, the Shadow 200 and the Shadow 600. It is unclear from published sources whether or not these improved versions were developed in collaboration with IAI.

The U.S. Air Force originally bought the Popeye, an air-to-ground standoff missile, directly off the shelf from Rafael. However, Rafael later formed a joint venture with Lockheed to continue upgrading and marketing the Popeye. These changed business arrangements for the same foreign system are discussed in greater detail in Chapter Five.

CONCLUSION

In conclusion, aerospace exporting on the weapon system platform level, which once involved the relatively straightforward sale and transfer of finished goods from the supplier/developer to the purchaser, has evolved to encompass a wide variety of complex business arrangements involving a range of activities, including countertrade, offsets, coproduction, foreign investment, marketing agreements, major cooperative R&D and modification efforts, and significant technology transfer issues. Major trends in U.S. combat aircraft exports since the 1950s include the following:

- A move away from lower-capability export aircraft and other systems to high-end aircraft and systems closer in capabilities to those in the U.S. inventory;

- The growing importance of industrial and technological offsets;

- An increasing trend toward FMS and licensed coproduction of the purchased item in the purchasing country;

- The increasing importance of direct commercial sales compared to U.S. government–administered FMS;

- The emergence of significantly modified variants developed by U.S. contractors, sometimes in collaboration with foreign contractors, solely for the use of foreign customers; and

- Growing involvement of the purchaser in R&D, combined with increased demand for access to U.S. technology.

Nevertheless, U.S. primes often believe they are at a disadvantage when competing with European contractors because of the perception of more restrictive and bureaucratic procedures imposed by the U.S. government for export control, technology transfer, and offsets.

On the import side, the U.S. government appears to have benefited from the rare cases in which it has imported major systems. In the case of the original Harrier, the United States benefited by buying off the shelf a unique technology developed overseas. Building on that technology, the United States subsequently developed much more capable variants. In both cases, standardization and interoperability were enhanced with a key ally, the UK. In the case of the Popeye and the Pioneer UAV, the U.S. armed forces were able to gain quick access to existing systems that had no exact equivalent in the United States. Later, U.S. industry was also able to build on and improve the technology from these imported systems.

The export and import of finished aerospace goods now involves all categories of cross-border business relationships and activities that we have identified in our typologies. The substantive program differences between the export of systems and subsystems on the one hand and cooperative development and cross-border investment on the other have continued to diminish. As a result, the regulatory regime and issues of technology security have become much more prominent and complex, as demonstrated by the UAE F-16 sale and the Korean F-X program.

However, unique concerns about national security have given rise to a host of policy instruments that may be affecting the development of the aerospace market and may possibly explain some of the patterns that we observe in the data. Some of these instruments seek to promote cross-border activities, while others—such as the International Traffic in Arms Regulations (ITAR), which set controls for U.S. exports of weapons and technology, the Buy American Act, which places limits on U.S. government purchases of foreign supplies; and the CFIUS process, which oversees foreign capital inflows—seek to restrict them. Whether these restrictive instruments create unnecessary or undesirable barriers to trade, investment, and other business relationships has been the subject of an ongoing debate that is discussed in Chapter Three. At the same time, other international programs, such as FMS and Foreign Military Financing (FMF), may serve to subsidize and encourage U.S. weapon exports.

Because the intent of these policy instruments is to protect national security, the central question for policymakers is not whether they affect cross-border trade, investment, and other business activities—they are intended to do so—but whether they affect such activities unnecessarily or undesirably. U.S. policy instruments, including those that seek to promote international transactions, may affect both the extent of cross-border activity and its character. Firms may be opting for or against particular forms of cross-border collaboration in response to the policy environment. In addition, other, more subtle market conditions, such as purchasers' attitudes, may affect firms' behavior as well. If purchasers in the United States and overseas are more comfortable buying domestically, it may be difficult for U.S. firms to enter foreign markets and for foreign firms to enter U.S. markets.

A key step in developing an Air Force strategy for managing globalization is to better understand why, in practice, certain types of activities seem to be associated with certain types of business relationships. It is of particular interest to clarify whether these relationships and activities generally support the three overarching Air Force objectives identified in Chapter One: enhanced market sector competition (with its attendant benefits, price reduction, and technical innovation), standardization or interoperability with key allies, and preservation of national security. This question is the focus of the chapter that follows.

Chapter Three

THE GLOBALIZING AEROSPACE INDUSTRY: OPPORTUNITIES AND CHALLENGES

INTRODUCTION

A review of DoD and Air Force policy documents identifies three overarching objectives that motivate Air Force concerns about globalization of the defense aerospace industrial base:

1. The need to equip aerospace forces with affordable yet highly capable weapon systems, both today and in the future (the economic and technological dimension);

2. The need to prepare the United States, its allies, and other friends to fight future wars as coalitions (the political-military dimension); and

3. The need to protect U.S. national security (the national security dimension).

These objectives are not necessarily presented in order of importance, and they do not necessarily conflict. In many cases, the same policy or policies can support all three. Policies promoting trade among allies in weapon systems and parts, for example, can lower costs, spur innovation, help close technology gaps, and enhance interoperability, thereby strengthening allied coalitions. Strong coalitions in turn strengthen national security. However, policies that create opportunities under some circumstances can create challenges in others; for example, if insufficiently monitored or controlled, trade can also facilitate weapon proliferation.

A review of recent studies of globalization reveals that most such analyses focus on the commercial sector. As a result, the standards these studies use to evaluate the pros and cons of globalization are often strictly economic. Consequently, these efforts—while useful for assessing the impact of globalization on the first objective listed above—do not and generally cannot address the second or third objectives listed above. Analyses of commercial sector globalization can help us assess globalization's potential effect on the cost, quality, and technical innovation of weapon systems but not its effect on the interoperability of allied equipment or its implications for U.S. national security.

More promising for our purposes are the much smaller number of studies that have explored the implications of defense sector globalization, many of which have been produced by and for the U.S. government, particularly DoD.[1] These studies examine the national security as well as the economic dimensions of defense sector globalization but generally say little about its implications for coalition warfighting capability. They also tend not to make strong distinctions between markets for relatively low-value components and markets for high-value items such as defense aerospace systems, subsystems, structures, and major parts. This distinction is important because we believe that the globalization of high-value activities is both more promising in terms of coalition operations and more problematic in terms of national security.

Another important issue sometimes missed by studies of the defense sector is the distinction between globalization of supply and globalization of demand, each of which poses a different set of opportunities and challenges to the Air Force.[2] National security considerations aside, there is nothing structurally different about the design,

---

[1]We acknowledge that as a practical matter, it is often difficult if not impossible to separate developments in the defense sector from developments in the commercial sector. Many Air Force contractors have direct ties to the commercial world through the sale of commercial products ranging from business jets to home appliances. Still more have indirect ties through the use of commercially derived technologies and inputs. Therefore, while this chapter—and, indeed, this report—focuses on the defense aerospace industry, the growing commercialization of that industry implies growing dependence on an already highly globalized commercial world.

[2]DSB (1999) does separately consider the globalization of demand, which it terms "product market globalization."

development, and production of combat aircraft as opposed to most high-technology commercial manufactures. In principle, defense aerospace prime contractors and their suppliers could operate from facilities all over the world even if DoD were their only client. While the national security implications of such a global diversification of supply would be significant, the economic costs and benefits would be the same as those for any commercial industry. The Air Force would benefit to the extent that production costs are lower in other countries and would lose to the extent that transportation and monitoring costs are higher. Coalition warfighting ability would not be affected because the achievement of interoperability is primarily a function of globalized demand, not supply.

The nature of demand for the products of defense industries, however, is inherently different from that of most commercial industries. Unlike the demand for automobiles, for example, where global expansion offers firms the opportunity to reach millions of autonomous consumers worldwide who have no reason to know or care about each others' resources or needs, the demand for weapons and weapon system platforms consists of a relatively small number of "consumers" made up overwhelmingly of national governments.[3] These governments have considerable control over the follow-on marketing of platforms and systems for which they are the principal funders. Thus, many of the benefits of globalization can be realized only if two or more governments choose to coordinate their requirements or if one or more governments choose and are permitted to adopt a system or platform selected by a first.[4]

To cite an example, studies often identify economies of scale as a major benefit of globalization for consumers. In the commercial sector, this is reasonable in that the globalization of supply and that of demand almost always move together. Suppliers from around the world seek to enter a large number of markets and thereby lower their unit costs of production. If these markets are competitive, consumers worldwide benefit from the resulting price declines. If

---

[3]The market for small arms much more closely resembles commercial markets in this respect.

[4]This is somewhat less true for design, because design innovations may be applicable to a wide range of aircraft.

worldwide growth in demand is slow or stagnant, however, globalization's potential for achieving economies of scale is limited. Because consumers have strong reasons not to want any individual supplier to become dominant, antitrust laws in most countries require that at least two or more firms compete for any market. This limits the potential for achieving full economies of scale in any single market.

As shown in the previous chapter, global demand for defense aerospace products—particularly for technologically advanced weapons and weapon system platforms—is dominated by the United States. Since U.S. demand for any particular system or platform is unaffected by the existence of a global supply base, all else equal, globalization of supply is not likely to offer the Air Force much in the way of economies of scale. As we discuss below, however, globalization of supply can offer a great deal in terms of labor cost and other types of savings. Further, all else may not be equal: Under the right circumstances, globalization of the supply base may actually encourage globalization of demand.

In this chapter, we use analyses presented in both the commercial and defense sector literature to assess what the extent and character of U.S. defense aerospace industry globalization may imply for all three of the Air Force objectives listed above. Although we discuss issues surrounding globalization of the low-value parts and components supplier base, our focus is on the globalization of the design, development, manufacture, and integration of high-value items.

ECONOMIC DIMENSIONS OF DEFENSE AEROSPACE GLOBALIZATION

A large body of literature documents the economic benefits provided by globalization of the U.S. economy. At the industry level, both the broadly commercial and the specifically defense-oriented literatures typically argue that market opening lowers costs, raises productivity, improves quality, and promotes innovation.

Although some of these benefits are one-time, others, such as those affecting productivity, have longer-term effects. Competitive pressure is key to delivering all of these gains, creating incentives for domestic firms either to improve or to go out of business. Foreign competition, or the credible threat of competition, can help dilute domestic firms' power in highly concentrated markets. Thus, from the Air Force's perspective, globalization may help mitigate some of the less desirable consequences of aerospace consolidation by increasing the number of firms bidding on contracts.

Globalization also presents economic challenges. Featuring prominently in anti-globalization arguments, for example, are concerns about unemployed workers and about unprofitable and underutilized plants and equipment.

At the macro level, globalization causes some industries to expand while others contract as resources shift in response to opportunities abroad and foreign competition at home. Workers in declining industries may become redundant if their skills do not match requirements in rising industries; manufacturing facilities may become obsolete if they cannot be retooled or refitted.[5] Although theory predicts that gains to the winners will outweigh losses to the losers, there is no assurance that losers will be compensated. Further, certain domestic design and manufacturing capabilities may be lost as foreign imports displace domestic products and U.S. firms relocate abroad. From a broad economic welfare perspective, this may not matter—although the point is heavily disputed. However, the loss of key defense industrial capabilities would have important national security implications, as discussed below.

International Trade

As we have seen in Chapter Two, total U.S. aerospace exports are high and imports quite low relative to the exports and imports of other high-technology manufactures. In stark contrast to the aerospace industry, for example, is the computer industry, where nearly half of all U.S. computer shipments are exported—yet imports account for more than 60 percent of the value of purchases. As described by CEA (2001, p. 146),

---

[5]Data from the 1980s show that competition from imports contributed at most 10 percent of the observed job displacements from manufacturing in the worst year of that decade (CEA, 1998, pp. 244–245).

The United States gains in both directions from two-way trade in computers and parts. U.S. computer firms can lower their costs by obtaining components from efficient foreign producers, and later profit from selling finished computers in the larger global markets.

By analogy to the computer industry, we would expect U.S. aerospace firms to take the lead in the design and integration of complete aircraft. Indeed, the data do show that U.S. exports of complete combat aircraft dominate the world market. This may be due to U.S. government promotion of defense aerospace systems through mechanisms such as the FMS and FMF programs as well as to "natural" comparative advantage. In any case, however—and with no attempt to analyze the cost-effectiveness of these types of export promotion programs—it is clear that strong exports are good for the Air Force on purely economic grounds. By allowing U.S. firms to achieve greater economies of scale in production, strong exports lower the costs of Air Force acquisition programs. They also help firms survive periods of low Air Force demand, making it possible to retain skilled employees and to maintain facilities that might otherwise be forced to close. They can, in addition, significantly lower the costs to the Air Force of holding legacy equipment in inventory by keeping production lines open (whether in the United States or elsewhere) for replacement parts and components. Finally, the potential for export sales lowers the risks to firms associated with failure to win particular Air Force contracts. This helps encourage new firms to enter the defense aerospace business and helps convince existing firms to stay in.

By the same computer industry analogy, we would also expect to see economically significant U.S. imports of aerospace products, especially at the level of components and small parts. These types of items are presumably less technically sophisticated than complete aircraft and should thus be well within the design and production capabilities of U.S. trading partners. In point of fact, however, we observe relatively few aerospace imports, whether of parts or complete aircraft, civil or military. This could be because our data do not capture major categories of imported inputs and therefore understate the true magnitude of foreign supply. Similarly, it could be that, for reasons of cost or quality or the desire to keep close control over suppliers, U.S. primes prefer not to work with foreign subcontractors. Yet it could also be the case that noneconomic factors—including government regulations, policies, and practices—have discouraged U.S. primes from utilizing foreign sources of supply.

The data presented in Chapter Two do not allow us to discriminate between these alternatives. In particular, the lack of a breakdown between civil and military aerospace inputs constrains an important potential avenue of investigation. As we show in Chapter Four, policies governing military imports are more restrictive than those pertaining to civil imports. Therefore, if the primary reason for low aerospace imports is government policy, we might expect to see a significant difference in the magnitude of imports of civil versus military aircraft and aircraft parts and equipment. We do see quite a difference between civil and military imports in the complete aircraft category. As illustrated in Figure 2.3, for civil aircraft the average import share between 1997 and 1999 was 37 percent. For military aircraft it was less than 1 percent. These descriptive statistics are consistent with our examination of the historical trends in U.S. defense aerospace imports, which revealed that with one possible exception, the United States has never deployed a jet fighter/attack aircraft developed in another country. Even off-the-shelf imports of much less complex items such as missiles have been quite rare.

Those data that are available suggest that this low level of dependence on foreign sources of supply may be as true for military inputs as it is for finished products. A recent DoD study of FY 2000 subcontracts for eight large weapon system programs indicates that the value of parts, components, and materials obtained from foreign sources accounted for less than 2 percent of the value of total subcontracts.[6] The only fighter included in the study, the F/A-18E/F Super Hornet, utilized foreign subcontractors for just $21.8 million of the $3.1 billion subcontractor effort, representing less than 1 percent

---

[6]This study, which was required under Section 831 of the FY 2001 National Defense Authorization Act, collected information on subcontracts valued at over $100,000 for U.S. suppliers and at more than $25,000 for non-U.S. suppliers, where a "U.S. supplier" was defined to be firms located in the United States or Canada (Under Secretary of Defense for Acquisition, Technology, and Logistics (USD[AT&L]), October 2001). The eight programs examined were the AH-64D Apache Helicopter Upgrade Program; the F/A-18E/F aircraft; the M1 A2 Abrams Tank System Enhancement Package; the AIM-120 Advanced Medium-Range Air-to-Air Missile (AMRAAM); the Patriot Missile Ground Station; the AGM-114L Longbow Hellfire Missile; the Joint Direct Attack Munition (JDAM); and the Advanced Amphibious Assault Vehicle (AAAV).

of the total. The program with the highest percentage of foreign sub-contracts by value (18 percent), the Patriot missile ground station, uses imported computer hardware components, microcircuitry, and ceramics. According to DoD, these items could all be obtained from alternative domestic or foreign suppliers without "significant cost or risk" (USD[AT&L]), August 2001, p. 17).

The DoD foreign sourcing study is also instructive because it identifies some of the potential benefits and costs associated with the global diversification of defense-related production. With respect to economic objectives, DoD states that appropriate use of non-U.S. suppliers

- Permits DoD to access state-of-the-art technologies and industrial capabilities;

- Exposes U.S. industry to international competition, helping ensure that U.S. firms remain innovative and efficient; and

- Encourages the development of mutually beneficial industrial linkages that enhance U.S. industry's access to global markets (USD[AT&L]), August 2001, p. 3).[7]

On the downside, the only economic concerns about foreign sourcing expressed in the study derive from possible negative impacts on the economic viability of the defense industrial base. According to DoD, such concerns are unfounded because of the small number and value of total program subcontracts let to foreigners. Of course, this argument cuts both ways: It is also hard to see how any significant benefits can be achieved with such a limited use of non-U.S. suppliers.

Is U.S. neglect of foreign aerospace suppliers due primarily to U.S. government policies that discourage imports? As we discuss in greater detail in the following chapter, there are relatively few direct formal legislative barriers to increased U.S. imports of foreign aerospace parts and components. "Buy national"–type legal provi-

---

[7]This last point presumably refers to the export opportunities created as a result of foreign sourcing, which, as we state above, are of unambiguous economic benefit to DoD.

sions have for the most part been waived with respect to the defense sector. One possibility is that laws and regulations designed to restrict technology transfers abroad for reasons of national security— that is, export controls—actually have the added, unintended effect of discouraging imports. This is because of the informational constraints they may place on U.S. firms seeking contract bids from foreign companies. Or, alternatively, U.S. primes may simply have avoided foreign sources in the past in the belief that using domestically based subcontractors would improve their chances of winning U.S. government contracts.

International Investment and Business Relationships

Using the typology established in the previous chapter, we consider the economic opportunities and challenges associated with the international opening of capital markets through the following arrangements:

- U.S. direct investment abroad—that is, U.S. mergers with and acquisitions of foreign firms, including the establishment of new affiliates;

- Foreign direct investment in the United States; and

- Marketing agreements, teams, and joint ventures involving U.S. and foreign partners.

On purely economic grounds, the opening of capital markets, like the opening of goods markets, should in principle benefit the Air Force. The acquisition of foreign firms or the establishment of new foreign affiliates should allow U.S. firms to source inputs more cheaply and effectively. Perhaps more important, U.S. direct investment abroad should expand U.S. export and overseas licensing opportunities by improving access to foreign government procurement programs. At the same time, foreign acquirers of U.S. firms often invest in new technologies, plants, and equipment, thereby improving U.S. productivity. Under certain circumstances, growth in the number of U.S. affiliates of foreign firms is also likely to stimulate competition for Air Force contracts.

This last point is, however, key. Is foreign direct investment likely to force U.S. firms to increase their efficiency and hasten their innovation, or will it tend to drive them out of the market? The answer depends on the type of transaction as well as the nature of the market. By definition, foreign direct investment can consist of either establishing new companies or acquiring or expanding existing ones. With respect to new establishments, Dunning (1990) argues that domestically owned firms are often well positioned to contend with foreign entrants if a country is technologically advanced. On the basis of this argument, new foreign direct investment in U.S. aerospace firms—including joint ventures with U.S. firms—seems likely to enhance domestic competition for Air Force contracts. On the other hand, the acquisition of existing operations by foreign firms may reduce the overall number of competitors. The U.S. Department of Justice and the Federal Trade Commission carefully monitor and control both foreign and U.S. domestic takeovers of U.S. firms in order to limit monopoly power in the defense as well as commercial sectors.

As we pointed out in Chapter Two, firms also create many business linkages that involve some degree of cross-border trade and investment but stop short of foreign direct investment, among which are subcontract arrangements, marketing agreements, and teams. How are these types of cross-border linkages likely to affect the Air Force's ability to equip aerospace forces with affordable yet highly capable weapon systems?

There is little evidence and relatively little theory on the relative economic benefits to consumers of arrangements such as cross-border marketing agreements, teams, and joint ventures—or, for that matter, parent/subsidiary or prime/subcontractor relationships. As a general rule, however, any type of business relationship will help the Air Force achieve its economic objectives to the extent that it encourages participating companies to be more innovative and to use resources more efficiently.

International teams and joint ventures, for example, both allow aerospace firms to bring their best efforts to a particular project or program or, more broadly, to a product line or market segment, but teams seem to allow more flexibility. GAO (September 2000, pp. 2 and 18) reports that U.S. firms prefer the flexibility of teaming as an arrangement that can temporarily add capabilities to enhance their competitiveness; "that can allow companies to choose new partners in each market in which they wish to compete"; and "that they can easily abandon should the alliance be unsuccessful in competing for new business or should an alliance with other companies offer greater potential for increased sales and revenue."

If successful, however, a team may lead to further collaboration or, eventually, to the formation of a joint venture. Teams can provide a venue for aerospace firms to try out a new relationship before taking steps to solidify it. Moreover, like forms of direct investment but with less formal involvement, teams and marketing agreements can help firms enter new markets, potentially paving the way for more local sales and trade. Although marketing agreements probably afford less opportunity for technology transfer and information sharing than do teams, in cases where U.S. or foreign enterprises obtain rights to modify or produce equipment, there can be considerable opportunity.

There is some question as to whether cross-border teams and marketing agreements can be anticompetitive.[8] Ultimately, as in the case of M&As, the outcome depends on the nature of the market and alliance. Teams can affect the market in several different ways. First, they can be anticompetitive if they result in fewer effective enterprises—that is, if firms that would have struck out on their own choose instead to ally themselves with a larger team enterprise. Second, they can reduce competition if they create barriers to entry, as may occur in an exclusive arrangement, by blocking other teams' access to unique capabilities or otherwise monopolizing crucial expertise. These two concerns are not specific to international teams. Third, they can be procompetitive if opening them to foreign entrants encourages more firms to create teams or vie for membership. The extent to which the Air Force would benefit from more subtier competition depends in part on whether the system integrators are themselves competitive and pass on gains. Fourth, they can enhance

---

[8]DoD (Under Secretary of Defense for Acquisition and Technology (USD[A&T]), 1999) raises this issue in a memo on anticompetitive teaming. Although not specifically addressing cross-border agreements, these concerns also apply to such agreements. Referring to exclusive agreements, the memo finds that "these teaming arrangements have the potential of resulting in inadequate competition for our contracts. While our preference is to allow the private sector to team and subcontract without DOD involvement, there are circumstances in which we must intervene to assure adequate competition."

competition if they yield stronger—though not necessarily more—teams, thereby fueling rivalries across teams.[9]

Finally, one factor to consider in evaluating the desirability of any of these relationships is whether they were initiated by the companies themselves. Generally speaking, industry-initiated relationships are likely to be more efficient than government-initiated relationships because they are presumably governed by economic as well as political considerations. A second factor to consider in evaluating cross-border business linkages is the extent to which they encourage the cost-effective exploitation of imports and the promotion of exports. As we have already suggested, two-way trade in defense aerospace products helps the Air Force achieve low-cost, high-performance combat aircraft. Mechanisms such as marketing agreements and teams can be used to circumvent political, informational, and sometimes regulatory barriers to simple subcontracting arrangements that send goods and services across national borders. For example, foreign companies often find it difficult to bring their products to the attention of domestic government procurement managers. This may be due to explicit obstacles, such as the existence of formal "buy national" requirements, or to less tangible obstacles, such as a lack of familiarity with domestic procurement processes. Marketing agreements, which link up foreign firms that have products to sell with domestic firms that have government access, provide a way to overcome both of these obstacles. The question, of course, is whether in so doing they violate important underlying rationales for limiting exports and imports in the first place.

POLITICAL-MILITARY DIMENSIONS OF DEFENSE AEROSPACE GLOBALIZATION

The ability to conduct air operations as part of an effective international coalition is a high priority for DoD—and for the NATO alliance

---

[9]Likewise, the effects of marketing agreements can play themselves out differently. Firms can use marketing agreements to gain access to local markets that might be otherwise difficult to enter, thereby enhancing competition. However, they can also use them to carve out discrete market territories or segments.

and other key allies. Although the implications of globalization for coalition warfare are not widely discussed in the literature, various studies have identified intermediate political-military goals for acquisition policy, including the following:

- Technical interoperability through commonality of U.S. and allied weapons and weapon system platforms (standardization of equipment);

- System- and subsystem-level technical interoperability of independently designed and developed U.S. and allied defense aerospace platforms through compatibility in areas such as command, control, communications, intelligence, surveillance, and reconnaissance (C^3ISR) systems and munitions; and

- Narrowing of the defense technology gap between the United States and NATO Europe and other key allies.

In addition, DSB (1999, p. iii) argues that globalization in the form of closer defense industrial links between the United States and NATO Europe could help avert protectionist "Fortress Europe" and "Fortress America" tendencies, which weaken NATO political-military cohesion.

For the same reason that globalization can enhance competition, however, it could also result in the proliferation of alternative systems as a consequence of the improved capabilities—and hence competitiveness—of both European and non-European industry. According to Hura et al. (2000), as late as 1980 U.S. designs made up the vast majority of the fighter inventories of all NATO European air forces except for those of France, the UK, and Portugal. Yet despite general agreement on the desirability of equipment standardization among NATO countries—and despite U.S. policymakers' long history of encouraging allies to purchase and field U.S.-developed equipment—NATO Europe has over time become increasingly reluctant even to coproduce U.S. aircraft designs, let alone import complete aircraft from the United States. Hura et al., for example, estimate that by the year 2010, the British and Italian air forces will have no

U.S.-designed fighter aircraft, while less than 20 percent of the German fighter fleet will be of U.S. design.[10]

In response to European resistance to purchasing U.S.-designed weapons and weapon system platforms (and vice versa), a supposedly more politically palatable approach to achieving commonality through reciprocal trade was tried in the 1970s and 1980s. Under this approach, sometimes referred to as the "Two-Way Street," U.S. and European industry were to specialize in different categories of finished weapons and weapon system platforms, each supplying each other's governments. A variation on the Two-Way Street was the "Family of Weapons" concept, which promoted the transatlantic development and production of complementary weapon systems. In theory, both the Two-Way Street and Family of Weapons approaches would have allowed the NATO allies to preserve certain, probably different, defense industrial capabilities while at the same time providing the economic benefits of scale economies and comparative advantage and the political-military benefits of interoperability.

Unfortunately, reciprocal trade agreements have proved to be largely unworkable in practice. Differences over requirements and the desire of larger NATO members to retain a full spectrum of industrial capabilities are among the causative factors. In the 1980s, for example, differences over requirements helped doom an agreement between the United States, Germany, France, and the UK to develop and produce complementary air-to-air missiles. While the United States went ahead with plans for the U.S.-designed AMRAAM, DoD soon differed with its European partners over technical goals for AMRAAM's short-range counterpart, the Advanced Short-Range Air-to-Air Missile (ASRAAM). In the end, France and Germany dropped out and ASRAAM became an all-British program. It was never purchased by the United States and thus far has not been taken up by any other NATO allies.[11]

---

[10]This is likely to change after 2010, when the UK, Italy, and other NATO allies and friendly nations start to bring the U.S.-designed JSF into inventory.

[11]For a short discussion of the problems associated with the AMRAAM/ASRAAM program, see Lorell and Lowell (1995). Although the UK and Australia are the only countries to have committed to ASRAAM as of late 2001, Greece, Spain, Switzerland, and South Korea have reportedly expressed interest.

By the end of the 1980s, achieving commonality of major weapons and weapon system platforms through trade seemed to be a distant if not actually receding goal within NATO owing to leaner defense budgets and diverging rates of technological innovation among NATO members, as well as to the greater diversity of possible NATO missions. Yet greater interoperability, either through commonality of equipment or through system- or subsystem-level technical interoperability, remains an important NATO objective. Some observers have expressed the hope that closer integration of the U.S. and European defense industrial bases may finally move NATO closer to that objective.[12]

Mergers, acquisitions, and other forms of collaborative business relationships between U.S. and NATO European defense firms have the potential to encourage interoperability both through equipment commonality and through subsystem- and component-level interoperability. With respect to equipment commonality, such relationships can make joint equipment purchases by national governments politically and economically more attractive. In the past, for example, cross-border armaments cooperation programs have been characterized by governmental matchmaking between their respective national firms. With firms now initiating their own cross-border relationships, however, some of the economic inefficiencies introduced as a result of this matchmaking should be reduced. This is because firms are generally better able than governments to select partners on the basis of complementary capabilities. Moreover, work shares and technical responsibilities negotiated in the marketplace are likely to result in a more efficient allocation of resources than those negotiated by governments.[13]

Closer integration of national defense industrial bases may also make it more likely that the United States and its NATO allies will purchase similar or even identical systems within the context of purely national weapon system procurement programs. By blurring the national character of individual firms, governments may be more comfortable purchasing designs or even finished equipment from

---

[12]See, for example, DSB (1999).

[13]Lorell and Lowell (1995) provide some evidence on the cost implications of international collaboration in weapon procurement.

abroad. Even arrangements that are relatively limited in scope, such as cross-border marketing agreements, may result in the unplanned coordination of equipment acquisition by national governments.

In addition to possibly encouraging international cooperation with respect to weapon system acquisition, purely economic considerations suggest that systems developed by firms involved in cross-border R&D teams and joint ventures—as opposed to simple marketing agreements—are likely to have important elements in common. This is because the sharing of design concepts, technology standards, and inputs is likely to be a major feature of these types of arrangements—provided, that is, that such arrangements are initiated by the firms themselves rather than by governments. The extent of the resulting interoperability will, of course, depend both on the nature of particular cross-border relationships and on the features of particular national programs, but subsystem-level solutions to achieving interoperability have several advantages over solutions that require commonality of major weapons and weapon system platforms. These include lower relative cost and greater flexibility of application, both of which are highly desirable in the post–Cold War era (see, for example, Hura et al., 2000).

These arguments notwithstanding, under certain circumstances globalization also has the potential to actually *decrease* NATO interoperability. As foreign firms become more capable as a result of increased access to U.S. technology and capital, competition between international supplier teams is likely to increase. The new consolidated pan European megafirms, for example, possibly working with U.S. subcontractors, may now have the capabilities and government backing to develop different but highly competitive systems in most market sectors. This could lead to the acquisition by European and other allied foreign governments of indigenously designed systems that are not standardized, and perhaps not even interoperable, with U.S.-developed systems. Chapter Five offers some evidence on this point.

Finally, it is important to stress that interoperability cannot be achieved without a NATO-wide commitment to defense modernization. Regardless of the form or character of transatlantic industrial cooperation, NATO European defense budgets must increase in order to bridge the U.S.-European technological gap. This is a key element of NATO's DCI. An onslaught of transatlantic teams, joint ventures, and other business partnerships all targeted toward the U.S. market will not overcome profound disparities in U.S.-European capabilities. Without proper controls, such an onslaught might, however, do damage to U.S. national security. One reason is the high degree of technology transfer—and the resulting potential for unauthorized resale to third parties—that is potentially involved in all of these cross-border relationships. For the United States, the greatest obstacle to making NATO forces truly interoperable may be the need to convince our allies to adopt the same type of export control regime as we ourselves have.

NATIONAL SECURITY DIMENSIONS OF DEFENSE AEROSPACE GLOBALIZATION

The Air Force faces at least four national security challenges associated with globalization of the U.S. defense industrial base:

- Loss of domestic defense capabilities and technologies and associated dependence on foreign sources of supply;

- Worldwide weapon proliferation;

- The acquisition of advanced conventional armaments by unfriendly nations or groups; and

- Foreign control over U.S. capabilities and potential lack of responsiveness to Air Force needs.

On the opportunities side of the ledger, globalization also

- Provides the Air Force with more "bang for the buck" as global competition forces costs down and quality up;

- Strengthens overall U.S. military capabilities by providing greater access to foreign technologies; and

- Strengthens overall U.S. military capabilities by improving the financial health of U.S. defense firms.

International Trade

The trade data presented in Chapter Two indicate that at current levels, there is little cause for concern over any broad loss of U.S. domestic defense aerospace capabilities and technologies resulting from imports. In fact, casual analysis suggests that if anything, U.S. industry is not taking full advantage of foreign technologies or possibly cheaper foreign sources of supply; there would appear to be ample opportunity to achieve more "bang for the buck" without compromising national security, especially at the level of parts and components.

From a national security perspective, however, this aggregate analysis could be cold comfort if even just a few militarily critical capabilities get transferred overseas, causing the Air Force to become dependent on foreign sources of supply. As a general rule, the United States should not depend on foreign suppliers if a supply disruption could seriously degrade its ability to field or operate military forces (Neu and Wolf, 1994). Fortunately, there is no evidence that this is the case: The DoD foreign sourcing study referenced above, for example, found no important classes of imported inputs that either could not be quickly and easily produced at home or were not being stockpiled in militarily significant amounts (USD[AT&L], October 2001). From 1962 to January 2001, there were just 25 "Section 232" investigations of the effects of imports on national security, only six of which concluded that imports did indeed threaten to impair national security, and all six of these cases involved crude oil and other petroleum products (BEA, 2001).[14] These findings seem to confirm the arguments of Neu and Wolf (1994, p. 41), who state that "[t]he U.S. economy is very broad, and given enough time, it is undoubtedly capable of producing any product manufactured anywhere in the world."

Of more concern, perhaps, is the potential for proliferation as U.S. industry continues to increase its dominance over world arms exports. Is the United States helping foster a worldwide arms race? Perhaps this may be the case, but the classic counterargument is that

---

[14]Two other cases did, however, lead to policy changes: increased stockpiling of chromium, manganese, and silicon ferroalloys, and the imposition of voluntary export restraints on metal-cutting and metal-forming machine tools.

if U.S. industry pulls back, other countries—particularly in Europe—will quickly step up to fill the breach. There is probably little that the United States alone can do to prevent countries from obtaining weapons and technologies that are available from multiple foreign sources. To counter this type of proliferation, an effective multilateral approach toward arms control is needed. The issues surrounding multilateral arms control are outside the scope of this report.

More important from a national security perspective is the extent to which the United States may be unintentionally arming its present and future enemies with advanced weapons and technologies that are not available elsewhere in the world. This speaks to the issue of technology transfer—that is, "the process of transferring, from an industry in one country to another or between governments themselves, technical information and know-how relating to the design, engineering, manufacture, production, and use of goods" (Defense Institute of Security Assistance Management [DISAM], 2000, Chapter 20). According to the U.S. government, the export of physical goods (including armaments) is a type of technology transfer. In addition, under U.S. law the term *export* can include activities such as transfers of technical information or know-how to foreign nationals within the United States ("deemed exports"), the electronic transmission of proprietary data to individuals abroad, or the return of foreign equipment to its country of origin after repair in the United States (15 CFR 730.5).

As we discuss at greater length in the following chapter, the United States imposes numerous restrictions on the type and nature of weapons, weapon system platforms, and parts and components that may be exported. The U.S. export control system also places clear restrictions on which countries or (rarely) subnational groups are authorized to receive them. The intent of these restrictions is not only to prevent unfriendly groups or nations from obtaining weapons they can use in the field, but also to prevent such entities from obtaining weapon technology through reverse engineering.

Globalization poses a threat to the U.S. export control system in large part because it increases the likelihood of third-party transfers—that is, the subsequent unapproved foreign resale of equipment and technology authorized for transfer to an approved party abroad. The more acute threat is from third-party transfers of technology, not equipment. This is because technology transfers, which help build enemy defense industrial capabilities, are a greater long-term concern than enemy acquisition of materiel—and reverse engineering is difficult. It is cross-border investments and business relationships, not trade per se, that have the greatest potential for increasing undesirable third-party transfers of technology. There is also a potential threat of the third-party transfer of unique weapons developed indigenously by a legitimate recipient of U.S. systems or technologies—one who has developed those indigenous systems in part or in whole by reverse engineering U.S. systems or employing U.S. technologies.

International Investment and Business Relationships

Some observers worry about the potential loss of key U.S. domestic defense industrial skills as a result of the offshore relocation of development and manufacturing facilities by foreign investors in U.S. defense businesses (Denoon, 1979). Most, however, agree with DSB (1999), which argues that the United States is more likely to *gain* needed skills from foreign investment, as foreign investors usually seek to establish an industrial presence in the United States in order to penetrate the U.S. market. Nevertheless, there are at least two reasons a foreign firm might purchase U.S. manufacturing facilities and then relocate them abroad: to obtain technology or to shut down a competitor. Although such actions are certainly not typical, GAO (September 2000, p. 12) cites the case of a European firm that purchased two U.S. firms, closed their operations, and moved specialized hardware and software to its European facility. One goal of the CFIUS approval process, discussed at greater length in the chapter that follows, is to prevent this from happening in the defense sector.

A more serious concern for the Air Force is whether foreign owners will run their U.S. operations like "real" American firms.[15] Will they be as responsive to Air Force needs as their U.S.-owned counterparts during a national emergency as well as during peacetime? Will they be less likely to engage in militarily important activities? With re-

---

[15]To some extent, this concern may also apply to joint ventures, but likely less so because of U.S. firms' participation.

spect to the first question, Neu and Wolf's (1994) review of the empirical literature suggests that there is no evidence of systematic differences in behavior between U.S.-owned and foreign-owned firms during peacetime. Also in a peacetime context, DSB (1999, p. 21) argues that "[i]n cases where DoD is the sole consumer of a particular product, it is likely to retain the same influence over the foreign supplier as it does over the U.S. contractor." In general, supplier responsiveness to DoD during peacetime is probably influenced more by the relative size of DoD contracts than by the nationality of the supplier.

Nevertheless, according to Moran (1993, p. 44), "[h]istory is full of attempts by governments to influence the sovereign activities of other nations by withholding supplies or issuing extraterritorial directives to the overseas affiliates of domestic firms." Moran provides several examples: U.S. attempts in the 1960s to prevent a French subsidiary of IBM from selling computer technology that might have aided France's nuclear program; the Reagan administration's retroactive order to the European subsidiaries of Dresser Industries and General Electric to cancel contracts for supplying gas pipeline technology to the Soviet Union; and the Japanese government's refusal to allow Dexcel, the U.S. subsidiary of Kyocera, to provide advanced ceramic technology to the U.S. Navy's Tomahawk missile program. As pointed out by Moran (1993, p. 45), the credible threat of denial or manipulation "leads to legitimate national security exceptions to liberal doctrines of free trade and investment."

Understandably, there is little empirical evidence to support conjectures about foreign supplier responsiveness during national emergencies simply because there have been so few. Under U.S. law, the President has the power to require that contracts in support of the national defense be accepted and performed on a preferential or priority basis over all other contracts (FAR Part 11.602). This means that foreign as well as U.S. domestic primes and subcontractors— including the U.S. subsidiaries of foreign firms—on authorized military programs may be required to drop other commitments in order to meet DoD demands. However, suppliers not connected with authorized programs have no such obligation.

A second question is whether the U.S. subsidiaries of foreign firms will be less likely to engage in militarily important activities. This is clearly most relevant in cases where U.S. firms already conducting militarily sensitive activities are purchased by foreign interests. Are such activities likely to be stopped once ownership changes hands? As described in more detail in the next chapter, all foreign purchases of U.S. firms are subject to review by CFIUS, a government committee set up to monitor and evaluate new foreign direct investment. If a particular acquisition or merger is perceived to have the potential to threaten U.S. capability and capacity to meet the requirements of national security, the transaction may be disallowed, even retroactively. The question, therefore, is not so much whether foreign-owned firms are likely to engage in militarily important activities but rather whether they should be allowed to do so.[16]

Finally, the growth in cross-border investment flows and related business tie-ups has prompted legitimate concerns about the growing potential for undesirable overseas transfers of dual-use and military technologies. In fact, as is now frequently seen in the commercial aerospace sector, even "conventional" prime/subcontractor relationships are no longer conventional in that they often involve much more significant sharing of concepts, design elements, and technologies than was the case in the past.[17] The very quality that is likely to make relationships such as teams and marketing arrangements most successful from the standpoint of economic and coalition warfighting benefits—a high degree of technology transfer—also poses the greatest challenges.

CONCLUSION

In sum, deeper economic integration and ensuing technology transfer is likely to be a double-edged sword for the Air Force: On the one hand, globalization presents an opportunity to enhance interoperability and strengthen coalitions, but on the other hand it poses significant security challenges. Overall, aerospace globalization is likely to promote important economic objectives such as lower

---

[16]They might be less interested in engaging in such activities if there were no compensating returns. Although addressing slightly different questions, Neu and Wolf (1994, p. 45) find "no evidence of systematic differences in behavior" between U.S.-owned and foreign-owned firms in the United States.

[17]See Lorell et al. (2000).

prices, higher quality, and increased innovation. Many different types of cross-border business relationships can help the industry realize those gains. For example, business partnerships such as marketing arrangements or international teams can help firms gain access to otherwise blocked markets, thereby achieving greater economies of scale. Even cross-border business relationships that target national programs may, almost inadvertently, promote interoperability of equipment.

On the demand side, formal collaborative purchase agreements between national governments—which may involve firms of different nationalities working together through joint ventures, teams, government-initiated work share arrangements, or various types of subcontract arrangements—expand markets as well, spreading production and sometimes RDT&E costs over a broader sales base. These business partnerships can also achieve important political-military objectives, such as enhancing interoperability and strengthening allied coalitions. They may also reduce costs, especially if they are industry-initiated.

However, there are also some economic, political-military, and national security–related hazards associated with globalization. For example, close cross-border business relationships, like close domestic business relationships, may serve to consolidate market power, thereby diminishing competitive incentives to reduce costs and to innovate. With respect to national security, ongoing economic integration may make it harder to control the spread of weapons and technology beyond our borders and those of our allies.

In the end, the key to success for any cross-border business relationship involving the United States as well as the larger NATO European countries, such as France, Germany, Italy, and the UK, will be the extent to which that relationship results in greater cooperative participation in design and development than would have been possible or practical in a world in which one slate of purely national firms competes against another. The legal, regulatory, and policy framework that governs the formation of such relationships is the subject of the following chapter.

Chapter Four

THE LEGAL, REGULATORY, AND POLICY FRAMEWORK FOR AEROSPACE INDUSTRY GLOBALIZATION

INTRODUCTION

In Chapter Two, we saw that the U.S. aerospace industry as a whole is quite active in international trade and investment markets, although it is heavily export-oriented. However, the U.S. military aerospace sector is less internationally integrated than the nonmilitary sector, with less than 0.1 percent of U.S. purchases of complete military aircraft originating overseas. Is this due to U.S. superiority in military aerospace technology, design integration, and manufacturing? Or could it be that U.S. government, DoD, or Air Force policies and practices are slowing military aerospace globalization—and thereby preventing full realization of the benefits of global economic integration? Do policies affecting defense globalization reflect higher priorities related to U.S. national security interests, or are they the result of outdated bureaucratic procedures or unnecessary protectionist legislation? In either case, to what extent is the Air Force constrained by these policies?

Using the three objectives identified in Chapter Three as an organizing framework, we briefly describe the policy instruments that either encourage or impede globalization of the defense industrial base. We pay particular attention to areas in which objectives—and therefore policies—can be at cross purposes. We conclude by reviewing trends in U.S. legal and policy activity, summarizing leadership perspectives within DoD and the Air Force as well as other U.S.

departments and agencies in order to provide an indication of the direction of future reforms.

EQUIPPING AIR FORCE WARFIGHTERS WITH SUPERIOR, AFFORDABLE WEAPON SYSTEMS

As its *Vision 2020* clearly states, if the Air Force is to remain the foremost aerospace force in the world, its warfighters must have superior training and equipment (U.S. Air Force, 2000). This in turn will be possible only if it is supplied by an extraordinarily capable and responsive industrial base. Yet with the array of potential aerospace threats expanding to include space warfare, information operations, ballistic and cruise missiles launched by rogue nations, and the like, U.S. and allied defense modernization funds are being stretched thin (AIAA, 2001). Therefore, a key Air Force objective is to obtain the "best value" for the warfighter. Put another way, the Air Force seeks to achieve superior warfighting capabilities at affordable prices.

One important step toward achieving this objective is to promote both innovation and efficiency within the defense industrial base. A review of DoD and Air Force policy and guidance suggests that competition is seen as central to achieving both goals (DoDD 5000.1, paragraph 4.3.3; AFPD 63-3). This position is consistent with the United States' long history of antitrust legislation beginning with the Sherman Antitrust Act of 1890, which provides authority for the government to block mergers, acquisitions, and other actions that tend to limit competition or create monopolies. Thus, the Air Force's and DoD's primary approach toward ensuring a healthy defense industrial base is to foster competition, monitor the results, and intervene only when a desired military capability appears likely to be downgraded or lost (DoD 5000.2-R, paragraph C2.9.1.1.2.1; DoDD 5000.60).

As evidenced by the data presented in the preceding chapter, products and technologies provided by foreign defense firms have not been an essential part of the Air Force's competition-based strategy for encouraging innovation and efficiency. This may be changing, however, in part because of the improved technical capabilities of foreign—particularly European—firms, and in part, perhaps more importantly, because of the recent rapid consolidation of the U.S. defense sector. Both factors have impelled DoD and the Air Force to try to expand the U.S. defense industrial base, first through greater participation by U.S. commercial sector firms, and second through greater participation by foreign defense and commercial sector firms, including foreign-owned companies located in the United States.

Promoting Competition Within the U.S. Domestic Industrial Base

U.S. federal law both directly and indirectly requires DoD and the Air Force to ensure a healthy defense industrial base by promoting competition. Many of these statutory requirements are captured in the FAR, the Defense FAR Supplement (DFARS), and the Air Force FAR Supplement (AFFARS) as well as in lower-level DoD and Air Force guidance. For example, U.S. Code (USC) Title 10, Section 2440, directs the Secretary of Defense to "prescribe regulations requiring consideration of the national technology and industrial base in the development and implementation of acquisition plans for each Major Defense Acquisition Program (MDAP)."[1] As implemented, the weapon system program manager, along with his or her staff and Milestone Decision Authority (MDA), is to consider the effects of programmatic decisions on the future health and capability of the industrial base, in addition to industry's more immediate ability to support their program. In practice, one of the effects of this statute and its implementing regulations is to make preserving competition a key criterion in the selection of contractors for weapon system acquisition programs.

The USD(AT&L) has reinforced the statutory requirement to enhance and protect the defense industrial base with several Directive Memoranda that establish DoD policy in this area. In 1997, then–Under Secretary of Defense for Acquisition and Technology

---

[1] In 10 USC Section 2430, an MDAP is defined to be a program "estimated by the Secretary of Defense to require an eventual total expenditure for RDT&E of more than $300,000,000 or an eventual total expenditure for procurement of more than $1,800,000,000, based on fiscal year 1990 constant dollars." Although most DoD acquisition programs are too small to be MDAPs, their managers still pay attention to the possible consequences of programmatic decisions for the industry base.

(USD[A&T]) Paul Kaminski introduced five initiatives to ensure that DoD has the knowledge and capability to monitor and deal with potentially reduced subtier competition (USD[A&T], 1997).[2] Two years later, USD(AT&L) Jacques Gansler issued a Directive Memorandum establishing policy and illustrating a variety of remedies to deal with anticompetitive teaming, while his Principal Deputy Under Secretary, David Oliver, issued a similar Directive Memorandum designed to ensure robust subcontractor competition (USD[A&T], 1999; Principal Deputy Under Secretary of Defense for Acquisition and Technology, 1999). In a July 2000 directive memorandum on future competition, USD(AT&L) directed Component Acquisition Executive Deputies to meet with the Deputy Under Secretary of Industrial Affairs (DUSD[IA]) to discuss areas where competition may be limited in the future (USD[AT&L], 2000).

Each of the policies established by these memoranda has been captured in the new 5000 series (DoD 5000.2-R, paragraph C2.9).[3] However, both the regulation and the original policy letters provide general rather than quantitative guidance on how to define a healthy industrial base—or a sufficient level of competition. Since the character of competition as well as the means to foster it will vary over time, between sectors, and between prime and subcontractor tiers, acquisition decisionmakers are instead directed to consider the impact of their decisions on the current and future industry base. They are also instructed to observe the industry sectors that they know best to look for signs of problems. Direct intervention to ensure a competitive environment is expected to be the exception rather than the rule (DoDD 5000.1, paragraph 4.3.3; DoD 5000.2-R, paragraph C2.9.1.1.2).

A more straightforward requirement to promote competition per se is found in 41 USC 418. This statute directs all federal agencies to establish Advocates of Competition responsible for "promoting full and open competition, promoting the acquisition of commercial items, and challenging barriers to such acquisition." The Air Force has re-

---

[2]USD(A&T) became USD(AT&L) in April 2000 as a result of DoDD 5134.1.

[3]The "5000 series" is a trio of DoD publications that forms the DoD acquisition manager's front-line authoritative guidance for planning and conducting a weapon system acquisition program. See Appendix A for a further description.

sponded to this requirement by issuing AFPD 63-3, which establishes the Deputy Assistant Secretary of the Air Force for Contracting (SAF/AQC) as the Air Force Competition Advocate General. Furthermore, AFPD 63-3 directs the "Air Force procuring activities" listed in AFFARS Subpart 5306.5 to assign Competition Advocates for their organizations. SAF/AQC, in his or her role as Air Force Competition Advocate General, is directed to encourage effective competition and the use of commercial items and practices as well as to manage the Air Force's competition program. All Air Force Competition Advocates are to promote competition in contracting and the use of commercial practices; monitor and track the number of acquisitions that are competitively awarded; identify barriers to competition and effective remedies; and track those barriers and remedies. Each of these actions is to be accomplished in coordination with relevant technical or program management staffs. Once again, however, no formal, objective definition of "effective competition" is provided.

Finally, civil-military integration has become a cornerstone of U.S. government, DoD, and Air Force competition policy (10 USC 2377; FAR Part 12; DFARS Part 212; AFPD 63-3). Through the adoption of commercial business practices and minimization of military-unique specifications and data requirements, DoD and the Air Force hope to make it easier and more attractive for commercial businesses to compete for DoD business.[4] In principle, civil-military integration should also permit foreign contractors to compete more easily. Desired benefits include avoiding—or at least sharing—the development costs for items having both commercial and military applications (dual-use items); eliminating certain administrative, contracting, and data-tracking costs; having access to manufacturing sources for components after the completion of weapon system production runs; and exploiting economies of scale. In particular, if the military can purchase existing systems or components as commercial off-the-shelf (COTS) items or as NDI, DoD may be able to avoid

---

[4]Civil-military integration is also seen as a way for traditional defense firms to broaden their market base by competing in commercial markets and thus lower costs.

the considerable schedule and cost risks normally associated with development programs.[5]

Competition Policy and the Role of Foreign Industry

Although the statutes, regulations, and policies described above focus on enhancing U.S. domestic competition rather than on defense industrial base globalization, they should in principle be heartening to foreign suppliers who want to compete for DoD contracts. Explicit support for increased participation by foreign industry can be found in the opening paragraphs of DoDD 5000.1, "The Defense Acquisition System," which states that DoD "must take all necessary actions to promote a competitive environment, including . . . ensuring qualified international sources are permitted to compete" (DoDD 5000.1, paragraph 4.3.3). More specifically, AFPD 63-9 lists several benefits of ICRD&A programs that parallel the benefits of civil-military integration. These include accessing a broader range of technologies, leveraging international investments, and enjoying economies of scale. AFPD 63-9 also states that ICRD&A fosters a more efficient market for trade in defense technology, goods, and services.

DoDD 5000.60, "Defense Industrial Capabilities Assessments," is also directly relevant to foreign suppliers. DoDD 5000.60 requires the Defense Components to conduct analyses when acquisition and inventory managers or buyers identify a risk to industrial base capabilities and to take necessary remedial measures. Responsible offices are tasked to identify the most cost- and time-effective options for preserving critical military capabilities. One of many options to be considered is to secure a foreign source of supply.

DoDD 5000.62, "Impact of Mergers or Acquisitions of Major DoD Suppliers on DoD Programs," provides a somewhat different perspective on the potential role of foreign contractors in the U.S. defense industry. This directive establishes policies and assigns re-

---

[5]NDI are products that require modest modifications to meet military requirements. Numerous DoD and Air Force publications extol the virtues and direct the use of civil-military integration, military standard and specification reform, COTS, and NDI. See, for example, Secretary of the Air Force for Acquisition (SAF/AQ) (1999) and the new 5000 series.

sponsibilities for assessing the potential impact of all proposed M&As involving a major defense supplier on DoD programs, including M&As involving foreign companies. USD(AT&L), DUSD(IA), and the DoD General Counsel are jointly responsible for identifying the impact on national security and on defense industry capabilities as well as for advising the Secretary of Defense regarding potential competition, cost, and other implications for DoD programs.[6] For each case, they receive input from designated offices within the affected component(s).

The Air Force activity tasked with executing DoDD 5000.62 is the Industrial Base Planning (IBP) Program within the Materials and Manufacturing Directorate of the Air Force Research Laboratory at Wright-Patterson Air Force Base. According to the IBP Program Manager, international cases are usually limited to those that involve foreign direct investment in the United States or mergers of foreign companies that have U.S. subsidiaries.[7] He summarizes the focus of the IBP Program's M&A studies in three questions related to the potential suppression of competition through vertical and horizontal integration:

- Do the two companies currently compete or are they likely to compete in the future?

- Does one company supply key components to a competitor of the other?

- Does an integrator-supplier relationship exist among the two firms?

The Air Force Secretariat provides the answers to these questions along with analysis of their implications for the Air Force and corresponding recommendations to DUSD(IA).[8] The Department of Justice and the Federal Trade Commission use DUSD(IA)'s synthesized results as one input in their analysis of the antitrust implica-

---

[6]In 2001, DUSD (IA) became the Deputy Under Secretary of Defense for Industrial Policy (DUSD[IP].

[7]Interview with Alan Taylor, IBP Program Manager, Air Force Research Laboratory, February 21, 2001.

[8]Specifically, the Systems Engineering Division (SAF/AQRE) tasks the IBRP and staffs the Air Force's responses to DUSD(IA).

tions of the proposed merger or acquisition. If one of the proposed partners is a foreign firm, the results may also support investigations by CFIUS, which is headed by the Department of the Treasury. The CFIUS investigation process is discussed at greater length below.

Finally, Congress and others have already taken some steps to mitigate the effects of major barriers to foreign competition in the defense market by providing exemptions to key "buy national" statutes. The Buy American Act (41 USC 10a–10d; FAR Part 25.2; DFARS Part 225.2) and the Balance of Payments Program (FAR Part 25.3; DFARS Part 252.3) each place restrictions on U.S. government purchases of supplies that are not domestic end products.[9] The former restricts purchases of foreign end products to be used in the United States, and the latter places somewhat different restrictions and evaluation procedures on the purchases of foreign end products to be used outside the United States.[10] However, treaties, international agreements, and "Determinations of National Interest" have resulted in numerous limitations and exemptions to these laws. Such exclusions are often related to trade with specific nations and bear direct relevance to the Air Force's acquisition of foreign military equipment.

Under the authority of the Culver-Nunn Amendment (10 USC 2457), for example, the Secretary of Defense has decided that it is *not* in the U.S. public interest to apply the Buy American Act or the provisions of the Balance of Payments Program to U.S. acquisition of defense equipment from the following nations: Australia, Belgium, Canada, Denmark, Egypt, Federal Republic of Germany, France, Greece, Israel, Italy, Luxembourg, the Netherlands, Norway, Portugal, Spain, Turkey, and the UK (DFARS Part 225, paragraph 225.872). DoD has thus entered into bilateral "Reciprocal Procurement" Memoranda of Understanding (MoUs) with these nations to preclude the application of any "buy national" requirements. On a purchase-by-

---

[9]Domestic end products are either raw materials and commodities mined or produced in the United States or end products that are manufactured in the United States, where "manufactured in the United States" applies to all items for which the cost of components mined, produced, or manufactured in the United States exceeds 50 percent of the cost of all its components (DFARS Part 225, paragraph 225.003).

[10]These laws generally do not prohibit foreign acquisition but rather provide source selection evaluation procedures that favor domestic products.

purchase basis, the same exclusions can be made for Austria, Finland, Sweden, and Switzerland.

Furthermore, in accordance with 10 USC 2533 and DFARS Part 225, paragraph 225.103, the Secretary of Defense, after careful consideration of several factors, can determine that it is inconsistent with the public interest to apply the Buy American Act to purchases of defense products from manufacturers in other countries. Procurements from nations that are not listed above, such as the Pacific Rim nations, could therefore be exempted as well. DFARS Part 225, paragraph 225.103, also explains that USD(AT&L) has determined that a public interest exemption is appropriate for information technology components that are substantially transformed in the United States.[11] This would include, for example, electronic hardware and software components that are manufactured in the Pacific Rim and integrated into computers and other hardware in the United States.

Most of the nations that could sell world-class weapon systems and components to the U.S. Air Force are already excluded or can be excluded from the provisions of U.S. "buy national" laws. In addition, U.S. prime contractors are not allowed to use these laws as a justification to preclude qualifying country sources from competing for subcontracts (DFARS Part 225, paragraph 225.872-8). Therefore, while the Buy American Act and the Balance of Payments Program may act as barriers to international trade in other industries, their impact on U.S. purchases of aerospace weapon systems and components from abroad should in theory be greatly mitigated.[12] Nevertheless, the United States' friends and allies—especially its European allies—apparently continue to consider them a barrier (U.S. General Accounting Office, 1998). This suggests that attitudes rather than statutory or regulatory obligations may be a key

---

[11]Specifically, this includes items covered by Federal Supply Groups 70 (Automatic Data Processing Equipment [including Firmware], Software, Supplies, and Support Equipment) or 74 (Office Machines, Text Processing Systems, and Visible Recording Equipment).

[12]However, DFARS Subparts 225.70 and 225.71 describe other, more narrowly focused statutes and DoD policies that do restrict the purchase of foreign military equipment. For example, 10 USC 2534 restricts U.S. purchases of certain ball bearings and roller bearings from nations other than Canada and the UK.

cause of low levels of U.S. imports of defense goods. This is a subject worthy of further research.

To conclude, the "buy national" provisions of U.S. law that were originally designed to limit U.S. government purchases from foreign suppliers probably do little now to limit those purchases in the area of defense. On the other hand, DoD and Air Force policies designed to promote an efficient and innovative defense industrial base have the potential to elicit increased foreign contractor participation in U.S. defense markets. In particular, policies designed to make it easier for U.S.-owned and U.S.-based commercial firms to participate in DoD and Air Force procurement programs should in principle benefit foreign commercial and defense sector firms as well.

PREPARING FOR COALITION WARFARE

A second major objective motivating Air Force concerns about globalization of the defense industrial base is the expectation that the United States will fight future wars as a member of coalitions. Both DoD and the Air Force believe that U.S. warfighting capability can be multiplied—and international support engendered—through the judicious employment of coalition operations with NATO allies or other friendly nations (Cohen, 1997; AFPD 63-9; AFI 16-110). Coalition operations are most effective if their equipment is common or at least interoperable and if training and tactics are also standardized or harmonized. Thus, defense cooperation—that is, assisting and cooperating with our allies and friends in the development, procurement, and support of weapon systems—is the cornerstone of the U.S. approach to interoperable coalition forces.[13]

There are two major categories of defense cooperation. The first, International Armaments Cooperation (IAC), consists of government-to-government cooperative armament development and acquisition programs. The second, Security Assistance, is defined as "the transfer of military and economic assistance through sale, grant, lease, or loan to friendly foreign governments" (DoD 5105.38-M, paragraph 10103). Note that all defense cooperation programs require some form of U.S. government involvement, including com-

---

[13]See, for example, Cohen (1997).

mercial sales of military equipment by U.S. private sector firms to foreign governments, which fall under the category of Security Assistance and require State Department approval of export licenses. The laws, regulations, and other forms of guidance regarding the various forms of defense cooperation are extensive owing to the variety and complexity of these international programs and to the direct and extensive involvement of the U.S. government.

The Deputy Under Secretary of the Air Force for International Affairs (SAF/IA) is the focal point in the Air Force for defense cooperation. However, other offices, including SAF/AQ, also have major responsibilities in this area. Specifically, Air Force Manual 16-101, paragraph 1.6, states that SAF/IA "develops, implements, manages, and supervises the U.S. Air Force's international affairs, international technology transfer control, and security assistance programs" and liaisons with OSD, the Departments of State and Commerce, and others (U.S. Air Force, 1995). This manual adds that SAF/AQ "is responsible for acquisition policy, program management, and execution of all major, complex Foreign Military Sales system acquisition cases administered by SAF/IA." Similarly, regarding IAC, AFI 16-110, paragraph 1.4, states that SAF/IA is responsible for Air Force IAC policies and procedures and manages Air Force IAC, while AFPD 63-9, paragraph 1.4, states that SAF/AQ is responsible for policy, resource advocacy, and oversight of Air Force participation in ICRD&A programs. At the DoD level, the Defense Security Cooperation Agency (DSCA) manages military Security Assistance programs, and the Deputy Under Secretary of Defense for International Cooperation (DUSD[IC]) oversees IAC.

International Armaments Cooperation

IAC generally includes all aspects of defense acquisition programs that are jointly conducted with one or more foreign nations or organizations. Facets of IAC include requirements harmonization, RDT&E, production, acquisition, and weapon system support. IAC programs are formalized through written international agreements between the United States and other governments or international organizations, but in practice they may be either government- or industry-initiated (Deputy Under Secretary of Defense for International and Commercial Programs, 1996, Chapter 5).

Within DoD literature, the categorization of IAC programs varies. The six composite categories briefly described below are bilateral forums; the Defense Data Exchange Program; the Engineer and Scientist Exchange Program; the Foreign Acquisition and Foreign Comparative Testing programs; International Cooperative Research, the Development, Test, and Evaluation (ICRDT&E) and International Cooperative Production programs; and the International Cooperative Support programs.   Of these, the ICRDT&E, International Cooperative Production, Foreign Acquisition, and Foreign Comparative Testing programs contribute directly to the globalization of the defense industrial base, while the other programs foster technical interaction and professional relationships that can also stimulate defense industry globalization.

- **Bilateral forums.** The United States is involved in a large number of formal bilateral and multilateral forums for discussing the breadth of IAC issues with our allies and friends. Most multilateral forums involve U.S. and European nations or English-speaking nations, while most bilateral arrangements involve Pacific Rim nations or Israel. AFI 16-110, Chapter 6, and DISAM (2000, Chapter 19) describe Air Force participation in these bodies.

- **Defense Data Exchange program.** This bilateral arrangement facilitates the mutually beneficial exchange of RDT&E data between the U.S. military and allied or friendly nations' defense components for the purpose of research and development.

- **Engineer and Scientist Exchange program.** This program consists of bilateral exchanges of U.S. and foreign defense agency engineers and scientists to fill technical positions in each other's R&D facilities. The program provides opportunities for these professionals to learn about each other's technologies, practices, management, and perspectives.

- **Foreign Acquisition and Foreign Comparative Testing programs.** According to AFPD 63-9, the Air Force can save time and development costs, take advantage of foreign technical expertise, and enhance standardization and interoperability by buying foreign-developed defense weapons and components. Foreign Comparative Testing programs facilitate the evaluation of foreign defense articles to meet U.S. defense requirements and can lead to foreign acquisitions.

- **ICRDT&E and International Cooperative Production programs.** These efforts are jointly managed and jointly financed RDT&E programs that work toward meeting common requirements. Ideally, cooperative R&D programs will transition through test and evaluation into cooperative production programs.

- **International Cooperative Support programs.** Cooperative support can include supplies, maintenance, and other aspects of logistics and sustainment for fielded systems. It can be a planned and integrated element of an international cooperative development and production program, or it can stand alone.

DoDI 5000.2, paragraph 4.7.1.3.2, shows a strong preference to engage in IAC programs when new weapon systems are procured. It directs acquisition decisionmakers to adhere to the following hierarchy of alternatives in identifying the course of action to acquire equipment:[14]

1. The procurement (including modification) of commercially available *domestic or international* technologies, systems, or equipment, or the additional production (including modification) of previously developed U.S. military systems or equipment *or allied* systems or equipment.

2. Cooperative development programs with one or more allied nations.

3. New joint component or government agency development programs.

4. New component-unique development programs.

Thus, to avert delays, risk, and cost, the first preference is to buy existing U.S. or allied COTS items, NDI, or inventory equipment.[15] If

---

[14]Emphasis added.

[15]Not all Air Force acquisitions involving international industry participation take place in the context of formal IAC Foreign Acquisition programs. For example, the Air Force can purchase weapon systems that contain components obtained from international sources from U.S. industry.

this is not possible and new equipment must be developed, an ICRDT&E program followed by an International Cooperative Production program is preferred over a U.S.-only development.

The Nunn Amendment to the FY 1986 National Defense Authorization Act allows the Secretary of Defense to enter into international cooperative research and development (ICR&D) with NATO and other "major allies" so long as the projects improve the conventional defense capabilities of NATO or the cooperative defense capabilities of the United States and its major non-NATO allies (10 USC 2350a; DISAM, 2000, Chapter 19). It also requires that DoD develop a "Cooperative Opportunities Document" for use by the Defense Acquisition Board for each MDAP. The Cooperative Opportunities Document delineates the opportunities for international cooperation and allows DoD acquisition decisionmakers to consider the opportunities for international cooperation early in the program, before major resources have been committed.

DoD 5000.2-R, paragraph 7.11, directs the MDA, in consultation with the Joint Requirements Oversight Council and legal counsel, to make a decision regarding the establishment of an international cooperative program as early as possible in the acquisition process, and it further directs that international cooperation continue to be considered at each milestone. Once a DoD component has decided to fully fund an international cooperative program, they are exhorted to remain faithful to that commitment and are directed not to reduce that funding by more than 25 percent without approval from USD(AT&L) or the Assistant Secretary of Defense for Command, Control, Communications, and Intelligence (ASD[C^{3}I]) as appropriate. USD(AT&L) or ASD(C^{3}I) may choose to insist that the component continue to provide some or all funding for the program.

An important question requiring further research is the extent to which formal government-initiated IAC programs encourage international teaming or other international business relationships that would not otherwise occur. This question is important in part because the extent to which government-initiated IAC programs foster the efficient use of U.S. national resources is debatable. Historically, for example, governments that have initiated ICRDT&E programs have often not only provided funds but also actively coordinated and directed the involvement of their own industry. Usually they demand that the value of their firms' contracts equal their own tax-payer-funded contributions to the program (often known as "work share"). Sometimes they have preselected their own national firm or firms, effectively telling those firms what their technical responsibilities will be.[16] In such cases, coalition interoperability may still be advanced. It is not clear, however, that innovation is encouraged, that the best technology is incorporated, or that delays, risks, and costs are reduced beyond what would have occurred in a U.S.-only development—where the winning firm or firms are presumably chosen on the basis of competitive advantage rather than other, primarily noneconomic criteria.

Security Assistance

Like IAC, Security Assistance encompasses several DoD programs and functions, taking as its goal the enhancement of collective security. Four DoD Security Assistance programs with significant influence on the defense industrial base are discussed here: Foreign Military Sales (FMS), Foreign Military Financing (FMF), Direct Commercial Sales (DCS), and International Military Education and Training.

- **Foreign Military Sales.** FMS is a government-to-government program in which foreign governments purchase defense articles, services, and training from the U.S. government. Since the foreign governments normally pay for the U.S. government's administrative costs as well as for the articles, the program does not require appropriated funds. The articles may be supplied from existing DoD stocks or may be new. The approval of FMS is dependent on several factors, including export restrictions, the purchaser's circumstances, and U.S. national security considerations. The U.S. government's management of the sale of defense equipment can add significant value for the customers, especially if they have not established a sophisticated acquisition system. Purchase agreements can include offsets and other arrangements, including coproduction of defense products.

---

[16]This can happen when a government wants to jump-start the technical capabilities of a firm chosen to be a "national champion." See, for example, cases presented in Lorell and Lowell (1995).

Appendix 4 of the DISAM Green Book provides an excellent comparison of the DCS and FMS methods of foreign nations purchasing U.S. defense articles (DISAM, 2000).

- **Foreign Military Financing.** FMF consists of loans or grants from the U.S. government to foreign nations to purchase U.S. defense articles through FMS or DCS, with the FMS avenue being the more common mechanism. DISAM points out that the practice of offering guaranteed and even forgivable loans has given way to grants.

- **Direct Commercial Sales.** DCS, including licensed coproduction, are also known as "commercial export sales." Interestingly, the U.S. government considers sales from U.S. industry to foreign governments to be a form of security assistance (DISAM, 2000, Appendix 4). Like FMS, these sales are subject to export restrictions under the Arms Export Control Act (AECA), so they too are subject to U.S. government approval. They are normally paid for by the customer, so congressionally appropriated funds are not required.

- **International Military Education and Training.** The International Military Education and Training program affords U.S. training to foreign military and civilian personnel and is paid for through Congressional appropriations. Although its primary function is not directly related to acquisition, it can promote U.S. exports. Through training, foreign personnel can develop professional relationships with U.S. personnel and can become familiar with—and perhaps establish a preference for—U.S. weapon systems, tactics, and procedures. This can result in FMS or DCS when these individuals return to their regular military duties in their home nations.

Note that FMS and DCS coproduction activities differ from the partnership production programs previously described as a form of IAC, which result from cooperative development programs. FMS coproduction falls under the Security Assistance umbrella and is a government-to-government program involving the manufacture of U.S.-developed defense equipment by foreign industry. DCS involving licensed coproduction requires that U.S. industry obtain a munitions export license, which allows foreign industry to manufacture U.S.-designed defense articles. DoD is involved in the export license approval process for licensed coproduction, but industry, not the U.S. government, manages the associated contracting.[17]

Both Security Assistance and IAC programs are designed to enhance U.S. national and collective security. By design, however, Security Assistance is primarily unidirectional. By standardizing equipment and training, U.S. policymakers believe they can help allies and other friends become more capable of defending themselves and become better prepared to fight in coalition with the United States.[18] The opportunity to build professional relations between militaries and to provide foreign decisionmakers with firsthand knowledge of U.S. weapon systems and tactics should enhance the United States' international relations and promote international sales of U.S. weapon systems.

Promoting the sales of U.S. military equipment abroad is a key component of security assistance. For example, while 22 USC 2321i directs that military personnel in U.S. missions abroad "should not encourage, promote, or influence the purchase by any foreign country of U.S.-made military equipment, unless they are specifically instructed to do so by an appropriate official of the executive branch," the Clinton administration's U.S. Conventional Arms Transfer Policy, issued by Secretary of State Warren Christopher in February 1995, stated that when an arms transfer decision has been made, U.S. mission personnel should support marketing efforts (DISAM, 2000, Chapter 1, Attachment 1). In harmony with this position, DoD's leadership has directed military personnel to encourage and promote sales of U.S. defense articles to foreign nations when those sales are consistent with established national security and foreign

---

[17]Chapter 10 of the *International Armaments Cooperation Handbook* (Deputy Under Secretary of Defense for International and Commercial Programs, 1996) provides additional details regarding the subtle but significant differences between cooperative production and coproduction. See also DoDD 2000.9.

[18]See, for example, congressional testimony by former Secretary of State Madeleine Albright: "As we saw several times during the past decade, when America's military is called upon to act, we will often do so as part of a coalition. Accordingly, I ask your support for our security assistance programs, which contribute to the health of America's defense industrial base, take advantage of opportunities to promote democratic practices, and help friends and allies to develop armed forces that are more capable and better able to operate with our own" (Albright, 2000).

policy goals.[19]   Military personnel are thus encouraged to endorse the sale of U.S.-built defense products to allies, which should also have a positive impact on the U.S. industrial base.

PROTECTING THE NATIONAL SECURITY

As we have seen, DoD monitors and interacts with the defense industrial base to ensure that it remains competitive, innovative, and responsive.   Given today's consolidating industry bases both here and abroad, these objectives are being met partly through closer international industry cooperation.   At the same time, DoD and the Air Force conduct IAC and Security Assistance programs to enhance U.S. and friendly nations' warfighting effectiveness, both alone and in coalitions.   These programs also provide considerable business to U.S. industry.

A third major objective evident in the defense guidance, however, is that any interaction with other nations or international industry must be consistent with U.S. national security policy.   That is, policies and programs designed to promote competition and international cooperation must not act to erode the technological advantage that U.S. military forces hold over potential adversaries or in any way reduce the effectiveness of U.S. military capabilities.   Unfortunately, the need to restrict transfers of militarily relevant technologies and to maintain U.S. control over key industrial capabilities tends to slow cooperative programs and complicate international relationships, creating some tension for governments and industry between the requirement for national security precautions and the desire to reap the benefits of defense cooperation and globalization.

Overview of Policies Toward Technology Transfer

Broadly speaking, U.S. laws and procedures governing technology transfers abroad consider three aspects of such transfers: the type of technology to be transferred, the characteristics of the intended end

---

[19]See, for example, former Secretary of Defense William Perry's 1995 memorandum, "Policy on Letters Encouraging Foreign Governments to Procure from American Sources," which encouraged endorsements, emphasizing gains from standardization, interoperability, and mutual security. In 1999, USD[A&T] Jacques Gansler and USD[P] Walter Slocombe jointly endorsed DoD support for international sales (USD[A&T] and USD[P], 1999).

user, and the nature of the intended end-use. Technologies with the potential to contribute significantly to military capabilities are controlled in order to protect the United States from countries or groups that might threaten U.S. national security.[20] Current export control reform initiatives, discussed at greater length below, may soon allow countries that meet certain requirement to be exempted from some (unclassified) export license requirements (DoS, June 2000).

As identified by DISAM (DISAM, 2000, Chapter 20), there are at least three main types of technologies: military technologies, dual-use technologies (i.e., technologies that may be used for both commercial and military purposes), and civilian or consumer technologies. Transfers of purely civilian technologies generally require only a shipping license, which in practice means no more than filling out a Shipper's Export Declaration form issued by the U.S. Census Bureau. U.S. automobile manufacturers, for example, need only obtain shipping licenses to sell their products overseas. At the other end of the spectrum, military technologies and components are almost always subject to export controls and foreign investment restrictions and, if classified, are also subject to National Disclosure Policy.

Within the constraints of national security and intellectual property rights considerations, DoD is supportive of domestic technology transfers, encouraging defense laboratories to transfer technology to U.S. industry in order to enhance competitiveness and improve the U.S. quality of life (AFPD 63-1). Internationally, DoD's security assistance and IAC programs promote technology transfers partly as a means of achieving greater interoperability between U.S. and allied forces.

While direct commercial sales and FMS-related exports are often thought of as the primary means by which defense-relevant technology, goods, and services are transferred abroad, other mechanisms are also viable (DoDD 2040.2, paragraph E3.1.12). International cooperative research development, test, evaluation, and acquisition (ICRDTE&A), marketing agreements, teams, information available on the Internet, transfers across business units of multinational corpo-

---

[20]However, transfers of nonmilitary technologies to certain countries and end users are sometimes controlled for foreign policy reasons. Commodities deemed to be in "short supply" may also be controlled through EAA 1979.

rations or between company employees of different nationalities, and foreign acquisition of U.S. businesses have also become increasingly important in recent years. All of these arrangements involve some type of technology transfer abroad.

Although issues do frequently arise with respect to the transfer of military technologies, the middle group of dual-use technologies poses special challenges for defense-related trade and investment policy. One reason is that this set of technologies is growing so rapidly. According to the DSB, for example (DSB, 1999, p. 8), "commercial software is pervasive, whether embedded within integrated weapons systems as components or subsystems, or purchased directly by the Department [of Defense] as full-up information systems." A related reason is that it is becoming increasingly difficult to differentiate between primarily military and primarily civilian technologies, as many satellite, sensor, and advanced electronics applications illustrate. A third reason is that the ability to transfer dual-use technologies abroad is increasingly important to U.S. firms' competitiveness in global civilian markets—or at least it is perceived as such by U.S. industry as well as by many elements of the policymaking community (DSB, 1999; DISAM, 2000). The tension between national security and healthy industrial base objectives is therefore increasingly pronounced with respect to export controls and other policies affecting transfers of dual-use goods, services, and technologies.

Controls on Defense-Related Trade

A variety of policy instruments, both statutory and regulatory, address the national security aspects of U.S. exports of defense-related goods and services and related technology transfers.[21] Table 4.1 summarizes the most important of these instruments at the federal level as well as the directives that establish organizational responsibility within DoD for ensuring that improper transfers do not occur.

---

[21]Although national security protections are designed only to restrict the outbound transfer of U.S. goods, services, and technology to foreign countries, as mentioned in the previous chapter they may also have a limiting effect on imports and inbound technology transfers.

Defense Goods, Services, and Technologies. As reported in Table 4.1, the 1976 AECA, as amended, provides the statutory basis for U.S. government control over the sale and export of defense goods, services, and related technical data. Thus, the implementing regulations for the AECA, the ITAR, cover most of the military Security Assistance and IAC programs described above, including DCS of defense articles and services, FMS, coproduction programs, licensing and data exchange arrangements, and cooperative research, development, test, evaluation, and acquisition (RDTE&A) programs.

The Office of Defense Trade Controls (DTC), a division of the DoS's Bureau of Political and Military Affairs, is responsible for designating which goods, services, and technologies are deemed to be defense goods, services, and technologies. This designation places them on the U.S. Munitions List (USML), which is contained in the ITAR (22 CFR 121). Each export of a USML item or technology must be licensed by DTC.[22] DTC also has primary responsibility for defining license application procedures. The majority of military export license applications are repeat cases or otherwise routine. DTC evaluates the national security and foreign policy implications of these applications without referring them to other agencies. A minority of cases are referred to DoD.

Although primary responsibility for the USML export licensing process rests with DTC, DoD plays a key role as well. USML designations are made "with the concurrence of the Department of Defense" (22 CFR 120.2), and DTC must consult with DoD before initiating the process of removing an item from the list. As part of the May 2000 Defense Trade Security Initiative (DTSI), discussed at greater length in the following section, DoD and DoS have jointly set up a four-year cycle whereby one-fourth of the USML will be reviewed each year. One of DoD's primary objectives for this process is to reduce the number of items on the USML by focusing only on truly sensitive and unique military technologies.[23]

DoD is also responsible for reviewing and making recommendations on applications for USML export licenses referred by DTC. In

---

[22]Except in cases where waivers have been granted, as described below.

[23]DTC website, DTSI initiative #17, http://www.pmdtc.org/docs/DTSI_17proposals. pdf.

Table 4.1

Summary of Statutes, Regulations, and Other Authoritative Guidance
Affecting Defense-Related Trade

Title and Implementing Regulations	Function
Arms Export Control Act (AECA), Pub.L. 94-329 (1976), 22 USC 2751–2799aa-2	Governs the sale and export of defense articles, services, and data. Establishes U.S. policy toward international programs and projects for the cooperative exchange of data, research, development, production, procurement, and logistics support to achieve specific national defense requirements. Establishes criminal penalties for failing to comply with this act.
International Traffic in Arms Regulations (ITAR), 22 CFR 120–126	Contain the U.S. Munitions List (USML), which defines the types of defense articles and services that require DoS's approval for export, and enumerates the entities that may request such approval and the general policies and procedures related to exports.
Export Administration Act (EAA 1979), Pub.L. 96–72, 50 USC	Governs the export of most unclassified articles and services not covered by the AECA, based on their impact on national security, foreign policy or supply availability.
Executive Order 12924 (1994)	EAA 1979 expired in 1994 but continued to operate under the authority of an executive order (1994–2000). (See 15 CFR 730.2 for a description of the President's statutory authority in this matter.)
Export Administration Modification and Clarification Act of 2000	Reauthorized EAA 1979 until August 20, 2001.
Export Administration Regulations (EAR), 15 CFR 730–774	Implement EAA 1979. Contain the Commerce Control List (CCL)(15 CFR 774), which covers civilian goods that can also enhance the military capability of the recipient (dual-use items).
DoDD 2040.2, International Transfers of Technology, Goods, Services, and Munitions (January 1984)	Defines fundamental DoD policy toward defense-related technology. Establishes working relationships among the Joint Staff, the services, and the defense agencies for the purpose of institutionalizing technology security responsibilities.
DoD 5105.38 M, the Security Assistance Management Manual (SAMM) (June 1, 2001)	Provides detailed guidance on security assistance programs administered by DoD.
Defense Capabilities Initiative (DCI) (April 1999)	NATO initiative designed to close the capabilities gap between the United States and NATO allies by enhancing flexibility, mobility, and interoperability.
Defense Trade Security Initiative (DTSI) (May 2000)	A joint DoS and DoD package of 17 export procedure reforms for unclassified information that are compliant with the existing statutory framework. These reforms are designed to improve the efficiency of international defense industry linkages, thus enhancing transatlantic competition and supporting NATO's DCI while preserving the export controls necessary to protect national security.

SOURCES: GAO (September 2000); DUSD(PS) (2000).

September 2001, responsibility for coordinating DoD's recommendations regarding export licenses was moved back from the Defense Threat Reduction Agency (DTRA) of USD(AT&L) to the reconstituted Defense Technology Security Agency (DTSA) within the Deputy Under Secretary of Defense for Policy (DUSD[P]).[24] DTSA is now the DoS's focal point within DoD for arms transfers and provides advice to senior Pentagon officials on technical aspects of technology security. DTSA receives input and assistance from numerous other DoD organizations for export license application reviews. These include

- The military services, which support DTSA with technical, intelligence, and operational information;

- The Joint Staff, which provides operational and military mission impact assessments; and

- The Defense Intelligence Agency, which, among other things, conducts end-user checks and intelligence reviews on particular transfer cases; assesses the foreign availability of technologies proposed for transfer; and provides intelligence concerning the total effect of technology transfers on U.S. security.

Dual-Use Goods, Services, and Technologies. While DTSA supports DoS in the control of military technologies, it supports the Commerce Department in the U.S. government export control regime for dual-use goods, services, and technologies. The Export Administration Regulations (EAR), the implementing mechanism for the 1979 Export Administration Act (EAA 1979), are administered by BXA. BXA establishes which commercial goods, materials, software, and technology (including data and know-how) have military applications and should therefore be listed on the Commerce Control List (CCL). Depending on the final destination, items on the CCL require a validated license. Validated licenses are granted only for specific orders, in specific quantities, and to certain destinations. The CCL is periodically updated by BXA with significant input from DoD, the intelligence community, and the Department of Energy. Under current legislation, however, the Commerce Department is

---

[24]Apparently some senior Pentagon officials felt that DTRA's primary mission—to prevent the proliferation of weapons of mass destruction—had led it to become too conservative in approving conventional arms exports (Muradian, 2001).

not required to consult with DoD when items are removed from the list.

Like the ITAR, the EAR apply to technology transfers as well as to the actual shipment of goods and provision of services to foreign countries. However, applying the EAR entails unique challenges because the CCL encompasses a broad and often ill-defined range of goods and technologies. For example, some types of products on the CCL—such as high-performance computers, lasers, and communications satellites—have the potential to add significant military capability to an unfriendly power yet are sold predominantly for commercial markets and applications. Further, many dual-use products are made from COTS parts and components.[25]

Another complicating provision of the EAR is the requirement that exporters submit individual validated license applications to BXA if they "know" that an export otherwise exempt from the validated licensing requirements is for "end uses involving nuclear, chemical, and biological weapons, or related missile delivery systems in named destinations listed in the regulations" (BXA, undated a). Pleading ignorance is not allowed: Both managers and employees of exporting firms are required to actively look for "red flags" that might indicate an inappropriate end use, end user, or destination for their product or technology. If any red flags are found, the exporter must obtain documentary evidence that can explain or justify them, which is often a long and costly process.

Finally, a serious concern for all U.S. defense firms—particularly those that are involved in business relationships with foreign firms—is the application of the "deemed export" rule to employees who are foreign nationals (15 CFR 730.5). Under the EAR's "deemed export" rule, a U.S. company that intends to employ a foreign national on a project involving controlled technology or software must acquire a license from BXA.[26] In addition to basic information about the em-

---

[25]How to handle products made by integrating COTS parts and components is also a growing issue for USML items.

[26]The "deemed export" rule does not apply to foreign nationals who either have permanent residence in the United States (a green card) or are considered "protected individuals" under the Immigration and Naturalization Act (BXA, undated b; 15 CFR 734.2).

ployee such as his or her name, address, citizenship, passport number, and immigration status, the firm must provide "an explanation of the process, product, size, and output capacity of all items to be produced with the technology or software, if applicable, or other description that delineates, defines, and limits the controlled technology or software to be transmitted" (BXA, undated b).

Restrictions on Foreign Direct Investment in the U.S. Defense Industrial Base

Mechanisms for overseas technology transfer such as DCS, FMS, and ICRDT&E are of concern to the national security establishment primarily because of their potential to narrow the technological gap between the United States and potential adversaries. This concern also holds true for foreign investment in U.S. industry, but here there are additional dimensions. Perhaps the most significant of these is that to the extent foreign direct investment in the United States allows foreign companies, nations, or nongovernmental organizations (NGOs) to exercise influence over the U.S. defense industrial base, it has the potential to undermine U.S. warfighting ability. Further, foreign direct investment in the United States could give foreigners access to sensitive or classified information. Finally, foreign direct investment in the United States has the potential to reduce competition for weapon system contracts.

Therefore, in addition to controlling foreign access to militarily significant technologies, the legal framework for addressing the national security aspects of foreign direct investment in the United States contains specific provisions for strictly limiting FOCI over U.S. defense firms. As shown in Table 4.2, the major statutes affecting the foreign acquisition of U.S. firms consist of Executive Orders 11858 and 12829, the Exon-Florio Amendment, and the Byrd Amendment. In addition, the United States' major antitrust legislation applies to foreign direct investment just as it does to domestic industrial activity.

In 1975, Executive Order 11858 established the CFIUS to monitor and evaluate foreign direct investment in U.S. activity. CFIUS is chaired by the Secretary of the Treasury and includes the Secretaries of State, Defense, and Commerce, the Attorney General, the Director of the

Table 4.2

Summary of Statutes, Regulations, and Other Authoritative Guidance Affecting Foreign Acquisition of U.S. Firms

Title and Implementing Regulations	Function
Executive Order 11858 (1975)	Established the interagency Committee on Foreign Investment in the United States (CFIUS) in 1975 to monitor and evaluate foreign direct investment in U.S. activity.
Defense Production Act of 1950, as amended (7 USC 721) by the Exon-Florio provision and the Byrd Amendment (1988, 1993)	Empowers the President to suspend, prohibit, or dissolve foreign acquisitions, mergers, and takeovers if he determines that the foreign interest has or is attempting to acquire control and might take action that threatens to impair U.S. national security. Also requires a CFIUS investigation whenever (1) the proposed acquirer is controlled by or acting on behalf of a foreign government; and (2) the acquisition could result in foreign control over interstate commerce affecting the national security of the United States.
Executive Order 12661 (1988)	Delegates the President's authority under Exon-Florio to CFIUS to investigate foreign direct investment activities and make recommendations to the President.
Executive Order 10865, "Safeguarding Classified Information Within Industry" (1960), as amended by Executive Order 10909 (1961) and Executive Order 11382 (1967)	Authorizes the Secretary of Defense to prescribe requirements, restrictions, and other safeguards necessary for industry to protect classified information.
Executive Order 12829, "National Industrial Security Program" (1993)	Establishes the National Industrial Security Program to safeguard classified information released to contractors, licensees, and grantees of the U.S. government. Also significantly amends Executive Orders 10865, 10909, and 11382.
DoDD 5220.22, "DoD Industrial Security Program" (December 8, 1980)	Authorizes DoD 5220.22-R, "Industrial Security Regulation"; DoD 5220.22-M, "The National Industrial Security Program Operating Manual"; and other implementing publications.[a]
Sherman Antitrust Act of 1890	Provides authority for the government to block mergers, acquisitions, and other actions that tend to limit competition or create monopolies.
Clayton Antitrust Act of 1914	Restricts various anticompetitive activities and strengthens the rights of laborers.
Hart-Scott-Rodino Act of 1976	Requires companies to report planned M&As.

SOURCES: Adapted from GAO (September 2000); and from source documents cited in this table.

[a]DoD 5220.22-M was originally entitled "The Industrial Security Manual for Safeguarding Classified Information," as authorized in DoDD 5220.22.

Office of Management and Budget, the U.S. Trade Representative, and the Chairman of the Council of Economic Advisers. Since 1988, committee membership has also included the Director of the Office of Science and Technology Policy, the Assistant to the President for National Security Affairs, and the Assistant to the President for Economic Policy. The committee receives notices of proposed foreign direct investment in U.S. companies; reviews each proposal to determine if it merits a full investigation; and conducts investigations if required.

Prior to 1988, CFIUS did not have a strong national security focus, and its activity was limited. However, the Exon-Florio provision of the Omnibus Trade and Competitiveness Act of 1988 dramatically increased Executive Branch responsibility for protecting the national security in the case of foreign mergers, acquisitions, and takeovers of U.S. firms.[27] Exon-Florio empowers the President of the United States to suspend, prohibit, or dissolve foreign acquisitions, mergers, and takeovers if and only if he determines that the foreign interest "might take action that threatens U.S. national security" and if "the provisions of law, other than the International Emergency Economic Powers Act (IEEPA), do not provide adequate and appropriate authority to protect the national security" (U.S. Department of Treasury, undated).[28] Pursuant to Executive Order 12661, the President in 1988 delegated some of his Exon-Florio responsibilities to CFIUS. Executive Order 12661 requires that the committee receive notices of foreign acquisitions of U.S. companies to determine whether an investigation is warranted; to undertake that investigation if warranted; and to make recommendations to the President at the conclusion of the investigation.

---

[27]Exon-Florio, as further amended by the FY 1993 National Defense Authorization Act (the Byrd Amendment), is codified as Section 721 of Title 7 of the Defense Production Act of 1950.

[28]The Byrd Amendment requires an investigation in all cases where "the acquirer is controlled by or acting on behalf of a foreign government" and "the acquisition could result in control of a person engaged in interstate commerce in the U.S. that could affect the national security of the United States" (U.S. Department of the Treasury, undated).

Exon-Florio defines the following five factors that the President or his designees may consider in their investigation of a proposed foreign investment (50A USC 2170):

1. Domestic production needed for projected national defense requirements;

2. The capability and capacity of domestic industries to meet national defense requirements, including the availability of human resources, products, technology, materials, and other supplies and services;

3. The control of domestic industries and commercial activity by foreign citizens as it affects the capability and capacity of the United States to meet the requirements of national security;

4. The potential effects of the proposed or pending transaction on the sales of military goods, equipment, or technology to any country that supports terrorism or proliferates missile technology or chemical and biological weapons; and

5. The potential effects of the proposed or pending transaction on U.S. technological leadership in areas affecting U.S. national security.

As necessary, the Secretary of Defense may be formally asked how a proposed foreign direct investment transaction should be viewed in terms of these five factors. In such cases, DUSD(IP) works with the appropriate component or components to assess the potential effects on the industrial base and develops a DoD position for the Secretary of Defense. In cases relevant to the Air Force, DUSD(IP) will task SAF/AQRE, who will in turn task the IBP Program to evaluate the case and develop recommendations. To the extent that these factors consider the impact and influence of the proposed foreign direct investment transaction on the health and capability of the U.S. defense industrial base, the Air Force's IBP Program employs many of the same tools and databases as those used for its other industrial base analyses, including many of the methods outlined in DoDD 5000.60 and DoDD 5000.62. Typically, CFIUS incorporates the DoD position into its analyses without further interaction with the Air Force.[29]

When a CFIUS investigation has been completed, the committee provides a report of their findings, along with recommendations, to the President. The President then has 15 days to review the committee's recommendations and then decide on and announce a course of action. The entire process from receipt of notice through the President's announcement must be completed within 90 days. Notifications of planned foreign direct investment transactions are voluntary; however, the President may conduct an investigation and take appropriate actions even after a transaction has been concluded. As prior notification could save industry unnecessary expense and effort should a transaction be revoked, there is a presumption that most if not all proposed transactions that could be relevant to the national security will be voluntarily reported.

There are other provisions in U.S. law that also apply to foreign defense firms operating or seeking to operate in the United States. The Sherman Antitrust Act of 1890, the Clayton Antitrust Act of 1914, and the Hart-Scott-Rodino Act of 1976 all seek to limit anticompetitive activities. All are administered jointly by the Department of Justice and the Federal Trade Commission. Therefore, with the sole purpose of protecting competition, many proposed M&As between foreign and U.S. firms are independently investigated by the Department of Justice or the Federal Trade Commission.[30] As described above, DoD and the Air Force are on occasion asked to provide input to the Department of Justice or the Federal Trade Commission as well as to CFIUS.

Finally, the President's decision to allow, halt, or require changes to a foreign direct investment transaction is not the only means of protecting U.S. national security with respect to FOCI firms. Established by Executive Order 12829 in 1993, the National Industrial Security Program (NISP) provides protection for classified informa-

---

[29]Interview with Alan Taylor, IBRP Director, February 21, 2001.

[30]These two agencies have overlapping jurisdictions but coordinate their efforts to avoid duplication. The Federal Trade Commission investigates most defense-related matters, while the Department of Justice handles most cases involving anticompetitive practices such as price fixing (U.S. Federal Trade Commission, undated).

tion and attempts to prevent foreign investors and owners from exerting influence or control over U.S.-based firms that deal with classified information. NISP is administered for a number of U.S. agencies by DoD's Defense Security Service (DSS), which is responsible for processing facility and personnel clearances for U.S. contractors requiring access to classified information. The National Industrial Security Program Operating Manual (NISPOM) describes NISP policies and procedures.

For cases that involve U.S. companies with access to classified information, the NISPOM requires that DSS conduct a separate industrial security review to determine how to preclude foreign access to that information. As defined by the NISPOM (Section 2-301-a), "a U.S. company is considered under foreign ownership, control, or influence whenever a foreign interest has the power . . . to direct or decide matters affecting the management or operations of that company in a manner which may result in unauthorized access to classified information or may affect adversely the performance of classified contracts."[31]   Without the adoption of appropriate negation measures, U.S. subsidiaries of foreign companies, joint ventures between U.S. and foreign companies, and many international marketing agreements and teaming arrangements could not operate effectively without compromising facility clearance eligibility. This is because of the risks they pose for unauthorized transfers of classified information and because important management positions tend to be held by non–U.S. citizens in these types of arrangements.

With respect to foreign acquisitions of U.S. companies, CFIUS and DSS industrial security reviews are carried out in two parallel but separate processes with different time constraints and considerations. CFIUS reviews are conducted on a case-by-case basis with specific requirements for timeliness, reporting, and announcements of decisions and findings. All told, the process cannot take more than 90 days from the date of notification. According to the NISPOM (Section 2-304), when industrial security concerns arise surrounding a case under review by CFIUS, an agreement should ideally be reached with the proposed foreign investor before CFIUS formulates

---

[31]DoD 5220.22-R, Section 2-202, and Section 2-302 of the NISPOM provide a more exhaustive list of factors to consider when determining if a company is under FOCI.

its recommendation (ASD [C³I], 1995). However, a security agreement cannot be signed until the proposed foreign investor legally completes the transaction. When a recommended security arrangement is rejected by the investor and alternative, mutually agreeable terms of such an arrangement are not apparent, further negotiations can be continued well beyond the original 90 days.

The security measures imposed on FOCI firms depend on the nature of the FOCI. If the issue is foreign control or influence rather than ownership, FOCI negation plans must ensure that the relevant foreign person or persons are denied access to classified information and cannot affect performance on classified contracts. Examples of such measures include the modification or termination of loan agreements or contracts with foreign interests; the diversification or reduction of foreign source income; and the physical or organizational separation of the facility component performing on classified contracts (NISPOM, Section 2-305-b).

If the issue is foreign ownership—which is always relevant in CFIUS cases—a security concern arises when a foreign shareholder has the ability to control or influence the election or appointment of one or more members of the board of directors of the U.S. firm. CFIUS commonly applies one of the following mitigation approaches (NISPOM, Section 2-306; DoD 5220.22-R, Section 2-205):

- Board resolutions are employed in cases where the foreign person's influence is insufficient to elect board members or be otherwise represented on the board of directors. In these cases, the board must identify the foreign shareholders and the type and number of foreign-owned stock. The board must acknowledge the applicant's obligation to comply with industrial security and export control requirements and must certify initially and annually thereafter that the foreign shareholder will not be involved with classified information or export-controlled technology. The FOCI company must distribute these resolutions to its board members and principal officers and must record the distribution in its corporate records.

- Voting trust agreements and proxy agreements are similar arrangements that can be employed when the foreign ownership is sufficient to gain representation on the FOCI firm's board of directors. Both arrangements require that the foreign owner's voting rights be vested with cleared U.S. citizens approved by the U.S. government.[32] The foreign owner is consulted on the sale or disposal of company assets as well as financial pledges, mortgages, mergers, reorganizations, dissolutions, and bankruptcies. In operational matters, however, the proxy holders or trustees are to direct the company uninfluenced by the foreign owner. These agreements preserve a company's eligibility to have access to classified information or to enter into classified contracts by severely limiting the foreign owner's control over the company.

- Special security agreements (SSAs) allow foreign nationals to serve on the FOCI firm's board of directors as representatives of the foreign owner ("inside directors") and to influence most aspects of company management. However, cleared U.S. "outside directors" are appointed to ensure that classified information is protected from unauthorized or inadvertent access by the foreign owners. Unlike proxy or voting trust agreements, SSAs impose operational restrictions on the FOCI firm's access to classified information. In particular, firms operating under an SSA can access classified information above the level of Secret only if the government contracting activity determines that it is in the national interest to allow them access to such information.[33] This judgment is rendered in a National Interest Determination (NID).

- A limited facility clearance can be granted to FOCI companies whose foreign owners are citizens of certain nations. Access is normally granted when the U.S. has entered into Industrial Security Agreements with the foreign owners' governments. In these cases access is limited to classified information required to fulfill the terms of a contract involving that government.

---

[32]According to DoD 5220.22-R, in a voting trust the foreign owners transfer legal title of their stock to the trustees, while in a proxy agreement the foreign owners transfer their voting rights to the proxy holders by means of an irrevocable proxy while retaining ownership.

[33]"Proscribed" information, as defined by the NISPOM, Appendix C. The U.S. government must also have a general security agreement with the foreign government involved.

SSAs are the most common form of FOCI negation measure (Ciardello, 2001). Under 10 USC 2536, the Secretary of Defense may allow the award of a contract involving classified information to a foreign entity (including firms operating under SSAs) if he or she determines that it is in the U.S. national interest. However, DFARS as well as DoD and Air Force guidance impose more rigorous national security requirements on the NID and therefore present a greater obstacle to foreign direct investment in the U.S. defense industry.

According to DFARS, a NID must include "(1) identification of the proposed awardee, with a synopsis of its foreign ownership (include solicitation and other reference numbers to identify the action); (2) [a] general description of the acquisition and performance requirements; (3) identification of the national security interests involved and the ways in which award of the contract helps advance those interests; (4) statement as to availability of another entity with the capacity, capability and technical expertise to satisfy defense acquisition, technology base, or industrial base requirements; and (5) description of any alternate means available to satisfy the requirement, e.g., use of substitute products or technology or alternate approaches to accomplish the program objectives" (DFARS Part 209.104-1[g][ii][C]). In addition, the NISPOM requires that the NID indicate why any U.S. company with the capability to produce the product should be denied the contract, as well as any reasons alternative means to satisfy the requirement are not acceptable. AFI 31-601 further states that the NID must "explain how the FOCI contractor's product or service is crucial or is the sole available source to the Air Force."

If the purpose of a NID is to ensure that contracts are awarded to a foreign company only when there is no U.S.-based alternative, these added requirements are simply extensions to the Title 10 requirement. The statute's stated purpose, however, is to ensure that the contract award advances the national security interests of the United States. As the DSB points out (1999, p. 17), these intensified requirements may be placing foreign firms at a significant competitive disadvantage. If DoD determines that it is in the national interest to use foreign companies—including U.S. subsidiaries of foreign-owned companies—to enhance competition, these more restrictive implementing requirements may be working against that purpose. Further research is required to determine if this is significantly limiting competition in practice and if national security concerns warrant such limitations.

NATIONAL SECURITY POLICIES: A LOOK AHEAD

U.S. policymakers and industry leaders agree on the undesirability of transferring military equipment and technology to countries that support terrorism or proliferate missiles or chemical and biological weapons. They do not all agree, however, on the extent to which U.S. laws, regulations, and policies designed to control militarily relevant technology transfer, limit foreign influence and control over the U.S. defense industrial base, and restrict access to sensitive or classified information reflect an appropriate trade-off between national security protection and other goals. In the discussion that follows, we outline industry, DoD and Air Force, and other government department and agency perspectives on how best to protect U.S. national security in the context of a globalizing defense industrial base. We also describe how differences in these perspectives may affect recent and ongoing efforts to reform U.S. laws governing defense and dual-use exports as well as foreign direct investment in defense-related industries.

U.S. aerospace industry leaders see the ability to participate actively in the global marketplace as vital to their companies' long-term health, competitiveness, and growth. Conversely, they see export controls—and, less critically, Exon-Florio—as impediments to partnerships with foreign firms that can provide them with increasingly valuable technological capabilities as well as foreign market access.[34] The aerospace industry would therefore like to see sweeping changes to U.S. national security policies, including the following:

- Limiting the USML to only the most militarily critical technologies;

- Limiting the CCL to technologies that have limited availability outside the United States;

---

[34]The reform of the export control system but not the CFIUS review process is listed in the AIA's top ten issues for 2001. See, for example, http://www.aia-aerospace. org/issues/topten_2001/topten_2001.cfm. See also AIA (2001).

- Reducing congressional notification for noncontroversial sales;
- Improving licensing approval times and reducing the unpredictability of approval for both USML and CCL items;
- Authorizing allies to retransfer U.S. parts and components if they have export controls comparable to ours;
- Ending the practice of publishing offset commitments to foreign governments on defense sales; and
- Expedited CFIUS reviews of proposed M&A activities (AIAA, 2001).

For the most part, OSD and the Air Force support these industry positions. In February 2001, SAF/AQ's Darlene Druyun strongly endorsed the conclusions reached in an aerospace conference she chaired entitled "Defense Reform 2001." In that conference, many panel members were highly critical of both ITAR and EAR controls (AIAA, 2001). In their widely cited 1999 Task Force Report on Globalization of the Defense Industry, DSB also concluded that current U.S. export licensing policy is outdated to the point of being counterproductive. DSB stated:

> Clinging to a failed policy of export controls has undesirable consequences beyond self-delusion. It can limit the special influence the United States might otherwise accrue as a global provider and supporter of military equipment and services. . . . Equally obvious, shutting U.S. companies out of markets served instead by foreign firms will weaken the U.S. commercial advanced technology and defense sectors upon which U.S. economic security and military-technical advantages depend (DSB, 1999, p. vii).

DSB added:

> [T]he more the United States depends on technology controls for maintaining the capability gap between its military forces and those of its competitors, the greater the likelihood that the gap will narrow. . . . [T]echnology controls ultimately will not succeed in denying its competitors access to militarily useful technology. . . . [A]t most, they will buy the United States time to engage in the further research, development and acquisition required to maintain its position of dominance (DSB, 1999, pp. vii–viii).

Overall, rather than urging tighter controls to protect it, DSB recommended that actions be taken to reinvigorate the U.S. defense industrial base in order to keep the newest and most innovative technologies and capabilities flowing to U.S., NATO, and other allied warfighters.

Two initiatives introduced since April 1999—the Defense Capabilities Initiative (DCI) and the Defense Trade Security Initiative (DTSI)—reflect this DoD priority, as do related efforts to extend country-specific ITAR exemptions to the UK and Australia through bilateral negotiations. DoD has also generally supported congressional efforts to authorize a less restrictive version of EAA 1979 and has opposed efforts to make the CFIUS review process more restrictive.

Defense Capabilities Initiative

By the end of the 1990s, experiences in Iraq, Bosnia-Herzegovina, and, most recently, Kosovo had convinced senior U.S. and NATO officials that alliance force structures were inadequate to meet 21st century security challenges (Cohen, 1998; NATO, 2000a). At the beginning of the Bosnian campaign, for example, NATO found that units from different nations could not talk to one another because of incompatible equipment. Kosovo further demonstrated that capabilities such as strategic lift, aerial refueling, support jamming, secure communications, and precision-guided munitions—all identified as key to mission success—were either weak or lacking in European allied forces (Kutner, 2000; and Robertson, 1999).

Spurred by the United States, NATO leaders launched DCI at their April 1999 Washington Summit. DCI identifies five functional areas in which alliance capabilities need to be improved:

- Rapid deployment of forces to locations where they are needed, including areas outside alliance territory (deployability and mobility);

- Maintenance and supply of forces far from their home bases and availability of sufficient fresh forces for long-duration operations (sustainability);

- Successful engagement of adversaries in all types of operations, from high to low intensity (effective engagement);

- Protection of forces and infrastructure against current and future threats (survivability); and

- Command, control, and information systems that are compatible with each other to enable forces from different countries to work together effectively (interoperable communications).

In each of these areas, DCI has two major objectives: closing the capabilities gap between the United States and its NATO allies, and enhancing the flexibility, mobility, and interoperability of allied forces (NATO, 1999). The achievement of these objectives, however, requires first that the European NATO nations increase their military capabilities—which will likely require increased spending on defense acquisition—and second that the United States assist the Europeans by sharing more technologies and capabilities. Thus, a major component of the United States commitment to implementing DCI is to reform its export procedures in order to enable its NATO allies to close the warfighting capabilities gap.[35]

Defense Trade Security Initiative

In May 2000, former Secretary of State Madeleine Albright announced the introduction of DTSI. DTSI is a package of reform measures jointly devised by DoD and DoS that are intended to streamline the U.S. defense export licensing process. Proponents of DTSI hope it will encourage U.S. defense firms to forge closer linkages with firms from friendly foreign nations (DoS and USD[AT&L], 2000). Although DTSI does not focus exclusively on NATO nations, it is the primary vehicle for implementing U.S. obligations under DCI.

DTSI consists of 17 proposed license reforms for transfers of unclassified information, equipment, and services. Although sometimes called "export reforms," these measures have the potential to affect many other types of business activities. DTSI's proposed reforms can be grouped in the following four categories:[36]

---

[35]DCI establishes policies to improve allied doctrinal and logistic interoperability as well as technical interoperability, but these concepts are not discussed here. See, for example, NATO (NATO, 2001) and Codner (1999).

[36]These categorizations and descriptions are summarized from "Defense Trade Security Initiatives," a DSCA background paper available at http://www.dsca.osd

- **The creation of new license authorizations (proposals 1–4).**
  DTSI creates four new "global" license categories for entire programs or projects. These categories are designed to eliminate
  authorized exporters' need to acquire individual licenses for
  transfers of defense hardware, technical data, services, and
  development, manufacturing, and logistical support when such
  items are part of a major program or project involving a NATO
  government, Japan, Australia, or Sweden. They cover U.S.
  government–sanctioned programs in which a U.S. company is
  the original equipment manufacturer; foreign government–
  sponsored commercial competitions; U.S. exporters performing
  activities in support of IAC programs; and qualified U.S. defense
  companies exchanging technical data with NATO, Japanese,
  Australian, or Swedish firms to explore opportunities for
  international business arrangements such as M&As, joint
  ventures, and teaming.[37]

- **Expanding the scope of existing license practices (proposals 5–
  9).** These expanded licenses will authorize overseas warehousing
  and preauthorize third-party transfers; will accelerate licensing
  in support of DCI-related programs; and will improve export license evaluation coordination between DoS and DoD.

- **Improving existing ITAR exemptions (proposals 10–14).** A key
  reform in this category is the authorization of an ITAR licensing
  exemption for unclassified material applicable to NATO allies
  and approved host-country defense firms that demonstrate export and licensing policies and procedures comparable to those
  of the United States. This category also extends ITAR exemptions
  to maintenance and training in support of allied equipment and
  technical data exchange with potential foreign bidding partners
  on proposals for DoD acquisition programs. It calls for more fre-
  quent use of existing DoD authorizations for ITAR exemptions as

---

.mil/dtsi/dtsi_links.htm. See Appendix B for a complete listing of all 17 DTSI reform
measures.

[37]Sweden was added in June 2001. See White House Office of the Press Secretary
(2001).

well as streamlined licensing of commercial satellite components and technical data for major allies.[38]

- **Improving transfers relative to government-to-government programs (proposals 15–17).** This category includes the elimination of license requirements for technical data and services in support of approved FMS sales as well as advanced retransfer consent to foreign governments that sign global end-use or retransfer assurances. In addition, the USML is to be completely reviewed every four years with the purpose of updating the list to include only military-critical items that are not widely available.

Since May 2000, DoD has taken several internal administrative steps to support the implementation of DTSI. To speed up license processing times, for example, DTSA is sending a large number of cases back to DTC without referring them to other DoD organizations. According to former DUSD(IA) Jeffrey Bialos, "Rather than having DTRA [now DTSA] refer 70 percent of incoming license requests at DoD to the services and other components, [DoD is] reversing that ratio and moving toward referring only 30 percent of the cases" (Bialos, 2000, pp. 9–10). More recently, former Deputy Assistant Secretary of State for Political/Military Affairs Gregory Suchan stated that processing times have dropped from 15 to 8 days for application licenses that are not referred to other agencies, and from 69 to 60 days for applications that are.

Although senior Pentagon officials have been strong advocates of DTSI, support from other U.S. government departments and agencies has been qualified. In an August 2000 report, for example, GAO argued that several of the DTSI proposals were based on incomplete data and perhaps faulty analysis. GAO further pointed to several areas where it perceived a lack of agreement between DoD and DoS, including the timeline for implementing the proposals, the nature and scope of the proposed interagency computer system, and the manner in which to set criteria or parameters for assessing the comparability of allied countries' export regimes. A key concern for DoS, according to GAO, was that even the closest of U.S. allies might not

---

[38]This DTSI provision fulfills the requirements of Section 1309(a) of the FY 2001 Foreign Relations Authorization Act.

have sufficient controls in place to prevent the reexport of military technologies to third countries (GAO, August 2000).

Concerns over the possible proliferation of technologically advanced U.S.-developed weapon systems as a result of the relaxing of export controls—whether through DTSI or through any other reform measures—are important and legitimate. To counter these concerns, DTSI's provisions require that importing nations have or adopt export and retransfer policies and practices that are comparable to those of the United States. These provisions are intended to reduce original exports of allied defense products as well as to eliminate the retransferring of sensitive U.S. defense articles to nations that the United States perceives as potential adversaries (DoS, 2000). Supporters of DTSI thus argue that if implemented correctly, DTSI should reduce proliferation, not encourage it. In their view, the DTSI proposal to extend ITAR exemptions on unclassified exports to countries that "share with the United States congruent and reciprocal policies in export controls, industrial security, intelligence, law enforcement, and reciprocity in market access" holds the potential to encourage dramatically closer defense industrial relationships between the United States and its major allies (DoS, 2000).

Bilateral Discussion with a View Toward Country-Wide ITAR Exemptions

In fact, well before the formulation of DTSI by DoS and DoD, DoD had already initiated bilateral discussions as a step toward encouraging greater integration of the U.S. and allied defense industrial bases. In February 2000, a nonbinding Declaration of Principles was signed by former Secretary of Defense Willam S. Cohen and the UK's Secretary of State for Defence, Geoffrey Hoon. A similar Statement of Principles between the United States and Australia was signed five months later. In both cases, it was possible to reach the negotiation stage because of agreement over the basic areas in which congruence and reciprocity are required. These areas, designated "the five pillars of cooperation" by former Deputy Secretary of Defense John Hamre, are as follows:

- Export control processes;
- Industrial security policies and procedures;

- Intelligence cooperation on matters of industrial security;

- Law enforcement cooperation; and

- Access to defense markets (Hamre, 2000).

It is too soon to know whether these two bilateral understandings can be further developed into binding agreements, but as of September 2001, some progress has been made. The January 2001 U.S.-UK Joint Statement on Defense Export Controls summarizes steps both nations have taken to explicitly address each of the five pillars (DoS, Office of the Spokesman, 2001). Confirming a high level of commonality between the USML and the UK's Military List, extending UK export controls to intangible transfers, and adding anti–third party transfer procedures to the UK licensing process are among the steps either taken or proposed.

A model for both understandings is the U.S. relationship with Canada, which is considered to be part of the U.S. defense industrial base for production planning purposes (DFARS Part 225, paragraph 225.870). Many factors have contributed to the development of such an open trading relationship, including harmonized policies and procedures related to the five pillars listed above.[39] However, even the U.S.-Canadian relationship requires attention and effort. In April 1999, for example, the United States temporarily suspended Canada's ITAR exemption after it found that Canadian firms had exported sensitive technology to Iran and China (DoS, Office of the Spokesman, 2000). In any case, the U.S.-Canada harmonization precedent may be difficult to duplicate with the UK and Australia by virtue of the far greater differences in these countries export control regimes.

The ultimate goal for DoD and perhaps other U.S. policymakers has been to extend bilateral discussions and agreements on export controls to multilateral discussions with NATO and other friendly nations (Bialos, 2000). The reasons are both pragmatic and strategic. Pragmatically, a bilateral agreement between the United States and the UK may have little impact given the consolidation of Europe's defense industrial base. Bilateral agreements cannot efficiently ac-

---

[39]See DoS, Office of the Spokesman (2000).

commodate the effective operation of major multinational weapon system integrators or the multinational workforces of many smaller European defense companies. Strategically, the culmination of many individual bilateral agreements would effectively be to create a new multilateral arms control arrangement based on the U.S. system. Given the perceived weakness of the current multilateral regime, the Wassenaar Arrangement, this could be highly desirable from a national security standpoint.[40]

Reauthorization of EAA 1979

DTSI and the bilateral discussions with the UK and Australia focus primarily on liberalizing the export control regime for military products, services, and technologies—that is, the ITAR. However, DoD also sees export controls on dual-use items as a major barrier to full defense cooperation with U.S. allies. DoD has therefore been broadly supportive of congressional efforts to revise and rewrite EAA 1979.

As a result of congressional differences over whether or how much it ought to be liberalized, the dual-use export control system mandated by EAA 1979 has been upheld since its expiration in 1994 through a series of temporary statutory extensions and by executive order under the authority of the IEEPA. This situation has been unsatisfactory to DoD as well as to others because, among other reasons, the IEEPA-based regime imposes lower penalties for violations and decreases the time available to DoD for license review from 40 to 30 days (Mancuso, 2000; U.S. Senate, April 2001).

After a failed attempt to pass a bill in FY 2000, a bill to reauthorize EAA 1979 was once again approved by the Senate Banking Committee in March 2001. Key national security features of EAA 2001 that differ from EAA 1979 are as follows:

---

[40]Although in principle an important tool for limiting transfers of conventional arms and arms technologies, most analysts agree that as of now, both structural and procedural shortfalls render Wassenaar ineffective for most U.S. national security purposes. See the congressionally sponsored Study Group on Enhancing Multilateral Export Controls for U.S. National Security (2001) for discussions of the Wassenaar Arrangement, its weaknesses, and ways it might be made more effective. DSB (1999) also briefly outlines reasons U.S. controls on conventional weapons—particularly dual-use technologies—are essentially unilateral.

- It establishes a National Security Control List for items that contribute to the military potential of other countries, or to stem weapon proliferation or deter terrorism;

- It requires the concurrence of the Secretary of Defense for items included on or taken off the list;

- It removes controls on items with foreign availability or mass-market status but allows the President to reimpose controls to advance U.S. national security;

- It creates an Office of Technology Evaluation within the Commerce Department to gather, coordinate, and analyze information on foreign availability and the mass-market status of items;

- It provides for enhanced controls on items, regardless of status, if the President finds that removing controls would pose a significant threat to U.S. national security;

- It establishes a five-level country tiering system for each controlled item or group of items;

- It establishes criteria for license review on the basis of the characteristics of the item, the threat to the United States from misuse or diversion of the item, and the effectiveness of national security controls on the item, and specifies new timelines for the initial review and referral process;

- It establishes an interagency dispute resolution process for disputed license applications; and

- It encourages U.S. participation in new and existing multilateral export control regimes.[41]

As of September 2001, the Senate was debating EAA 2001. One of the most salient issues for legislators who oppose the new bill is its apparent presumption that commercial concerns should be given weight equal to or even greater than that of national security concerns. Senator Richard Shelby, for example (U.S. Senate, April 2001),

---

[41]This list describes major provisions of S. 149, the Senate version of EAA 2001, which is the basis for all four of the versions of EAA 2001 introduced into the House. See U.S. Senate (January 2001 and April 2001).

has argued that the new bill "provides overly broad or exclusive authority to the Secretary of Commerce on important procedural issues such as commodity classifications, license and dispute referrals, license exemptions, and development of export administration regulations." Shelby and others are particularly concerned about the need for DoS and especially DoD to be given more authority and a larger role in the export licensing process.[42]

DoD officials have indeed argued in the past that the Commerce Department refers too few commodity classification requests to the agency for review. According to Mancuso (2000), out of 2723 commodity classification requests sent to the Commerce Department in FY 1998, just 12 were referred to DoD for review. DoD leaders believe, however, that EAA 2001 will allow for a "timely, transparent, and disciplined process for Department of Defense review of commodity classifications" (Tarbell, 2001).

DoD is further convinced that attempts to control many of the items on the CCL are futile. According to DSB (DSB, 1999, p. 8), "the commercial sector, which pays scant attention to national boundaries, is now driving the development of much of the advanced technology integrated into modern information-intensive military systems." For this reason, even under the current legislation, BXA cannot effectively control mass-market commercial-grade microprocessors, for example, even when they are incorporated as components of sophisticated missile guidance systems. Instead, the integrated guidance systems are included on the USML (22 CFR 120.3). One reason is that unilateral U.S. export controls on mass-market microprocessors would be extremely difficult to implement in that large quantities of simple general-use microprocessors are manufactured overseas and sold through multiple international distribution channels.[43] Furthermore, stand-alone commercial components such as microprocessors have little military value without

---

[42]Opponents of the bill also do not like the mass-market, foreign availability, overseas production, or incorporated parts provisions of the bill, which could significantly reduce the number of items controlled under the new regime (U.S. Senate, April 2001).

[43]However, general-purpose, high-performance microprocessors, as well as certain application-specific microprocessors, have greater potential to increase military capability and are controlled under the EAR (White House Office of the Press Secretary, 1999).

the added technical knowledge that is required to integrate them into military products.

Nevertheless, whether and how to impose export controls is a difficult question for "high performance" items that are rapidly gaining mass-market status. Between January 1993 and January 2001, for example, export controls on high-performance computers were revised six times as the power and capabilities of widely available computing systems continued to surpass control levels. In recognition of this widespread availability, a major revision of U.S. export control policy occurred in January 2001, when then-President Clinton granted license exceptions for shipments of high-performance computers to qualified end users and users in qualified countries (BXA, 2001). At the time of this last revision, the Clinton administration also recommended that Congress repeal those provisions of the FY 1998 National Defense Authorization Act that control high-performance computer exports to countries such as India, Pakistan, Russia, China, Vietnam, and certain Middle Eastern and Central European nations (Reuters, 2001). An even more liberal treatment of high-performance computer exports is a key feature of the debate over EAA 2001.

Trends in Foreign Direct Investment and Industrial Security Policies

Consistent with its intent to foster closer industrial linkages with key allies, DoD's position on foreign direct investment and FOCI in important segments of the defense industry appears to have liberalized over the last decade.[44] In FY 2000, DoD reviewed more than 60 CFIUS cases, several of which involved significant transactions that affect the U.S. defense industrial base. Among them were the following:

- The acquisition of Lockheed Martin's Aerospace Electronics Systems and Control Systems businesses by the British firm BAE Systems;

- The creation of U.S. subsidiaries of the multinational EADS;

---

[44]One former senior DoD official told us that the U.S. government had decided to allow greater foreign direct investment in the U.S. defense industrial base in return for foreign promises to abjure bribery and to tighten up on third-party transfers.

- The acquisition of Racal Electronics PLC and its U.S. subsidiary, Racal Communications, Inc., by the French firm Thomson-CSF (now Thales);

- The merger of Electro-Optics Industries Ltd. (ELOP) and its U.S. subsidiary, Kollsman, Inc., with Elbit Systems Ltd. of Israel; and

- The acquisitions of the Fairchild Defense Division of Orbital Sciences Corporation and the TI Group by the British firm Smiths Industries (DUSD[IA], 2001).

Although DoD did seek NISP risk mitigation measures in cases where the U.S. firms being acquired had access to classified defense technologies, this list nevertheless represents a major liberalization of policy since the early 1990s, when Thomson-CSF (now Thales) was forced to halt its attempted acquisition of LTV in part as a result of opposition from DoD.

An important question with respect to both the CFIUS process and NISP restrictions is the extent to which these measures have actually discouraged desirable as opposed to undesirable foreign investment—or any foreign investment at all. According to GAO, 1300 (or about 17 percent) of the nearly 7400 foreign acquisitions of U.S. companies reported to the Commerce Department between 1988 and 1999 were also reported to CFIUS (GAO, June 2000). From 1988 through spring 2001, just 20 out of 1356 cases reviewed were subject to presidential investigations (Ciardello, 2001). Moreover, there was just one forced divestiture, which involved a Chinese aerospace firm's acquisition of a parts manufacturer in 1989, and there were only two major voluntary withdrawals. GAO further reports that CFIUS was not informed of at least three foreign acquisitions of U.S. companies that had been identified by DoD, DoS, or the Treasury Department as having potential implications for national security. GAO also argues that there may have been more such cases, pointing to possible defects in the process CFIUS uses to identify foreign acquisitions with possible effects on national security (GAO, June 2000, p. 29). Nevertheless, it would seem that CFIUS and Exon-Florio are not major threats to friendly-nation companies' attempts to invest in the U.S. defense industry.

Another important question concerns the extent to which the U.S. export control regime together with Exon-Florio have encouraged

U.S. and foreign firms to form business relationships designed to evade or minimize the effects of regulation. For example, are U.S. and foreign firms choosing relationships such as teaming agreements rather than conducting more formal M&As in order to avoid the provisions of Exon-Florio? And, if so, what are the implications? GAO (GAO, September 2000, p. 2) found that the companies it reviewed did not "consider the U.S. legal and regulatory environment to be a major impediment to forming an alliance or a principal determinant of the type of alliance chosen." However, these companies were concerned about the effects of slow technology transfers— especially U.S. controls on third-party transfers—on their current alliance operations and future alliance sales. They also appeared concerned about costs imposed as a result of the regulations. There is, in addition, some evidence that contradicts GAO's findings. For example, it would appear that Europe's largest satellite manufacturer, Astrium, may be considering a teaming arrangement in order to avoid case-by-case export control scrutiny (Pasztor, 2001).

Summary and a Look Ahead

The Air Force and OSD both believe that the key to equipping Air Force warfighters with superior yet affordable weapon systems is competition. Although expanding the field to foreign industry has not become the major thrust of Air Force and OSD competition strategy, laws and regulations require and encourage acquisition personnel to allow international sources to compete, and the more general competition-promotion policies do have the potential to encourage greater competition from abroad. Further relaxation of domestic source restrictions such as the Buy America Act and 10 USC 2534 should also encourage greater foreign participation in Air Force contract competitions—although the limited number of restrictions on defense products that have not already been waived suggests that the effects of further relaxation may be small. Overall, attitudinal changes may be more necessary than regulatory changes in creating a more level playing field for products and technologies provided by foreign defense firms.

A second and probably more significant objective guiding Air Force and OSD policy toward defense globalization is preparation for coalition warfare. The Air Force and OSD believe that effective coalition operations require greater interoperability of equipment—a goal that can best be achieved through well-coordinated ICRDT&E programs and International Cooperative Programs (ICPs), foreign acquisitions, and the sale of U.S. equipment abroad. They are therefore actively seeking to lower unnecessary barriers to IAC and Security Assistance programs such as these, including barriers resulting from national security precautions.

The third and final objective guiding Air Force and OSD policy toward defense globalization is protection of the national security. Export control regimes such as the ITAR and EAR are designed to prevent the technological advantage of U.S. military forces from eroding. Restrictions on foreign direct investment in the United States through the CFIUS process and the NISP are designed to prevent foreigners from exerting undue influence over the U.S. defense industrial base as well as to keep them from inappropriately accessing classified information.

The Air Force and DoD now believe, however, that at least some of these national security–related constraints have become ineffective and even counterproductive since the end of the Cold War. DoD has therefore supported—and in some cases initiated—several important proposed reforms to the national security policies governing the globalization of international trade and investment markets. Reforms aimed at the ITAR include DTSI as well as bilateral negotiations with the UK and Australia; reforms aimed at the dual-use export control regime include support for EAA 2001, which is currently embroiled in congressional debate. Less visibly, DoD has also liberalized its position on foreign direct investment and FOCI by major allies in important segments of the defense industry.

Finally, the question remains to what extent DoD competition, defense cooperation, and especially national security policies discourage or encourage globalization in general and certain types of cross-border business relationships in particular. For example, to what extent do the two U.S. export control regimes discourage international trade involving licensed production of U.S. military technologies? Are U.S. and foreign firms choosing relationships such as teaming instead of equity-based linkages in order to avoid the CFIUS process? Finally, what types of cross-border business relationships should the Air Force prefer given its competition, defense cooperation, and national security objectives? Future case studies and those reviewed in the following chapter should help answer these questions.

Chapter Five

THE NEW CROSS-BORDER BUSINESS RELATIONSHIPS: CASE STUDY FINDINGS AND PROPOSED FUTURE RESEARCH

INTRODUCTION

As noted in Chapter One, interviews and recent surveys of U.S. aerospace management views point to a growing consensus that the U.S. aerospace industry must continue to "go global" and must pursue that objective much more aggressively. Yet according to these sources—and as indicated in the preceding chapter's discussion of U.S. government reform initiatives—industry executives often remain uncertain about what strategies to pursue and continue to be concerned about U.S. government policy barriers. For example, according to one study:

> Although globalization is viewed as an imperative, most [aerospace and defense] executives surveyed are still searching for the most effective way to overcome the constraints and enter new markets. Furthermore, the majority of [aerospace and defense] executives perceive their current global capabilities to be weak relative to their primary competitors. Executives [who] do have a clear picture in mind are looking to forge strategic alliances with partners overseas (Deloitte & Touche and Deloitte Consulting, 1998, p. 4).

The previous chapter discussed the extensive U.S. legal and regulatory regime that helps shape the response of the U.S. defense aerospace industrial base toward globalization. Also examined were recent U.S. government reform initiatives aimed at restructuring and streamlining that regime. Critics contend that the existing regulatory regime, which is designed to provide technology security and to protect domestic defense industrial base capabilities, impedes U.S. industry–initiated attempts to gain the benefits of greater globalization. One important goal of DoD reform measures is to reduce such impediments. It is unclear, however, how effective these reform measures will be either at enhancing globalization or at protecting U.S. national security.

U.S. industry and U.S. government leaders alike seek to reap the greatest possible benefit from increased globalization of the U.S. defense industrial base. Yet both are entering untrodden territory, and neither is entirely sure how to proceed. This chapter reports the initial findings we derived from our survey, using open-source published materials, of 38 recent innovative approaches toward aerospace defense industry cross-border relationships.[1] The purpose of this exercise is threefold.

First, it seeks to illustrate in more concrete detail the key characteristics and evolving nature of the major types of business relationships that have come to dominate cross-border interactions. Although all these business relationships can be categorized by means of the broad RAND typology presented earlier in this report, an examination of actual cases is necessary to gaining ground-level insight into what they may mean for the Air Force.

Second, it offers some initial insights into the factors that are promoting the creation of these types of cross-border relationships. A particular focus is whether or not the U.S. regulatory regime and the reform measures discussed in Chapter Four have positively or negatively affected the formation and functioning of such relationships.

Third, it provides an initial analysis of whether and to what extent these nontraditional cross-border relationships appear to be

---

[1]The specific cases are listed later in the chapter. Included in this number are the complex export and import cases discussed in Chapter Two. The focus of the cases in this chapter is on industry-initiated business relationships, but other types are included as well. Changes in business relationships involving the same basic product or program and the same firms are treated as different cases. In other words, when a teaming arrangement is changed to a joint venture but the program and industry participants remain the same, it is counted as two separate cases.

promoting the overarching Air Force globalization policy objectives already discussed in this report: (1) providing affordable and capable weapon systems for the Air Force; (2) enhancing the ability of the Air Force to operate effectively in combined operations with European NATO and other key allies; and (3) protecting key national security objectives, particularly with regard to technology security and domestic industrial base capabilities.

The selection criteria for the cross-border business relationships and programs presented herein were as follows: First, most of them represent recent cross-border agreements—the majority of which are industry-initiated—that are characterized by unusual or innovative elements aimed at responding to the new imperatives of globalization. Second, most are related to aerospace combat or combat support platforms or to important munitions or command, control, intelligence, surveillance, and reconnaissance (C^2ISR) programs.[2] Many are related to the capabilities identified in the NATO DCI. A substantial number of these cases also raise unique questions or issues regarding either claimed benefits or concerns regarding globalization.

The remainder of the chapter presents detailed descriptions of most of the 30-plus cross-border business relationships and programs we examined. These cases are presented according to the broad typology of cross-border trade, investment, and other cross-border business relationships presented in Table 2.1 of Chapter Two: marketing agreements, teams, joint ventures, and parents/subsidiaries.

MARKETING AGREEMENTS

As defined in Chapter Two, marketing agreements are agreements between two or more companies to distribute an existing product— i.e., a product that has already been developed by one of the partners. Marketing agreements may include the eventual modification of the item as well as the licensed production or coproduction of the item by the nondeveloping partner.

---

[2]A few nonaerospace defense programs have been included that exhibit great novelty or creativity in their business structures.

Although marketing agreements are sometimes components of offset agreements or are combined with other types of business relationships, the central reason for their creation is market access. Such agreements are usually made between two technologically advanced countries when market access to either country is difficult to attain without the assistance of a domestic firm. The partner that developed the item is willing to transfer technology and permit licensed coproduction by the nondeveloper partner in order to gain access to a new foreign market or to leverage existing market relationships of the nondeveloper partner. Once a sale is made, marketing agreements may be supplemented by teaming agreements or joint ventures for the production of the weapon system. Marketing agreements may also lead to teaming or joint venture agreements aimed at joint or single-party development of an upgraded version of the original item, followed by coproduction.[3] Typical examples of recent marketing agreements are shown in Table 5.1.

Lockheed/Rafael Popeye and Python

Two interesting recent cases are the marketing agreement between Israel's Rafael Armament Authority and Lockheed for the Popeye and Python 4 missiles and that between Rafael and Northrop Grumman for the Litening II targeting pod. Each of these agreements is designed to permit access to the U.S. market and to third markets through a powerful U.S. contractor. In return for certain third-country sales rights, the U.S. contractor modifies or upgrades the system, coproduces it, and markets it to the U.S. government.

A good example of this approach is the Popeye, a 3000-lb. precision-guided air-to-ground missile (AGM) that was originally an off-the-

---

[3]Cross-border marketing agreements are sometimes referred to as teaming agreements and may also be associated with import or export agreements and other types of business arrangements, as noted in the main text. However, we argue that there are significant business and technological differences between agreements involving items that have already been developed by one partner and those involving the cooperative development of a new item or items. In our taxonomy, we have therefore chosen to distinguish between marketing agreements, which we define as agreements in which an item usually has already been developed by one partner, and teaming agreements, where an item or items are usually planned for cooperative development.

Table 5.1

Examples of International Marketing Agreements

Firms	Items
U.S. company marketing/producing foreign-developed item	
Lockheed/Rafael	Python 4 missile, HAVE NAP/Popeye
Northrop/Rafael	Litening II targeting/navigation pod
Boeing/IAI	Arrow ATBM system (negotiations)[a]
Foreign firm marketing/producing U.S. or third-country item	
Alenia Marconi (MBDA)/Boeing	JDAM
BAE Systems/Saab	JAS Gripen

[a]ATBM = Anti-Theater Ballistic Missile.

shelf purchase of a foreign item by the U.S. Air Force.[4] Rafael developed the Popeye for use on the McDonnell Douglas F-4E by the Israeli Air Force. In the late 1980s, the U.S. Air Force viewed the Popeye as a short-term, stopgap, precision-powered munition that it could buy off the shelf from Rafael until U.S. industry developed more advanced smart munitions. Rafael worked with Boeing to qualify the Popeye for use on U.S. Air Force B-52s. The Air Force initially purchased all its Popeyes directly from Rafael as straight imports, designating the weapon the HAVE NAP and, later, the AGM-142.

In the hopes of continuing sales to the U.S. Air Force as well as to third markets, Rafael negotiated a marketing agreement with Lockheed.[5] Lockheed modified the Popeye to make it more compatible with the B-52 and other U.S. Air Force platforms as well as with the U.S. Air Force logistics system. Manufacturability was also improved, and performance capabilities were enhanced through the use of a new imaging infrared seeker and an I-800 penetrating warhead. Other modifications were also made.[6]

---

[4]The Popeye was also mentioned in the section in Chapter Two dealing with trade and is discussed again in the section in this chapter on joint ventures.

[5]It is possible that this was associated with F-16 offset agreements, but the open published literature does not address this issue.

[6]It is unclear from the open published literature whether these modifications were conducted collaboratively with Rafael or solely by Lockheed.

On a roughly 50-50 basis, Rafael and Lockheed formed a new joint venture, the Orlando, Florida-based Precision Guided Systems United States (PGSUS) LLC, to coproduce the higher-performance version of the missile in the United States for the U.S. Air Force and third countries.[7] This newly modified version was called the AGM-142 Raptor.

Interestingly, the formation of PGSUS appears to have led to a situation in which Rafael ended up competing against itself. When the Australian Air Force issued a requirement for a precision-strike standoff weapon, the three main contenders were the Rockwell (now Boeing) AGM-130; Rafael's Israeli version of the Popeye as a pure commercial sale; and the PGSUS LLC AGM-142 Raptor. The PGSUS LLC AGM-142 won the competition. It can be argued that Rafael's joint venture with Lockheed permitted that firm to penetrate a market it might not otherwise have been able to access without Lockheed's marketing prowess and technical upgrades. At the same time, the basic Popeye provided the U.S. Air Force and Lockheed with a product that presumably required less nonrecurring investment than would have been the case with a new start. It also broadened Lockheed's portfolio of precision-guided weapons available for export to third parties such as Australia.[8]

The Python 4 marketing agreement between Rafael and Lockheed is equally interesting from the perspective of maintaining competition and innovation in the U.S. aerospace industry. Since the 1997 Raytheon/Hughes/Texas Instruments mergers, Raytheon has exercised a virtual monopoly on U.S. Air Force and Navy tactical air-to-air missiles. Raytheon manufactures the standard U.S. short- and long-range air-to-air missiles (the AIM-9M, AIM-9X Sidewinder, and AIM-120 AMRAAM) as well as the Navy's long-range AIM-54 Phoenix. According to credible open sources, the Rafael Python 4

---

[7]See the discussion on joint ventures below.

[8]Lockheed and Rafael reportedly have also cooperatively developed a smaller version of the Popeye I HAVE NAP called "Popeye II HAVE LITE" for use on smaller F-16-class fighters. Press reports claim that Rafael has also negotiated a joint venture agreement with Turkish companies to produce and market HAVE LITE. Finally, unconfirmed press reports claim that a very long range, turbojet-powered Popeye variant labeled "Popeye Turbo" has been developed exclusively by Rafael for use as an Israeli nuclear-capable submarine-launched cruise missile.

with helmet-mounted sight is highly capable as well as competitive with the comparable AIM-9X, which has recently entered low-rate production. Although the Python 4 has not been purchased by the U.S. services, its active marketing by Lockheed may have placed significant competitive pressure on Raytheon in its development of the AIM-9X.

Rafael recently announced the development of the Derby missile, a new-generation beyond visual-range (BVR) air-to-air missile with an active radar seeker. Rafael claims that this missile provides lock-on after-launch capability as well as advanced programmable electronic counter-countermeasures (ECCM). Its manufacturer further contends that the Derby missile is competitive with the Raytheon AMRAAM and is expected to compete directly with AMRAAM for worldwide sales.[9] This is significant in that Raytheon effectively monopolizes the long-range BVR missile market in the United States. Raytheon also heavily dominates the global market, facing only minor competition from the French MICA, some Soviet missiles, and possibly Derby, at least until the European Meteor completes development over the coming decade (see below). If Rafael includes Derby in its marketing agreements with Lockheed, significantly greater competition may well be injected into the U.S. and global BVR air-to-air missile markets.[10]

On the other hand, both the withholding and the proliferation of sophisticated air-to-air missile technology have led to political, military, and industry-related problems for the United States. Some published accounts claim that Israel launched the development of Derby because the United States denied Israel access to ECCM software technology on AMRAAM and because it had become clear that the United States was likely to sell AMRAAM to Arab countries as well as to Israel. Israeli officials were allegedly concerned that Israel could not ensure the supply of AMRAAMs from the United States in a crisis, nor did it possess the information necessary to counter

---

[9]Rafael claims that Derby is lighter than AMRAAM and has a more technologically advanced programmable ECCM system. See Associated Press (2001).

[10]Perhaps as a counterweight to its extensive relationship with Lockheed, Rafael signed an agreement with Raytheon in mid-2001 to market its Black Sparrow medium-fidelity ballistic target missile to the United States and other countries. See Sirak (June 2001).

AMRAAMs that might be employed by opposition Arab air forces. This allegedly led to the development of Derby.

In addition, the existence of both Python and Derby means that highly advanced and capable air-to-air missiles may be proliferated to potential future opponents of the United States. According to press reports, the Chinese F-8 fighter that collided with the U.S. Navy Lockheed EP-3C Orion in early 2001 was equipped with Python 3 missiles or Chinese-manufactured derivatives thereof.

Finally, according to several open sources, Python and Derby have placed Israeli and U.S. industry into fierce competition with each other for third markets, thereby causing considerable friction between the two countries. In early 1998, after a bitter competition, the Australian Air Force selected the Matra BAe Dynamics AIM-132 ASRAAM over the competing Python 4 and the U.S. Raytheon AIM-9X. Ironically, the European ASRAAM's highly sophisticated infrared seeker is based on U.S. technology that was transferred to the UK earlier, when ASRAAM was a collaborative program between Germany and the United States.[11]

Raytheon also plays a key if not dominant role in precision-guided air-to-ground munitions with major products such as the AGM-154 Joint Standoff Weapon (JSOW) and the older AGM-88 High-Speed Anti-Radiation Missile (HARM); the GBU-12 Paveway laser-guided bomb (LGB); and the AGM-65 Maverick. Boeing and Lockheed are increasingly important players as well with their GBU-31/32 JDAM and Wind-Corrected Munitions Dispenser (WCMD) strap-on glide kits for dumb bombs; Conventional Air-Launched Cruise Missile (CALCM); Joint Air-to-Surface Standoff Missile (JASSM); AGM-130; and AGM-84H Standoff Land Attack Missile—Extended Response (SLAM-ER) standoff-powered air-to-ground munitions. However, most of these munitions do not directly compete with each other. It is possible that Lockheed/Rafael's upgrading and marketing of the AGM-142 Raptor have provided important competitive pressures

---

[11] See also Chapter Three.

that have had beneficial effects on programs such as Raytheon's JSOW and Boeing's upgraded versions of the AGM-130.[12]

For these reasons, it would be beneficial to learn how the Popeye and Python marketing agreements as well as the Rafael/Lockheed joint venture may have affected competition and innovation in the air-to-air and air-to-ground missile markets for the U.S. Air Force. This suggests the need for further detailed investigation and case study analysis.

Northrop Grumman/Rafael Litening II

Rafael has also teamed with Northrop Grumman to bring a high-quality foreign product into the U.S. market that appears to have resulted in reduced costs as well as increased U.S. service and allied equipment standardization. The product in question is the Litening II targeting and navigation pod. Like the Popeye missile, the original Litening I was developed by Rafael for the Israeli Air Force. It was designed to surpass the capabilities of Lockheed Martin's first-generation LANTIRN pods in a significant way while at the same time being cheaper, more reliable, and more maintainable.[13]

In 1995, Northrop Grumman signed a marketing agreement with Rafael to upgrade and sell the Litening pod to the U.S. government and other customers. This marketing agreement designated Northrop Grumman as the prime contractor for sales to the U.S. government and called for cooperative production between the U.S. firm and Rafael. Northrop Grumman upgraded the basic Litening I pod with third-generation forward-looking infrared (FLIR) sensors and laser marker technology, software upgrades, and other improvements, resulting in the Litening II Precision Attack Targeting System (U.S. Air Force Air Combat Command, no date). The Air Force recognized that Litening II would be a low-cost means of providing

---

[12]In terms of Air Force mission use, the AGM-142 probably competes most directly with the AGM-130. However, the AGM-142 remains the U.S. Air Force's only bomber-qualified, conventional long-range powered standoff munition.

[13]LANTIRN is an acronym for Low-Altitude Navigation and Targeting Infrared for Night. LANTIRN began development in 1980 and entered full-rate production for the U.S. Air Force in 1986. LANTIRNs were later adapted for use on U.S. Navy F-14s to provide a precision laser air-to-ground munition delivery capability.

older-model Air Force Reserve and Air National Guard F-16s with third-generation day/night under-the-weather standoff precision munition delivery capability.[14] According to some published accounts, Air Force testing showed that Litening II provided better capability along with much-improved reliability and maintainability when compared to LANTIRN.[15]

The Air Force purchased the pods as an off-the-shelf NDI after extensive testing and began receiving the first operational units in early 2000.[16] Published accounts claim that Rafael manufactures the forward sensor section while Northrop Grumman manufactures the aft section with most of the electronics. It is not clear from published sources whether Rafael gained access to the technology improvements incorporated in the improved Litening II variant by Northrop Grumman; nor is it clear whether collaborative R&D was undertaken.

In July 2000, Northrop Grumman reported receiving another major Litening II contract from the U.S. Marines for use on the AV-8B Harrier. This contract also included some units for Italian Navy and Spanish Navy Harriers. In September 2001, after extensive testing on the Harrier by the U.S. Navy, Northrop Grumman announced a second Litening II sale to the U.S. Marines—a sale that was three times larger than the first.

In the late 1990s, the U.S. Air Force initiated its competitive Advanced Targeting Pod (ATP) program for the acquisition of a third-generation pod to equip F-16CJ Block 50 fighters in regular Air Force units. Because this program hopes to provide ATPs for all regular Air Force F-16 squadrons and possibly F-15E squadrons as well—and because it may eventually be used in the National Guard and Reserves—this was clearly the most important competition of all for developers of third-generation tactical fighter targeting pods. A major requirement of the ATP program was that the pod had to be already developed and qualify as NDI. Northrop Grumman, teamed

---

[14]Air Force fact sheets report that the Litening II pod costs $1.4 million per unit compared to $3.2 million for the LANTIRN targeting pod and $1.38 million for the LANTIRN navigation pod.

[15]For example, see Clarke (1999). This is not surprising, since in many respects the LANTIRN is based on 30-year-old first-generation FLIR technology.

[16]The U.S. Air Force designation is AN/AAQ-28 Litening.

with Rafael, entered its Litening II+ pod in this competition. Ranged against the Litening II+ were two formidable competitors: the Raytheon Terminator ATP, derived from the Terminator Advanced Tactical FLIR (ATFLIR), which entered development in 1997 for use on U.S. Navy F/A-18C/Ds and E/Fs; and the Lockheed Martin Sniper Extended Range (XR), which is based in part on technology being developed for the Lockheed JSF design. In August 2001, the Air Force announced the selection of the Lockheed Martin Sniper XR as the winner (Erwin, 2001; Lockheed Martin Missiles and Fire Control, 2001).

Although the Litening II lost the ATP competition, it almost certainly contributed to the intense competitive pressure placed on Lockheed Martin and Raytheon during the selection process. In addition, published accounts suggest that the Litening II program provided a low-cost, high-quality interim solution that required no government R&D expenditures while greatly improving the attack capabilities of Air Force National Guard and Reserve F-16s as well as the Marine Harriers.[17] Furthermore, it provided for some increased cross-service equipment standardization as well as for greater standardization with at least two NATO allies that deploy Harriers.[18]

Published sources do not reveal what arrangements would have been implemented for work share, technology sharing, marketing, technology security, and third-country transfers for the Litening II. With the selection of the Lockheed Martin Sniper XR as the definitive ATP for F-16s, it is also unclear what the future role of the Litening II pods will be in the Air Force. Litening II may, however, end up competing with both the Sniper and the Terminator on international markets. Thus, although it has contributed to greater competition in the U.S. market, the Litening II pod may not promote greater equipment interoperability and standardization with allies or even within and among the U.S. services.

---

[17]For the use of Litening II pods in Operation Enduring Freedom in Afghanistan, see Loeb (2002).

[18]The Litening has been tested by the Norwegian Air Force and is already in use by six other foreign air forces, including that of Germany.

Boeing/Alenia Marconi Systems JDAM, Hellfire/Brimstone

Marketing agreements can, of course, be put in place to access foreign as well as U.S. markets. The recent joint marketing and teaming agreement signed between Boeing and Alenia Marconi Systems, for example, is a "reverse" marketing agreement that is particularly germane to Air Force interests and objectives. Alenia Marconi Systems, which specializes in aircraft munitions and defense electronics, is a 50-50 joint venture between the UK's BAE Systems and Finmeccanica of Italy (Hoyle, 2001). This marketing agreement appears to apply primarily to the Boeing JDAM, a low-cost guidance kit that attaches to "dumb bombs," transforming them into Global Positioning System (GPS) precision-guided unpowered standoff weapons.[19] Boeing provides Alenia Marconi with access to JDAM and derivative technology for use in the UK Precision-Guided Bomb program as well as for use in other potential markets. Boeing in turn gains access to European markets for JDAM through Alenia Marconi as well as access to the Diamond Back wing kit for JDAM.[20]

The two companies also plan to modify and jointly market the Boeing Hellfire anti-armor missile to fulfill the British Royal Air Force (RAF) Brimstone requirement for a precision antitank air-to-ground missile for use on fixed-wing fighter attack aircraft such as the Eurofighter.[21] In our cross-border business relationship typology, this could also be considered an R&D teaming agreement, since new development work is expected (see below). Alenia Marconi in the UK will be responsible for the seeker and for final missile assembly.

By signing the marketing and teaming arrangement with Alenia Marconi, however, Boeing is not merely cooperating with an Anglo-Italian company. In October 1999, British Aerospace (now BAE Systems), Aerospatiale Matra (now part of EADS), and Finmeccanica agreed to form a joint company called MBDA that will specialize in missiles and missile systems. The company, which will be headquar-

---

[19]See the section on teaming below for a discussion of the other teaming aspects of the agreement.

[20]Diamond Back is a wing developed by Alenia Marconi that attaches to the basic JDAM bomb/guidance kit combination to extend the range of the unpowered standoff munition. JDAM with the AMD Diamond Back is called JDAM ER.

[21]The existing Hellfire is used on attack helicopters but not on fixed-wing aircraft.

tered in London, will be formed by merging Matra BAe Dynamics (a joint venture of BAE Systems and EADS), Aerospatiale Matra Missiles (fully owned by EADS), and Alenia Marconi. Plans also include the possibility of adding Germany's two main missile makers through a joint venture between LFK-Lenkflugkopersysteme GmbH, owned by MBDA and its parent EADS, and Bodenseewerk Geraetetechnik GmbH (BGT), owned 20 percent by EADS and 80 percent by Diehl. Also included will be a Spanish joint venture company made up of the CASA missile affiliate of EADS, as well as the Spanish-owned Indra electronics company and the Izar shipyards, making MBDA "the Airbus of the missiles business." Press reports claim that MBDA will be close to Raytheon in missile sales revenues and ahead of Boeing and Lockheed Martin in this market segment (Taverna, 2001).

The implications for U.S. technology security and third-party transfers after this mega-merger takes place are not clear. Instead of allying merely with an Anglo-Italian firm, Boeing will be collaborating at least indirectly with virtually every major missile company in Western Europe, including those of France, Spain, and probably Germany. The complex web of relationships introduced as a result of the marketing and teaming arrangement between Boeing and Alenia Marconi suggests that further research into this relationship is warranted.

BAE Systems/Saab Gripen

Many intra-European marketing agreements also exist. BAE Systems, for example, was an original subcontractor on the Swedish Saab JAS Gripen fighter, with responsibility for designing and developing the wing. In 1995, the two firms formed a joint venture company called Saab-BAe Gripen AB to market, modify, manufacture, and support the Gripen for sale to third countries. In 1998, BAE Systems acquired a 35 percent ownership stake in Saab Aircraft of Sweden. The UK-based company will manufacture 45 percent of the airframes of all export units.[22] In September 2001, the two companies strengthened their marketing agreement by forming a new joint

---

[22]U.S. firms provide up to 30 percent of the Gripen's content by value, including much of the modified General Electric 404 engine used in the fighter.

venture called Gripen International, headquartered both in Sweden and in the UK. BAE Systems has fully integrated the Gripen into its marketing portfolio, placing it strategically between its lower-end Hawk advanced trainer/light attack aircraft and its high-end Eurofighter Typhoon.

The impressive marketing power of this alliance, which permits package deals of a much wider variety of products from the two companies, was demonstrated when the Gripen won its first export breakthrough to South Africa in 1999. In March of that year, the South African Air Force announced a package deal for 28 Gripens and 24 Hawks. In September 2001, the Swedish/UK joint venture stunned U.S. officials with an upset victory over Lockheed Martin in the Hungarian fighter competition. It had been widely believed that Hungary would select the U.S. Lockheed Martin F-16, but the Gripen was chosen instead (*Aerospace Daily*, 2001). As of September 2001, the Gripen also appeared to be the probable choice for the Czech Republic and was providing significant competition for the Lockheed F-16 in the battle for modernizing the Polish Air Force fighter inventory.[23]

The Saab/BAE Systems joint venture marketing alliance has proven to be a powerful tool for promoting third-country sales. It has resulted in a much more serious competitor for U.S. fighter prime contractors in Europe, Latin America, South Africa, Australia, and elsewhere. More significantly, it has seriously undermined the U.S. vision for interim air force equipment standardization based on the Lockheed Martin F-16 among second-rank and new NATO members.[24]

---

[23]In December 2001 the Czech Republic entered final contract negotiations with Saab/BAE Systems for the Gripen.

[24]The U.S. Air Force long-range vision for standardization within NATO air forces focuses on the acquisition of the Lockheed Martin F-35 JSF, which has just begun its system development and demonstration phase.

TEAMING FOR CROSS-BORDER COOPERATIVE DEVELOPMENT OF NEW SYSTEMS

The RAND typology of common defense aerospace relationships laid out in Chapter Two defined teaming as an agreement between two or more companies to work together, often to pursue a specific project. Teaming is by far the most common—and perhaps the broadest—category of cross-border defense industry business relationships. Teaming agreements can cover the full spectrum of business activities shown in Table 2.2. Since there are far more examples of teaming and a greater richness in the variety of relationships, we discuss more case studies in this subsection than in any other.

For our purposes, the most revealing teaming arrangements involve the cooperative development of new systems or subsystems as well as the cross-border outsourcing of subsystems or components. Such outsourcing can involve substantial equity investment and R&D by the subcontractor, or it can merely pertain to an agreement with a subcontractor to "build to print" an item designed and developed by the prime contractor. The trend in the aerospace industry, however, has been toward the former rather than the latter.

The most comprehensive and innovative teaming agreements entail major investment and developmental efforts by the leading team members, usually for a specific project, and constitute what is generally referred to as codevelopment. Both teaming and joint venture business arrangements that involve codevelopment are among the most important types of activities for analysis not only because they are the most difficult to implement efficiently but also because they exhibit the greatest potential for mutual cross-border savings and other benefits, at least in principle.[25] Theoretically, cross-border teaming for the cooperative development of major systems not only should provide the most economic benefits but should also best promote equipment standardization and interoperability, as true interoperability begins at the design stage.

Unfortunately, governments have in the past initiated many of these agreements in a manner that has undermined both their economic

---

[25]This is because both the development and production costs are shared by the partners, and R&D technology assets are often shared.

and interoperability benefits. Governments typically have begun cross-border codevelopment projects by negotiating each government's financial contribution to R&D and the quantities of each government's planned procurement of the developed item. Subsequently, government negotiators have often designated industry "national champions" or key national firms that must participate in the project team. Furthermore, governments have typically negotiated and designated precise work share and work content for their participating national industries for both the R&D and production phases. In this context, the value of work share has almost always been determined by the concept of "juste retour"—that is, a participating country's industries have received work share whose value has been equal to the participating government's financial contribution to each phase of the project.

In the past, then, the entire cross-border business structure—including the firms participating in the teaming arrangement, the work shares, and the work content—were often negotiated by the participating governments. Broad national economic objectives, national technology acquisition goals, and various political factors usually played a central role. Standard commercial business practices related to relative economic advantage, such as the competitive selection of suppliers on the basis of best value, cost, and technological capabilities, generally played lesser roles. The result was often a loss in economic efficiency. Indeed, because of such government-imposed economic inefficiencies, some early European codevelopment programs reportedly cost each participant more than a comparable all-national program (Lorell and Lowell, 1995).

Two major innovations in cross-border business relationships established for these types of comprehensive codevelopment teaming arrangements have emerged in recent years. In the first, two or more international teams compete for the same project. In the second, governments grant more authority to cross-border industry teams to negotiate the details of their own business relationships, including the selection of team members or subcontractors as well as work share and work content.

A variety of recent attempts to try new business approaches toward cross-border codevelopment teaming—approaches that enhance competition, promote best business practices, transfer more business decision authority to the participating firms, and the like—are of particular interest for our analysis. We have divided these potential case studies into three broad categories, as shown in Table 5.2. Within those categories, there are some extremely innovative and unusual variations—such as the JSF and the XM777 utltralightweight howitzer, both discussed below. The most important of the cases have aimed at increasing NATO alliance equipment standardization and interoperability, thereby upgrading NATO European allies' capabilities in line with the objectives of DCI while at the same time reaping the theoretical economic and technological benefits of cooperative development and production. Unfortunately, however, at this writing the most significant examples either have failed to bring about the desired results or are too preliminary to allow for definitive judgments on their efficacy.

NATO Airborne Ground Surveillance[26]

In November 1995, the Conference of National Armaments Directors (CNAD) established the NATO Alliance Ground Surveillance (AGS) program. This program called for the acquisition of a core capability jointly owned and operated by NATO and supplemented by interoperable national assists.[27] Currently, the United States is the only NATO member that possesses a highly capable fixed-wing aerial surveillance aircraft with a ground moving target indication (GMTI) radar. This aircraft is the E-8C Joint Surveillance Target Attack Radar System (JSTARS), which mounts a Northrop Grumman GMTI radar on a refurbished Boeing 707 airframe.[28] In the 1990s, the Air Force began serious discussions with Northrop Grumman for the development of a new, more capable AESA radar and other electronics for

---

[26]Major past and ongoing RAND Project AIR FORCE studies examine many of the cost, budget, technical, and operational aspects of the NATO alliance airborne C^2ISR problem. See Hura et al. (2000).

[27]This concept draws on the precedent of a similar existing NATO AWACS program using 17 NATO jointly owned and operated Boeing E-3 Sentry AWACS. The UK and France deploy seven and four nationally owned E-3 Sentries, respectively. The U.S. Air Force has 35 in its inventory.

[28]The French and Italians have fielded less capable GMTI surveillance radar systems on helicopters.

upgrading JSTARS. This program was originally known as the Radar Technology Insertion Program (RTIP).

To promote interoperability and reduce costs by increasing the production run, the U.S. Air Force and Northrop Grumman in early 1997 offered a reduced-cost E-8C JSTARS for procurement by NATO. In November 1997, the CNAD rejected the U.S. offer and requested that "fresh options" be examined. The next month, the U.S. offered a JSTARS RTIP radar on the platform of NATO's choice. In April 1998, after an analysis of this offer, the CNAD authorized a concept definition study based on RTIP sensor technology. One year later, the CNAD authorized a two-year project definition study at a Project Definition Office in Brussels. This became an official NATO project called the NATO Transatlantic Advanced Radar (NATAR) program.

NATAR did not, however, immediately attract the major NATO European powers owing to concerns over U.S. willingness to transfer technology and the potential domination of the program by U.S. contractors, among other issues. The British never directly participated in AGS or NATAR because of an earlier decision to develop a national surveillance radar platform called the Airborne Standoff Radar (ASTOR) program, as discussed below. Instead, the leading continental European powers formed their own joint venture technology demonstration effort called the Standoff Surveillance and Target Acquisition Radar demonstrator (SOSTAR-X) program, also discussed below. Thus, although the United States encouraged all NATO members to join the program, the U.S.-led NATAR effort initially attracted only the second-rank NATO powers: Belgium, Canada, Denmark, Luxembourg, and Norway.[29]

ASTOR

The British had been planning a national solution to their aerial ground surveillance radar platform requirement for many years. In 1978, the British Ministry of Defence (MoD) initiated a study called the Corps Airborne Standoff Radar. In the mid-1980s, the MoD issued a requirement for a surveillance radar aircraft with GMTI and

---

[29]See more on NATAR below.

Table 5.2

Examples of Innovative Cross-Border Codevelopment Teaming Arrangements

Program/Market Sector[a]	Description[b]
Foreign-led versus U.S.-led cross-border teams competing for specific systems	
BVRAAM	AMRAAM versus Meteor; a UK-led, mostly European cross-border team defeats a U.S. Raytheon-led transatlantic team for the RAF BVR missile.
XM777 lightweight howitzer	An unusual program with a UK prime and U.S. subs for the development of a 155mm gun for the U.S. Army, the U.S. Marines, the UK, and Italy.
Multiple international teams competing to codevelop specific systems	
ASTOR	Three U.S./UK teams compete for a UK government contract for a standoff surveillance radar.
NATO TMD Study Contract	Four U.S.-led transatlantic teams compete in the hopes of winning full-development contracts from NATO.
JSF	Two U.S./UK/other European teams compete for a contract from collaborating governments, led by the United States. Firms must "earn" a position on the team and work share.
FSCS/TRACER	Two U.S./UK teams compete for a contract on a cooperative U.S./UK light armored vehicle program.
Cross-border teaming for entire market sector	
Euro Hawk and other UAV and surveillance technologies; EW technologies	A Northrop Grumman/DASA (EADS) team competes for various U.S. and European government contracts.
JDAM derivatives, Brimstone, Small Diameter Bomb (SDB)	Boeing/Alenia Marconi.
Foreign-foreign versus U.S.-led cross-border teams competing for entire market sector	
IAI/EADS UAVs	Israeli/European team competes successfully against a U.S./European team (Eagle versus Global Hawk, B-Hunter versus Predator).

[a]BVRAAM = Beyond Visual Range Air-to-Air Missile; ASTOR = Airborne Standoff Radar; TMD = Theater Missile Defense; FSCS = Future Scout and Cavalry System; TRACER = Tactical Reconnaissance Armored Combat Equipment Requirement.

[b]Discussions of cases in the text do not follow the same order as the listing of the cases in this table.

synthetic aperture radar (SAR) modes. This eventually became known as ASTOR. As in the case of the NATO AGS program, the United States offered the UK a Northrop Grumman RTIP technology solution for ASTOR. Largely for reasons related to domestic employment and the national industrial base, however, the British MoD rejected this offer in favor of a new development program that called for a competition between two UK/U.S. industry teams—one led by Lockheed Martin Tactical Systems UK and another led by Raytheon Systems Ltd., both British subsidiaries of the U.S.-based companies. These two contractor teams received study contracts in 1995 (Worthen, 1998).

Northrop Grumman and the U.S. government heavily lobbied the MoD to permit Northrop, which had now teamed with British companies, to reenter the ASTOR competition with a new proposal based on its RTIP AESA technology. The U.S. government and the U.S. Air Force apparently hoped to reduce the costs of the RTIP program, to enhance interoperability with the UK, and to increase the prospects for the adoption of RTIP technology on upgraded JSTARS or other platforms that might be used in the NATO AGS and ASTOR programs.

In November 1998, apparently under U.S. government pressure, Northrop Grumman teamed with Raytheon (formerly Hughes El Segundo) on a 50-50 basis for the development of the radar sensor portion of RTIP, with Northrop remaining in the role of prime integrator. This may have represented an attempt to improve the prospects for ASTOR's selection of RTIP technology, since Raytheon was a key competitor on the British program. Furthermore, Northrop began offering a scalable version of its radar array that could be mounted on smaller, business-jet-size platforms, which the Europeans preferred.

At about this time, the British relented under U.S. pressure and permitted the Northrop Grumman team to reenter the ASTOR competition. However, this was only about three months before the "best and final offers" from the competing contractors were due. The Northrop Grumman team now included numerous British members, including BAE Systems. However, the radar proposed by the Northrop Grumman team remained the Northrop Grumman RTIP technology solution funded by the United States. Some sources claim that the British continued to encounter resistance from the United States with regard to transferring the RTIP technology to a British firm.[30]

In contrast, the Lockheed team proposal designated the British firm Racal (now a subsidiary of Thales of France) as the lead integrator for its radar. Ironically, Racal selected a variant of an existing Raytheon TI–developed radar—a radar based on technology from Raytheon's Advanced Synthetic Aperture Radar System-1 (ASARS-1) used on the U.S. Lockheed U-2R—as the antenna for its radar proposal for the Lockheed-led team. The Raytheon team also proposed that a British firm, Marconi Electronics Systems (now part of BAE Systems), serve as the lead on the AESA antenna. Like Racal, Marconi selected an improved version of the ASARS-2 radar in use on the U-2R. Although the ASARS radar reportedly uses a less sophisticated passive phased array, there are plans to eventually upgrade it with an AESA. Raytheon hoped that the ASARS-2 would eventually be used on the Northrop Grumman Global Hawk UAV as well.

Interestingly, the United States is reported in the press to have already released ASARS technology to British companies. Both of the British-preferred teams, Lockheed/Racal and Raytheon/Marconi, had selected a British contractor as the prime radar integrator, yet both were planning to base their antennas on the same Raytheon ASARS technology that had already been released to the UK. Northrop Grumman, with its more advanced RTIP AESA technology, did not pick a British company to act as the radar prime integrator; instead, it elected to play that role itself, raising questions about technology transfer to the UK. The UK was thus faced with picking the more advanced Northrop Grumman technology team but having doubts about technology transfer, or picking either the Lockheed or the Raytheon team and gaining full access to Raytheon ASARS technology and future upgrades in either case. The British also allegedly expressed concerns with the Northrop Grumman offer because of U.S. restrictions on third-country sales and technology transfer stemming from the U.S. arms transfer regulatory regime.

---

[30]For example, see *Defense Daily Network Special Reports* (1998).

Not surprisingly, in June 1999 the British MoD picked the Raytheon/Marconi-led team to develop ASTOR, which was to be integrated on a modified Canadian Bombardier Global Express business jet.[31] This apparently ended the possibility of British funding of—or participation in—the U.S. Air Force–preferred JSTARS upgrade based on Northrop Grumman RTIP technology.

Later NATAR Developments

After the ASTOR loss, the Air Force and Northrop Grumman restructured the program and renamed it Multi-Platform RTIP (MP RTIP), implying a scalable array and radar technology that could be used on many different platforms sizes.[32] This clearly represented an attempt to keep Northrop RTIP technology in the running for the NATAR program and other foreign markets, which might be looking at business-jet-size solutions rather than JSTARS 707-class aircraft. There may also have been a concern that the British government and the Raytheon team would market their ASTOR-based ASARS-2 technology to NATO allies for the NATAR program. There was even some speculation that it could be marketed for a JSTARS upgrade.[33]

In December 2000, the U.S. Air Force demonstrated its ongoing confidence in the Northrop Grumman/Raytheon MP RTIP program for JSTARS and NATO AGS by awarding a three-year, $303 million contract for the development of three MP RTIP prototypes: the smallest for use on the Global Hawk UAV; a second version for a "wide-area surveillance platform" (a larger JSTARS-type radar); and a third to meet the NATAR requirement (Northrop Grumman Corporation, 2000). Nonetheless, DoD appeared frustrated at the apparent inability of Northrop Grumman and Raytheon to hammer out the details of their MP RTIP collaboration and present a united front to the

---

[31]Twenty-five percent of the Global Express is built by Bombardier Aerospace's Shorts subsidiary in Belfast, Northern Ireland. Bombardier acquired Short Brothers PLC from the British government in 1989.

[32]During the competition, as noted earlier, the Northrop Grumman team did offer an ASTOR proposal based on a scaled-down RTIP technology radar that could be mounted in a Gulfstream V business jet.

[33] By 1999, Raytheon was reportedly marketing an export version of its ASTOR-based ASARS-2 radar in direct competition with Northrop Grumman's export version of its MP RTIP. See Morrocco and Taverna (1999).

Europeans for a NATO AGS/NATAR solution. DoD officials appeared determined to advocate the use of RTIP technology for upgrading JSTARS, for the Global Hawk UAV, and for the NATAR program. There even seemed a hope of migrating RTIP technology back to the ASTOR program during an upgrade phase (Fulghum, 2000).

SOSTAR

The SOSTAR-X technology demonstration program was seen as yet another major barrier standing in the way of an RTIP-based, standardized NATO AGS. SOSTAR-X is intended to demonstrate an all-European airborne GMTI and SAR surveillance radar technology capability using an advanced AESA antenna. SOSTAR was promoted by France, Germany, Italy, the Netherlands, and Spain as an alternative to the Northrop Grumman RTIP-based NATAR and was approved as an official program in 1998. In early 2001, these countries established a joint venture consortium called SOSTAR GmbH that was based in Friedrichshafen, Germany, and consisted of EADS/Dornier (28 percent), Thales (28 percent), Alenia Difesa's FIAR (28 percent), Indra of Spain (11 percent), and Fokker Netherlands (5 percent). One of the primary reasons for SOSTAR, according to the Netherlands State Secretary of Defense, was that the "restrictive U.S. export policy for defense technology would make it impossible for European nations to gain access to all technology of the U.S. ground surveillance radar."[34] At least some of the SOSTAR participants claim, however, that the program is not directly competing with the Northrop Grumman RTIP technology for NATAR but is instead intended to give the major European countries greater leverage in bargaining for their terms of entry into NATAR. Nonetheless, some observers are concerned about the possibility that SOSTAR could evolve into a European alternative to an RTIP-based NATAR or that ASTOR could be eventually accepted as the NATO AGS solution, leaving the U.S. Air Force standing alone with its MP RTIP program.

---

[34]Henk van Hoof, quoted in *Jane's International Defense Review* (2001).

Northrop Grumman/EADS Strategic Alliance

One way Northrop Grumman is attempting to counter these problems with its MP RTIP technology for NATAR is through a strategic market sector alliance it has formed with DaimlerChrysler Aerospace AG.[35] In April 2000, the two companies signed an MoU to explore the possibility of pursuing broad cooperative programs in "ground surveillance systems; high-altitude, long-endurance unmanned aerial vehicle (UAV) technology; maritime UAV technology, including real-time signal processing; airborne radar for military transport; naval radars and wide bandwidth data link technology for reconnaissance."[36] This is a particularly interesting teaming relationship because it encompasses entire market sectors rather than single specific projects or programs.

By 2001, the Northrop Grumman/DaimlerChrysler Aerospace (EADS) team was offering a joint transatlantic proposal to "kick start" the stalled NATO AGS NATAR program. In early June, the NATO defense ministers meeting in Brussels endorsed a NATO staff plan to merge the two competing NATO AGS programs into a transatlantic joint technological development effort. Some observers assumed that a collaborative industry effort would be built around the existing Northrop Grumman/DaimlerChrysler (EADS) relationship and a Thales/Raytheon joint venture for upgrading the NATO air defense system (Hill, June 2001).[37]

Northrop Grumman and DaimlerChrysler (EADS) responded by signing an MoU at the Paris Air Show that was aimed specifically at working toward a common technology solution that would bring together the RTIP-based NATAR and SOSTAR programs. The MoU established a working group to jointly study a common architecture for the NATO AGS. The two firms said that the study was open to other SOSTAR and NATAR companies, including Thales and Raytheon, if they chose to join (Morrocco, 2001).[38]

---

[35]This teaming relationship is expected to continue as the German company integrates into EADS.

[36]See, for example, Andrews Space and Technology (2000).

[37]See the section below on joint ventures.

[38]The second MoU related to the joint marketing of existing and new EW systems.

The two firms also agreed to continue work on the collaborative Euro Hawk program, which envisions equipping the Northrop Grumman (formerly Teledyne Ryan Aeronautics) Global Hawk high-altitude/long-endurance UAV with reconnaissance payloads developed by EADS. While this could become an important collaborative program, it may not support the U.S. Air Force's apparent desire to standardize JSTARS and Global Hawk with MP RTIP radar technology (Mulholland, 2001). Indeed, some EADS officials have expressed the desire for Euro Hawk to become the NATO Hawk, perhaps in competition with NATAR and SOSTAR.

Israel Aircraft Industries/EADS UAVs

Another complicating element is the competition posed by teams containing non-U.S. and non-European members. In the case of UAVs, for example, Israel Aircraft Industries (IAI) has also teamed successfully with EADS (France). In the past, IAI has provided UAV airframes and engines, while European firms have provided the avionics and sensors. When teamed with the French Alcatel company and other European firms, IAI sold the B-Hunter UAV to the Belgian military. The sensors and avionics of this UAV differ from those of the IAI Hunter that is coproduced with TRW for U.S. forces.

More recently, IAI has teamed with EADS (France) in order to introduce the Eagle-1 medium-to-high-altitude/long-endurance UAV to the European market. The Eagle is a modified and upgraded version of the IAI-developed Huron UAV. UAVs make up a market sector in which the Europeans remain weak, as has been emphasized by the NATO DCI. In May 2001, France chose the Eagle-1 over the U.S. General Atomics Predator used by U.S. forces. IAI further claims that it is developing GMTI and SAR radar capabilities that could be mounted on the Eagle or on modifications of that platform. Indeed, there has been mention in the press of such an upgraded platform, called the Eagle-2. Such a UAV could directly compete with either Global Hawk or Euro Hawk (Rosenberg, 2001).

It is unclear from the open literature what determined the French decision to select the IAI/EADS team, but it would not be surprising if technology transfer issues were involved. With France already deciding against Global Hawk or even Euro Hawk, this decision may make NATO RSI in this area much less likely.

Another interesting twist is that the IAI/EADS France teaming arrangement appears to be in competition with the proposed Northrop Grumman/EADS (German) proposed Euro Hawk. Which one EADS will promote most firmly remains to be seen, but the French selection of the Eagle does not bode well for NATO RSI.

The stunning complexities of the NATO AGS program—complicated as it is by the ASTOR, NATAR, SOSTAR, Euro Hawk, and Eagle efforts as well as by the Northrop Grumman/EADS strategic teaming agreement, the Raytheon/Thales joint venture, and the IAI/EADS team—make it a fascinating and potentially revealing case study on globalization trends, technology transfer issues, RSI, DTSI and DCI, and the manner in which the Air Force should try to influence such efforts. NATO AGS is also the highest-priority program in DCI, while the RTIP program is very important to the future of U.S. Air Force C^{2}ISR. Taken together, these cases thus constitute optimal areas for further research.

NATO Theater Missile Defense

Another related and interesting industry-initiated transatlantic teaming competition recently took place with the launching of several NATO Theater Missile Defense (TMD) feasibility studies. Although the initial TMD study contracts are relatively small (standing at $13.5 million), once the development phase is initiated in 2004 they could lead to one of the largest NATO collaborative programs in history. The initial contracts essentially call for the assessment of a "system of systems" architecture. Despite the limited scope of the initial study contracts, the potentially large long-term payoff led to an intense competition between four transatlantic teams.

Lockheed, whose Theater High-Altitude Area Defense (THAAD) system and other programs are prominent in U.S. theater and national missile defense, assembled the first team, which was composed of Matra BAe Dynamics (MBDA), TRW, and several other European firms.[39] A second team coalesced around the existing Raytheon/

---

[39]As mentioned early, Matra BAe Dynamics is expected to merge together most of Europe's remaining major independent missile manufacturers to become MBDA.

Thales NATO Air Command and Control System (ACCS) joint venture.[40] Later, a third team led (during the feasibility study phase) by Science Applications International Corporation (SAIC) was formed with Boeing, a French part of EADS, and British, German, and Dutch defense research organizations. Finally, Northrop Grumman's Logicon division formed a fourth team.

In mid-2001, NATO revealed that the Lockheed- and SAIC/Boeing-led teams had been selected as the finalists. This paper competition will continue until the 2004–2005 time frame, when a decision will be made regarding whether to enter into full-scale development (*Los Angeles Times*, 2000; Hill, May 2001). Whether or not a two-team transatlantic competition would continue after this point is unclear.

BVRAAM/Meteor

Two munitions programs also illustrate the problems currently confronting U.S. policymakers in promoting the NATO DCI and greater standardization and interoperability within NATO. The first is the British BVRAAM/Meteor program, which is intended to develop the main long-range air-to-air armament for the Eurofighter. The second is the Boeing/Alenia Marconi team agreement discussed below.[41] Like the NATO AGS program, the BVRAAM program pitted the United States' desire for NATO standardization and interoperability, as well as for European burden sharing of American weapon system development and procurement costs, against Europe's desire to consolidate and develop its own indigenous industry and capabilities together with its suspicion and anger toward U.S. export policies and controls. The result was essentially a competition between a nearly all-European team and a U.S.-led transatlantic team.

On the European side, a British-led consortium was formed that was originally composed of MBDA, Alenia Marconi Systems, DaimlerChrysler's LFK-Lenkflugkopersysteme (EADS), and Saab Dynamics. This was the European solution supported by Germany, France, Italy, Spain, and Sweden for BVRAAM. The European Meteor

---

[40]See the section on joint ventures.

[41]See also the section on marketing agreements.

consortium offered a highly advanced, new-generation long-range ramjet-powered missile concept.

On the U.S. side, Raytheon offered a time-phased program with a variety of staged upgrades to the latest version of the U.S. AMRAAM missile. The U.S. government strongly supported the Raytheon offer for reasons of standardization, interoperability, and cost sharing on further AMRAAM development and procurement. The AMRAAM is the standard long-range BVR missile on most U.S. fighter attack aircraft. The UK's European allies, however, placed great pressure on the British government to turn to a European solution, insisting that the Meteor program was crucial both for the consolidation of the European missile industrial base and for the maintenance of advanced technical capabilities in European industry.

The competition became high profile and intense. The Europeans pulled off a coup in late 1999 by signing on Boeing to the Meteor team. This countered U.S. accusations that Meteor represented a turn toward "Fortress Europe." Boeing's main role on the program originally appeared to be limited to integrating the missile on U.S. aircraft and assisting in marketing efforts in the United States as well as in other countries having U.S. aircraft in their inventories. Boeing may have seen the agreement as a means of countering Raytheon's near-monopoly on BVR missiles, just as Lockheed may have teamed up with Rafael on the Python 4 to counter Raytheon market dominance in other types of air-to-air missiles (Morrocco, 2000; Boeing Company, 1999).

A central argument made to the British government by the European team was that U.S. export regulations would permit the U.S. government to slow, delay, or block the export of the missile. The team argued that this could in effect undermine exports of the Eurofighter Typhoon itself, which would not be of much use without its missile. There appeared to many European observers to be an unacceptable conflict of interest for the Americans, since the Eurofighter directly competes with several existing and future U.S. fighters. The United States tried mightily to overcome these concerns. Raytheon, for example, recruited many European companies onto its team. The U.S. government and Raytheon eventually proposed the codevelopment of a radically new version of AMRAAM with the British acting as equal partners. In 1998, the U.S. Secretary of Defense personally assured the British Defence Secretary that the United States would not unfairly block sales of the Eurofighter through withholding of U.S. BVRAAM technology.

Yet while the Raytheon solution would likely have been both cheaper and less risky from a technological standpoint, European pressure ultimately proved overwhelming, and the British chose Meteor. Some observers allege that as compensation to the deeply disappointed Americans, the British MoD decided to lease Boeing C-17s for the short-term solution to its airlift requirements, until the planned Airbus A400M military transport completed development. Some characterized this a "sop to the Americans" to compensate for the Meteor decision (*Defense Systems Daily*, 1999; Morrocco, 2000).[42]

Although the UK's decision may have lessened the prospects for RSI within NATO on long-range air-to-air missiles, Meteor's marketing agreement with Boeing may yet improve the competitive environment for the U.S. Air Force in this market sector. As noted earlier, Raytheon enjoys a near-monopoly on air-to-air missiles, particularly in the long-range BVR category with its AIM-120 AMRAAM. Especially if it is marketed in the United States by Boeing, Meteor could provide healthy competitive pressure. Press reports also claim that Boeing has expanded its role by engaging in studies of the development of an anti-radiation missile variant of Meteor for suppressing enemy air defenses. Such a development would provide competition to Raytheon's HARM, which currently has a monopoly in the U.S. market (Hoyle, 2001). In addition, a Meteor-based anti-radiation missile developed by Boeing would be far more acceptable to the Europeans than an all-Raytheon proposal.

Boeing/Alenia Marconi Systems

As discussed earlier, the Boeing/Alenia Marconi broad-based teaming agreement may enhance competition and possibly contribute to greater standardization and interoperability in air-to-air and air-to-ground munitions. It will be recalled that this relationship includes a marketing agreement for JDAM as well as the joint modification and

---

[42]It is assumed that the UK will join the all-European Airbus A400M military transport program to fulfill its long-term airlift requirements.

production of a Boeing Hellfire missile variant to satisfy the UK's Brimstone requirement. This could lead to Boeing marketing efforts to push Brimstone in the United States and elsewhere, thus possibly placing more competitive pressure on such munitions as the venerable Raytheon AGM-65 Maverick series, which has been a dominant player in the market for years. The Small Diameter Bomb (SDB) program is a U.S. Air Force effort to develop very light (in the 250-lb. class), accurate GPS/inertial navigation system (INS)-guided bombs, with later upgrades to more accurate guidance systems (*Inside the Pentagon*, 2001; Hebert, 2001). Under the Bush Administration, this program has grown considerably in priority; Boeing, Lockheed, and Raytheon are all interested in the effort. Two contractors are expected to be selected to compete in an initial concept development phase late in 2001. The Boeing/Alenia Marconi strategic teaming agreement gives Boeing a preexisting vehicle for entering into European and other markets if it continues in the SDB program. In principle it also gives Boeing the opportunity to leverage Alenia Marconi technologies and other resources. Additionally, it provides Alenia Marconi with potential access to an advanced new U.S. munitions program, thereby increasing the chance that the munition could be successfully marketed in Europe.

Joint Strike Fighter

The JSF program is a particularly innovative international effort by virtue of the freedom it grants the prime contractors to structure their international business relationships on the basis of their own internal business assessments. Rather than representing a full code-velopment effort, JSF could be characterized as a U.S.-led program with significant foreign outsourcing at the second and third tiers. However, major foreign team members such as BAE Systems will play important developmental roles during the system development and demonstration (SDD) phase.[43] In addition, the JSF program concept development phase had two cross-border teams competing for the SDD contract—one led by Boeing and the other by Lockheed Martin.

---

[43]Formerly called engineering and manufacturing development. Foreign participants during SDD will include the UK and possibly Italy, Turkey, the Netherlands, Canada, Norway, and Denmark.

One of the most significant innovations of the JSF program with respect to cross-border relationships lies in the U.S.-UK policy dictating that foreign subcontractors must "earn" their way on the program and "earn" their work share through direct negotiations with the prime contractors. As noted earlier, government participants in traditional collaborative programs have historically negotiated work share percentages and content on the basis of government financial contribution and national technology acquisition objectives. Often governments have also designated which of their national firms must participate.[44]

In accordance with DoD's acquisition reform concept of cost as an independent variable (CAIV), the JSF program has very strict average unit production price objectives. The two prime contractors, locked for four years in an intense competition for what may ultimately be the largest procurement program in U.S. history, have been incentivized to select partners and subcontractors, whether domestic or foreign, in accordance with the commercial concepts of best value and price. As a result, projected foreign industry work share does not always equal anticipated foreign government contributions.

The British government, for example, is expected to contribute approximately 10 percent of the cost of the SDD phase of JSF, but the expected value of British firms' work share on both the Boeing and Lockheed teams is significantly greater than this. In other words, British industry is likely to get more work than it would have had in a traditional collaborative development program, where industrial participation tends to be in exact proportion to the foreign government contribution.

As a result of this novel policy, the specific British companies involved in JSF and the work tasks they undertake vary significantly between the two prime contractor teams. This is, of course, the result of the prime contractors' and other suppliers' having been granted the authority to determine foreign industry participation indepen-

---

[44]In Europe, this traditional approach toward collaborative development still appears to be the norm. In October 2001, for example, the eight European participants on the A400M military transport development program agreed to divide up work share in precisely the same proportions as the value of the planned national procurements of the aircraft. See Lewis (2001).

dently on the basis of their own business criteria and best business practices. The selection of foreign firms, for example, was based on best-value standards and on each team's technical and best-value needs. Thus, the specific companies and specific work tasks vary between the two teams, but the overall foreign representation by country is roughly the same.[45] This innovative approach may greatly reduce some of the economic and technical inefficiencies associated with prior international collaborative development and coproduction programs. For this reason, JSF remains an important case for further research.[46]

XM777 Ultralightweight Field Howitzer

An unusual new joint Army/Marine program is worth mention because it represents a unique situation in which a foreign-based contractor is serving as the prime contractor, developer, and integrator for an important U.S. weapon system requirement. The system is the XM777 Ultralightweight Field Howitzer (UFH), a 155mm towed howitzer that is essentially being designed and developed by a foreign-based firm to U.S. Marine and U.S. Army specifications. The prime developer is the UK's BAE Systems RO Defence, formerly the Armaments Group of Vickers Shipbuilding and Engineering Ltd.

BAE is delivering all eight SDD units from the UK. About 70 percent of the value of the production articles will be manufactured in the United States. The U.S. firm United Defense LP will be responsible for final assembly and test for delivery to U.S. customers. The U.S. Army and Marines are slated to procure nearly 700 XM777 howitzers, while the British Army plans on buying 65 and the Italian Army 70. In short, the XM777 is essentially a critical weapon system requirement whose design, development, and integration has been awarded

---

[45]On October 26, 2001, DoD announced the selection of Lockheed Martin as the winner of the concept development and risk reduction phase of the JSF program and awarded a contract for the beginning of SDD.

[46]On the other hand, while there was no formal requirement for industrial participation by firms from the countries whose governments joined the JSF program, in practice the two prime contractors knew that the inclusion of participating foreign countries' contractors could improve their chances of winning the competition. This is especially true in the case of the UK, since the British government has a role in the final downselect decision.

to a foreign contractor because that contractor offered the best technical solution for the best price. To the authors' knowledge, this is virtually unprecedented in the post–World War II history of U.S. major weapon system procurement (*Aerotech News and Review*, 2000). In addition to the economic benefits it offers, the program is clearly promoting equipment standardization with the British and Italian armies.

FSCS/TRACER

Most of the U.S. initiatives discussed above have shown strong industry involvement in the structuring of new forms of cross-border relationships to satisfy national technology and security objectives while at the same time maintaining or even increasing competition. The U.S. government has also attempted to proactively promote more innovative cross-border business relationships for more traditional, platform-specific programs initiated on a government-to-government basis.

The Future Scout and Cavalry System (FSCS)/Tactical Reconnaissance Armored Combat Equipment Requirement (TRACER) program is a cooperative U.S.-UK program for the development of a light armored combat vehicle, jointly called the Armored Scout and Reconnaissance Vehicle (ASRV). The effort is innovative by virtue of the actions taken by the participating governments to maintain competition in a transatlantic program in the early phases: Two transatlantic industry groups were assembled to compete during the technology demonstration/concept development phase of the program.

Of particular interest is the fact that the two groups chose to pursue different business relationships: One became a transatlantic joint venture subcontracting to a second transatlantic joint venture, while the other chose to remain a team. The first, SIKA International, is a 50-50 joint venture between BAE Systems and Lockheed Martin. It subcontracts to a second-tier joint venture called Vehicle Armour and Armament Ltd., a 50-50 joint venture between the British firm Vickers Defence Systems and the U.S.-based General Dynamics Land Systems.

The second industry group, called the LANCER team, was a prime contracting organization. Originally headed by GEC-Marconi as prime contractor, it included Raytheon Systems, Alvis Vehicles, GKN Defence, and United Defense LP. With the purchase of GEC-Marconi by BAE Systems, however, both SIKA International and the LANCER team included BAE Systems in leadership roles. This caused some concern over the competition on both sides of the Atlantic. Eventually the two governments required the establishment of "firewalls" between the two opposing BAE Systems teams.[47] In February 1999, SIKA International won the competition to develop the FSCS/TRACER.

This program provides an interesting example of competitive transatlantic teaming using different business approaches (joint venture versus team) and illustrates one of the possible effects of a merger in the middle of the process that places the same key player on both teams. The latter situation, however, is not unique. The MEADS program, for example, has some of the same key European players on both competitive cross-border teams. In addition, the FSCS/TRACER program has evolved into a much more traditional transatlantic program since the downselect and has experienced a variety of technical, political, and funding problems. On October 16, 2001, the U.S. and UK governments officially canceled the program after joint expenditures exceeding $230 million. One published account claimed that U.S. Army requirements had changed, noting that in the future international collaboration should "take place at the subsystem level, such as engines," rather than at the large system platform level (Barrie and Tiboni, 2001).

JOINT VENTURES

Table 2.2 defines a joint venture as a separate legal entity, either a partnership or a corporation, that two or more companies form to pursue a particular program or a larger market segment. While a team is usually informal and based on company-to-company MoUs, a joint venture tends to connote a deeper, more permanent relation-

---

[47]With the continuing consolidation of European and U.S. industry, this is becoming increasingly common, as in the case of BAE Systems and Rolls-Royce on JSF and BAE Systems on the Medium Extended Air Defense system (MEADS) program.

ship involving more significant amounts of cross-border investment. Like teams, however, joint ventures in the defense world can be formed to conduct a range of activities, from marketing to cooperative modification or development of a single system to cooperative R&D over an entire market sector. The first two joint ventures shown in Table 5.3, discussed earlier in this chapter, began as marketing agreements and evolved into more complex and lasting relationships. FSCS/TRACER, also discussed earlier, included a transatlantic competition between a cross-border joint venture and a cross-border team for the development and production of a specific system.

Medium Extended Air Defense System

The MEADS program, which involves the United States, Germany, and Italy, is one of the earliest examples of an effort in which governments have tried to inject greater competition into international development programs through competitive cross-border industry groupings during the project definition phase. As with FSCS/

Table 5.3

Examples of Cross-Border Joint Ventures

Companies	Description
Pioneer UAV, Inc.(AAI/IAI)	Joint venture to market, modify, and coproduce Israeli UAVs for the U.S. government.
PGSUS LLC (Lockheed/Rafael)	Joint venture to coproduce, upgrade, modify, and market the HAVE NAP AGM-142 Raptor.
FSCS/TRACER (SIKA, Inc.)	Joint venture in competition with a cross-border team to develop and produce a light armored vehicle.
MEADS	Air defense system; two competing U.S./German/Italian joint ventures established for a single program.
Air Command Systems International (Thales/Raytheon)	Joint venture formed to upgrade the NATO ACCS.
Thales Raytheon Systems	Joint venture formed to compete in a range of radar and command-and-control market sectors.

TRACER, MEADS also illustrates the difficulties involved even in innovative government-mandated business relationships.

The MEADS case represents one of the first times that two separate transatlantic joint ventures were formed to compete against each other for the same project. Two U.S. companies, Lockheed Martin and Raytheon, led the competing joint ventures. Interestingly, some of the key German and Italian members were the same for both teams, but different groups within each European company were "walled off" from each other in order to work with the two competing U.S. lead contractors. The Raytheon team was originally made up of a U.S. joint venture between Hughes and Raytheon called H&R Company. It integrated with a European joint venture called EuroMEADS which was composed of Finmeccanica of Italy and LFK-Lenkflugkopersysteme GmbH and Siemens AG of Germany. The Lockheed joint venture called itself MEADS International and consisted of Lockheed Martin of the United States, DaimlerChrysler Aerospace of Germany (EADS),[48] and Alenia Marconi Systems of Italy.[49] In May 1999, the selection of the Lockheed team was publicly announced. MEADS has, however, experienced numerous political, funding, and technology transfer disputes, and its final outcome is still in doubt.

Thales Raytheon Systems

The recently formed 50-50 joint venture between Thales and Raytheon, called Thales Raytheon Systems, is an innovative, industry-initiated effort to go beyond single projects and encompass entire market sectors.[50] Raytheon's Chief Executive Officer, Denis Ranque, has characterized Thales Raytheon Systems as "herald[ing] a new era in transatlantic relations" because it "takes us beyond a program-by-program arrangement to one that will create a long-term, stable relationship of benefit to our customers and our respective companies alike." According to Ranque, the new joint venture "is truly a unique initiative" because it "constitutes the first transatlantic initiative to

---

[48]LFK-Lenkflugkopersysteme GmbH is now part of EADS.

[49]As noted earlier, Finmeccanica owns half of Alenia Marconi.

[50]Northrop Grumman's teaming with DaimlerChrysler (EADS) is similar but has not taken on the legal formality of a joint venture.

build up a structural [joint venture] alliance in the defense sector" (*Aerotech News and Review*, 2001; *Aerotech News and Review*, 2000).

Thales Raytheon Systems grew out of a history of project-specific collaboration between the two firms, the most important of which was aimed at upgrading the NATO ACCS. In December 1996, Thales (then Thomson-CSF) and Raytheon formed a 50-50 joint venture based in Paris called Air Command Systems International (ACSI) that was aimed at winning the NATO ACCS Level of Operational Capability 1 (LOC1) improvement program. In July 1999, the NATO Command and Control Management Agency awarded the ACCS LOC1 contract to ACSI.

One and one-half years later, Thales and Raytheon announced the formation of Thales Raytheon Systems. The initial market sectors covered by the joint company are high priorities in the NATO DCI effort: air defense and command-and-control centers, ground-based air surveillance systems, and weapon-locating radars.

According to some published sources, the specific terms of the joint venture took many months to negotiate, mainly because of U.S. government controls over and concerns about technology transfer. In June 2001, however, the joint venture company announced that it had received all necessary governmental approvals on both sides of the Atlantic. The company has been structured in a manner that will help satisfy technology security concerns. Thus, for example, the joint venture company operationally consists of two subsidiaries: one in Fullerton, California, which is 51 percent owned by Raytheon, and one in Paris that is 51 percent owned by Thales. Program leadership and work are not expected to be split equally between the two subsidiaries; rather, they will be determined on a program-by-program basis. Company officials claim that there will be a free flow of information and technology within the company but that the customer will have to adhere to the regulatory regime of the country in which the lead subsidiary for a specific program resides (Lake, 2001).

Raytheon officials explicitly viewed this new joint venture company as a means of widening their market access to NATO and other European programs. Thales officials made it clear that entry into the U.S. market was their primary motivation. They noted, however, that a major advantage of a joint venture over the outright purchase of a subsidiary in the United States was that it circumvented some of the regulatory and oversight issues involved in purchasing a fully owned subsidiary.[51] Thales officials also noted that the French company entered the British market in a similar manner, starting first with project-specific teams, then forming joint ventures, and finally proceeding with the purchase of a major subsidiary, Racal Electronics, which was one-quarter of Thales' size. In principle, joint ventures such as Thales Raytheon could contribute substantially to NATO equipment standardization and interoperability in a variety of contexts. However, further research is necessary to determine if they will be effective in this area. Yet the Thales Raytheon joint venture is clearly one of the most innovative and unusual transatlantic business linkups in recent history, and it is in a key area stressed by DCI. It thus deserves to be a high-priority candidate for future case study research.

PARENT/SUBSIDIARY

The final category of cross-border investment and other business relationships listed in Table 2.2 is parent/subsidiary. A subsidiary is defined as an enterprise that is wholly owned or effectively controlled by a parent company physically located in another country, formed either as a new establishment or as a purchase of or merger with an existing establishment.

As discussed earlier, the most sensitive and high-profile subsidiaries from the United States perspective have historically been those that have resulted from the outright purchase of an existing U.S. defense contractor by a foreign company. The formation of such subsidiaries raises questions regarding access to U.S. classified information, technology transfer, security of supply, the investment strategy of the new foreign owners, and competition and innovation. Table 5.4 pro-

---

[51]In a widely publicized CFIUS case in 1992, Thomson-CSF was effectively blocked from purchasing the LTV Missile Division in Texas. See Center for Security Studies (1992).

Table 5.4

Examples of Overseas Subsidiaries Acquired Through Acquisition of Existing Firms

Companies	Description
Foreign firm/target U.S. firm	
Thomson-CSF/LTV Missiles (1992)	Purchase attempt withdrawn under U.S. government pressure.
Rolls-Royce/Allison (1995)	Purchase approved with SSA and proxy company; first approved foreign purchase of "crown jewel."
BAE Systems/LMAES (Sanders), LMCS (2000)[a]	Very sensitive EW developer; makes BAE Systems one of DoD's largest suppliers.
U.S. firm/target foreign firm	
United Defense LP/Bofors	U.S. firm acquires leading Swedish armament maker.
General Dynamics/Santa Barbara ENSB	Leading U.S. tank manufacturer acquires Spanish firm producing main foreign competitor's tank.
TRW/Lucas Verity	TRW, a major U.S. defense avionics and IT contractor and automotive manufacturer, acquires Lucas Verity, a British firm with similar specialties.

[a]LMAES = Lockheed Martin Aerospace Electronics Systems.

vides some examples of recent foreign subsidiaries that have been acquired through actual or attempted acquisitions.

Some OSD officials argue that there has been a "sea change" over the past decade in DoD's attitudes toward the foreign acquisition of U.S. defense contractors.[52] This change is illustrated by comparing the first three cases in Table 5.4.

Thomson-CSF/LTV Missiles (1992)

In 1992, Thomson-CSF (now Thales) attempted to buy LTV's Vought missile division. Because of concerns over technology security, this

---

[52]Based on interviews with OSD officials. Official documents, however, do not indicate such a change.

attempted purchase met with considerable opposition in DoD and elsewhere in the U.S. government. Eventually the CFIUS process produced a compromise that would in principle have permitted the purchase had it been accompanied by a strict SSA and by the establishment of a proxy firm. The conditions were so stringent, however, that Thomson-CSF withdrew its purchase offer.

Rolls-Royce/Allison (1995)

In late 1994, Rolls-Royce Engines made an offer to purchase Allison Engines of Cincinnati. DoD technology experts considered Allison to be a defense technology "crown jewel" because of its possession of unique, cutting-edge technologies. Much of its expertise was gained as a result of its heavy involvement, as a team member with General Electric Aircraft Engines Division, in the Integrated High-Performance Turbine Engine Technology (IHPTET) and Joint Advanced Strike Technology (JAST) programs[53] for the development of the next-generation gas turbine engines and fighter aircraft.

It was reported that the Air Force strongly opposed the approval of this deal because of concerns that IHPTET technology would migrate to Rolls-Royce commercial engines. The Air Force argued that Pratt & Whitney could be so financially undermined in its commercial turbofan jet engine sales that it might threaten the firm's position as a leading designer, developer, and producer of military gas turbine engines for U.S. fighters and other military aircraft. The Air Force's position was that at least two financially healthy, robust U.S. military engine developers and manufacturers (GEC and Pratt & Whitney) were necessary for the competition to maintain innovation, quality, and price.

OSD agreed with the Air Force evaluation, but after four months of assessments it concluded that safeguards could be put in place that would allow Allison's acquisition by Rolls-Royce to move forward. These safeguards included an SSA that imposed restrictions on uncontrolled transfers of information and technology between Allison and Rolls-Royce. In addition, programs classified above Secret, as well as the IHPTET and JAST programs, were placed in a separate,

---

[53]JAST later evolved into JSF.

newly created proxy company called Allison Advanced Development Company, Inc. (AADC). This company was governed by a separate proxy agreement, separate management, and additional security procedures. Even visits between representatives of Rolls-Royce and Allison and AADC required prior approval from the appropriate authorities. As a result, Allison and AADC became wholly owned subsidiaries of Rolls-Royce.[54]

Five years later, OSD concluded that it had overregulated the deal. OSD determined that Rolls-Royce had acted responsibly and that the threat to Pratt & Whitney's commercial viability no longer existed. In early 2000, DoD therefore dropped the requirement for a separate proxy company. AADC was dissolved, but an SSA remained in place. Apparently the Air Force concurred with this decision.

A key aspect of the Rolls-Royce/Allison deal was that it was the first time DoD had approved the acquisition of a "crown jewel" defense firm by a foreign company. This established a major precedent that was soon confirmed by the BAE Systems/Lockheed Martin deal.

BAE Systems/LMAES (Sanders), LMCS (2000)

In mid-2000, BAE Systems North America, the wholly owned U.S. subsidiary of the UK's BAE Systems, finalized an agreement with Lockheed Martin for the purchase of its Aerospace Electronics Systems (LMAES), sector, which includes Sanders. Sanders is widely considered to be the world's premier supplier of highly sophisticated and technologically sensitive EW equipment for combat aircraft. OSD and Air Force technology specialists clearly viewed Sanders as a "crown jewel" of the U.S. aerospace industry. Yet during the OSD and Air Force review process of the proposed purchase, there were allegedly very few major objections raised against the deal (*Aerotech News and Review*, 2000).

As one OSD official pointed out, this deal also represented a sea change when compared to the Allison deal. This time there was a clear bipartisan consensus that close allies, especially the UK, Canada, and Australia, would be permitted to buy virtually any

---

[54]See Assistant Secretary of Defense for Public Affairs (1995).

"crown jewel" of the aerospace industry with relatively few CFIUS restrictions. The BAE Systems/LMAES (Sanders) deal did not require a proxy firm as had been the case with Allison, although there were some required mitigation measures. Since the experience of Kosovo, the consequent recognition of allied technological equipment short-comings, and the launching of the NATO DCI, a consensus had emerged within DoD that such acquisitions by close, trusted allies were desirable because they could help enhance interoperability with U.S. forces and reduce the capability gap between NATO and U.S. forces.

As a result of this acquisition and earlier purchases such as Lockheed Martin Control Systems, BAE Systems has arguably become the world's largest defense contractor and one of the most important suppliers to DoD. This acquisition will make BAE Systems the world leader in the highly sensitive area of EW, perhaps rivaled only by Northrop Grumman.

Prior to the acquisition, Lockheed's Sanders unit had been experi-encing financial and programmatic problems with such key efforts as the Lockheed F-22 fighter program. Some observers have argued that BAE Systems' acquisition of Sanders could strengthen the unit financially and tighten up management, providing DoD with a more capable firm and a better competitor for Northrop Grumman. Others, however, are concerned about the sensitivity of the EW tech-nology, especially with regard to highly classified sources and meth-ods for EW intelligence. Concerns have also been raised about what some consider to be the inflated price paid by BAE Systems for LMAES and the huge debt the British company has run up with this acquisition and others both in Europe and in the United States (Aponovich, 2000; Sirak, January 2001).

There is little decisive evidence in the open literature demonstrating that these acquisitions by foreign firms have contributed signifi-cantly to increased alliance standardization and interoperability. The principal customers of these subsidiaries remain the U.S. gov-ernment, not allied governments. It is also clear that the main rea-son foreign companies acquire U.S. companies as subsidiaries is to gain easy access to the U.S. defense market through existing U.S. programs. Whether advanced technology is migrating to the mother companies in Europe and contributing to closing the U.S.-Europe capabilities gap is not discernible from published sources. On the other hand, Rolls-Royce Allison is an important partner on the JSF program, providing the lift fan subsystem for the Lockheed short takeoff and vertical landing (STOVL) design and several components for the Boeing STOVL design. It could be argued that British ownership of Allison encouraged British participation in JSF and willingness to procure significant numbers of the STOVL variant, thus promoting allied equipment standardization, but this remains speculation.

Raytheon/Kollsman

Two smaller but potentially revealing CFIUS cases are worthy of relating to illustrate recent technology investment and security issues as well as to highlight the problems that sometimes arise when non-British firms enter the U.S. market through acquisitions.

The first case involves the proposed acquisition by a small company called Kollsman of two former business units belonging to Hughes Aircraft and Texas Instruments (TI), both of which were acquired by Raytheon in 1997. The government required that Raytheon divest these two units after its acquisition of Hughes and TI in order to maintain adequate competition in the defense arena in the areas of focal plane arrays (FPAs) and electro-optics (EO). The former TI FPA unit was considered by some technical analysts in OSD to be a "crown jewel." Raytheon packaged the two units together and intended to sell them to Kollsman, its "chosen purchaser."[55]

OSD viewed Kollsman as inappropriate for two reasons. First, Kollsman was not seen as having the expertise or the resources to maintain cutting-edge technology development in the area of FPAs. This is because Kollsman is a relatively small company (about 600 employees and $100 million-plus annual turnover) that specializes in military laser-based EO systems and basic avionics but has little or no experience in cutting-edge FPA technology. Second, Kollsman was owned by ELOP, an Israeli EO defense firm. Some DoD officials

---

[55]In divestiture cases, "chosen purchasers" can be a DoD concern because of the belief that the divesting mother company may have an incentive to spin off the divested units to a new owner that will not pose a serious competitive threat.

believed that the Rolls-Royce/Allison deal had established a precedent for the acquisition of "crown jewels" by the UK but not by other countries. The CFIUS process ultimately resulted in a rejection of this proposed acquisition, and Raytheon sold off the units to another company. Ironically, in 2000, Elbit, another larger Israeli military avionics firm, bought out ELOP, including Kollsman. The new, combined firm has annual revenues close to three-quarters of a billion dollars and does 25 percent of its business with DoD and 30 percent of its business with NATO and other European Union (EU) countries (Berger, 2000).

ASM Lithography Holding/Silicon Valley Group (SVG) Inc.

Another interesting case involves the difficulty that the Netherlands' ASM Lithography Holding recently experienced in acquiring Silicon Valley Group (SVG) Inc. in San Jose, California. A number of concerns were expressed in the United States with regard to this issue, especially over the foreign acquisition of SVG's subsidiary, Tinsley Laboratories, which manufactures high-technology mirrors and lenses for military reconnaissance satellites and other military users. For a brief period, the episode caused considerable friction between the Dutch and U.S. governments. On the basis of press accounts, however, it would appear that opposition to the acquisition came primarily from several members of Congress, not from OSD. Eventually the deal was approved. Nonetheless, because congressional actions and concerns can critically affect both the CFIUS process and the entire question of technology and arms transfer, they may warrant further examination in the context of this case or similar cases.[56]

U.S. FIRMS AND FOREIGN SUBSIDIARIES

Historically, U.S. companies have preferred to form project-specific cross-border teams or joint ventures with European firms rather than to acquire entire foreign companies or units as foreign subsidiaries, as it is argued that this approach provides greater strategic flexibility. In addition, U.S. firms have traditionally maintained that because the

---

[56]See, for example, Simpson (2001).

European market was so fragmented, the forging of teaming arrangements and joint ventures often provided market access to more countries than the acquisition of a subsidiary in a single country (GAO, August 2000). An exception to this rule is the UK, where many leading U.S. defense contractors—such as Boeing, Raytheon, Lockheed Martin, Northrop Grumman, and General Dynamics—have long-established subsidiaries. Recently, however, the move toward consolidation of the European industrial base and the possible emergence of greater EU collaboration on requirements and procurement have led some U.S. firms to reexamine this strategy in the rest of Europe (DUSD[IA], 2001).

United Defense/Bofors

Bofors of Sweden and Santa Barbara ENSB (Empresa Nacional Santa Barbara de Industrias Militares SA) of Spain are two recent high-visibility European acquisitions by U.S. firms in countries other than the UK. In June 2000, United Defense LP, one of the two leading U.S. manufacturers of armored combat vehicles and naval gun systems, bought out Sweden's Bofors Weapon Systems, a division of Saab-Celsius. Bofors is a leading European manufacturer of artillery systems, naval guns, combat vehicles, and smart ammunition. The acquisition of Bofors gives UDLP a major entrée into the European market at a time when the U.S. armored combat vehicle market is stagnant (Foss, 2000).

General Dynamics, the other major manufacturer of armored fighting vehicles in the United States, including the M-1 Abrams Main Battle Tank (MBT), followed a similar strategy through its acquisition in mid-2001 of the principal Spanish MBT manufacturer, Santa Barbara ENSB.[57] This deal may give General Dynamics access to some of the leading European MBT technologies as well as better market access to the European market. Nonetheless, this was a controversial takeover in Europe.[58] To seal the deal, General Dynamics

---

[57]General Dynamics is a broad-based multidivision firm that also manufactures naval vessels, submarines, small commercial jet aircraft, and other products.

[58]Santa Barbara produces the German Leopard tank under license. The Santa Barbara acquisition was reportedly blocked for some time by heavy German lobbying

had to pledge to make a considerable investment in improving Santa Barbara's capital assets. The deal supports the earlier acquisition by General Dynamics of a major share of Austria's Steyr-Daimler-Puch Spezialfahrzeug AG, a privately owned shareholding company of which General Dynamics owns 25 percent. General Dynamics also has marketing and production rights for Steyr products, including the Pandur wheeled armored vehicle (*Washington Post*, 2001).

TRW/Lucas Verity

A major U.S. defense aerospace acquisition was completed in May 1999, when TRW acquired Lucas Verity of the UK for $9 billion. Both TRW and Lucas Verity are also major automotive parts manufacturers. In 1999, Lucas Verity logged roughly half the total sales of TRW. Following the acquisition, TRW reorganized into an automotive division with about 100,000 employees and an aerospace, defense, and information systems division of approximately 35,000 employees.

Although Lucas Verity is a typical acquisition for a U.S. defense aerospace firm in that it is headquartered in the UK, the British firm has a major marketing and manufacturing presence in several other countries in Europe and elsewhere (DUSD[IA], 2001). Lucas Aerospace, which became TRW Aeronautical Systems after the acquisition, has long been a world leader in engine controls and other sophisticated aerospace subsystems as well as in repair and overhaul. The acquisition of SAMM in France, a subsidiary of the PSA Peugeot Citroen group, made it a leading supplier of flight control actuators on the European continent. Thus, along with the United Defense acquisition of Bofors and the General Dynamics acquisition of Santa Barbara ENSB, TRW's acquisition of Lucas Verity may suggest that U.S. firms are starting to more vigorously pursue European acquisitions outside the UK.

Nonetheless, European penetration of the U.S. defense market through acquisitions remains much more striking than the reverse. More significantly, acquisitions launched from both sides of the Atlantic appear to be driven primarily by the desire to take over an

from Krauss-Maffei Wegmann of Munich, the manufacturer of the Leopard I and II MBTs.

existing foreign national market segment as an easy means of gaining market access. It is unclear from published accounts, however, whether such acquisitions contribute in any significant way to increased equipment standardization and interoperability. The newly acquired foreign subsidiaries tend to continue to do most of their business with their own foreign national governments and to focus on their existing national or cross-national programs.

SUMMARY OVERVIEW AND FUTURE RESEARCH

The initial findings from this review of a large number of recent cross-border business agreements and other types of collaborative arrangements are as follows:

- U.S. aerospace defense contractors are much more active and aggressive than has previously been the case in initiating cross-border business relationships on the basis of their own internal business and market calculations.

- Many of these relationships are innovative and vary from the types of business relationships—often imposed by governments—that were typical in the past.

- The extent to which the regulatory environment and the ongoing reform of that environment are influencing these new types of industry-initiated cross-border business relationships is not fully discernible from the published literature, but that influence appears to be significant.

- In-depth analysis of the relative advantages and disadvantages, from the Air Force's perspective, of the various types of new industry-initiated cross-border relationships cannot be fully discerned solely on the basis of the published literature.

- Further detailed research focused on primary source case studies and interviews with relevant industry and government officials is necessary to gain the information required to formulate policy options for the Air Force on optimally managing the new types— and greater numbers—of industry-initiated cross-border relationships.

We believe that field research based on interviews with relevant government and industry officials both in the United States and abroad, combined with in-depth case analyses of a carefully selected number of case studies, could fill the gaps in our knowledge and support the formulation of meaningful policy recommendations for the Air Force.

On the basis of an initial review of the wide number of cases discussed in this chapter, we find that the types of programs that realistically appear to show the most promise for promoting the potential military-political and economic benefits of globalization are those that have some or all of the following characteristics:

- They are voluntarily structured and sometimes initiated by defense firms rather than by governments on the basis of internal business calculations of market conditions and best business practices.

- They are painstakingly structured to satisfy the existing U.S. arms export and technology security regulatory regime and CFIUS.

- They often focus on promoting existing products or modifications thereof or on specific product market sectors.

- They often focus on subsystems, munitions, or discrete components or areas rather than on large, complex programs for the development of entire weapon system platforms.[59]

- They are designed to gain and expand active reciprocal market access through new programs.

- They are often motivated by a desire to add to a company's product portfolio a highly competitive product in a market sector dominated by another firm or firms. Thus, they inherently promote greater competition.

---

[59]Following the cancellation of the U.S.-UK FSCS/TRACER program in October 2001, one journalist noted that the program "highlighted many of the pitfalls of trans-Atlantic cooperation at the platform level" and reported that a senior British official observed that "in the future, collaboration at the subsystems level might be more fruitful." See Barrie and Tiboni (2001).

- They are characterized by mutual perception of balanced and complementary bilateral market access opportunities and technology transfer.

For further research, we suggest an examination of case studies for in-depth analysis to better illustrate the issues and problems involved with greater globalization, as well as the menus of policy options the Air Force has to manage them.

Two proposed case studies are shown in Table 5.5. These cases illustrate many of the most important emerging trends in cross-border business relationships as well as some of the formidable barriers and issues that must still be overcome if the U.S. Air Force is to realize the potential benefits of globalization. The first is the Northrop Grumman/EADS (Germany) market sector teaming arrangement for Global Hawk/Euro Hawk, EW, radar, and other product sectors. The second is a broader study of the overall NATO AGS program.

The two central questions we seek to answer in any follow-on research are as follows:

First, what types of new industry-initiated cross-border business relationships and cross-border activities are most likely to promote the claimed benefits of globalization?

- Greater competition in the interests of encouraging technological innovation and reduced equipment procurement costs to the Air Force;

- Greater cross-border procurement RCI with key U.S. allies;

- Achievement of the goals and priorities laid out in the NATO DCI; or

- Protection of key national security interests regarding technology transfer, security of supply, and R&D investment?

Second and most important, what "lessons learned" will provide the most guidance to the U.S. Air Force on how to effectively promote procurement efficiencies and achieve greater interoperability with our allies while protecting vital national security interests?

Table 5.5

Case Studies of Cross-Border Strategic Market Sector Collaboration

Program	Business Structure	Activity	Competition[a]	Globalization Issues
Surveillance radar, command and control	U.S. French market sector joint venture	Codevelopment, coproduction	Variable	Tech transfer, tech security, work share, NATO RSI,[c] competition
NATO alliance ground surveillance	To be decided	Codevelopment, coproduction	Euro Hawk, ASTOR, SOSTAR, Eagle+, NATAR[b]	NATO RSI, tech transfer, tech security, interoperability

[a]The "Competition" column indicates separate programs that are clearly in competition. See the main text for a detailed discussion of specific programs.
[b]ASTOR = Airborne Standoff Radar; SOSTAR = Standoff Surveillance and Target Acquisition Radar; NATAR = NATO Transatlantic Advanced Radar.
[c]RSI = rationalization, standardization, and interoperability.

We believe that further in-depth case study analysis of the types of cases listed above, along with more extensive interviews of relevant government and industry officials, will fill the gaps in our research to date and help us answer our basic policy questions for the U.S. Air Force.

Chapter Six

CONCLUSIONS AND PROPOSED FUTURE RESEARCH

In this chapter we present the principal findings of our study and describe the direction of our future research efforts. The main findings are organized into two sections. First, we consider how U.S. industry has responded to globalization, the consolidation of European industry, and other trends. Then we focus on the broader implications of these trends, particularly with regard to opportunities for expanding U.S. and European cross-border business relationships. At the end of the chapter, we identify gaps in current research that will be addressed in the follow-up report for this project.

THE RESPONSE OF U.S. INDUSTRY TO GLOBALIZATION

* **Numerous innovative cross-border strategic market sector agreements initiated by U.S. companies are emerging.** Leading U.S. aerospace prime contractors and subcontractors are aggressively seeking creative new forms of cross-border linkages in efforts to gain or maintain foreign market access. The most innovative linkages appear to be long-term strategic teaming or joint venture agreements aimed at entire market sectors rather than the more traditional approach focusing on specific projects or systems. While most of these relationships are in the very early stages, they appear to have a high potential for promoting equipment standardization and interoperability as well as for promoting cost and innovation benefits through economic rationalization. There are indications, however, that these rela-

tionships are very difficult to structure, especially with non-UK companies, because of the U.S. regulatory environment.

- **U.S. aerospace firms are not significantly increasing their acquisition of foreign defense aerospace firms and wholly owned subsidiaries.** There are few indications that U.S. defense aerospace firms have dramatically increased their interest in acquiring wholly owned foreign subsidiaries, although there seems to be some increase in U.S. M&A activity overseas in the defense industry as a whole. As noted above, the preferred industry-initiated cross-border business relationships appear to be teams and joint ventures. There are some indications that this preference is driven in part by the U.S. and European regulatory environments. Historically, U.S. firms have apparently favored teaming because of the flexibility it provides and because of its lack of long-term commitment. This may be changing, however. It is unclear what the benefits and costs of this preference are from the perspective of the U.S. government and the U.S. Air Force.

- **Teaming and joint ventures with non-UK and non-Europe-based firms are increasing.** In the past, most U.S. direct investment abroad as well as other types of U.S. industry-initiated cross-border investment and other business relationships have involved UK firms. This was in part because U.S. government technology security and third-party transfer concerns were often more easily resolved with UK companies than with companies from other countries. Over the past several years, however, there has been an apparent increase in M&As, teaming, and joint ventures with non-UK-headquartered European companies as well as with non-European companies. It is unclear from the open literature what the implications of this trend are for technology security and equipment standardization issues. Depending on the circumstances, they sometimes contribute to standardization and interoperability and sometimes do not. More often they appear to contribute to greater market competition and greater choice available to the Air Force, as well as to reduced procurement costs.

IMPLICATIONS OF EUROPEAN CONSOLIDATION AND INCREASED AEROSPACE GLOBALIZATION

- **U.S. industry collaboration with one country's firm increasingly means collaboration with many countries' firms.** The European defense aerospace industry is in the process of consolidating down to one or two dominant European transnational companies in nearly every major product sector. The three leading European companies—BAE Systems, EADS, and Thales—are interlocked with each other and with many other European firms through a complex web of joint ventures, collaborative programs, cross-ownership, M&As, and the like. Other important foreign industrial bases, such as those of Israel and Korea, are also consolidating and are increasingly forming strategic links with the new European megafirms (as well as U.S. firms) and with many other foreign firms located in different parts of the globe. The result is that it is increasingly unrealistic for U.S. government policymakers and industry leaders to think in terms of bilateral collaborative relationships between the United States and specific European or other foreign countries. The traditional U.S. government and U.S. industry approach of negotiating bilateral, country-specific agreements, which is continuing under the DTSI reform initiative, may have to be modified or adjusted as European and other foreign national defense aerospace firms transform into truly multinational megafirms.[1] This may also affect the United States' traditional emphasis on cross-border business relationships and investment with the UK. These changes may have significant implications for U.S. technology security issues.

- **Consolidated European and other foreign firms mean potentially more equal partners as well as stronger competitors.** The consolidation of the European defense aerospace industry is producing pan-European companies of roughly the same size and sales turnover as the leading U.S. firms in many product sectors. These new, pan-European companies seek to be more financially and technologically competitive in more product ar-

---

[1]U.S. government examination of issuing umbrella program-wide export licenses is one approach that helps deal with this situation.

eas with the leading U.S. firms. Such firms are eager to offer European solutions for European and third-country weapon system requirements that are fully competitive with U.S. products. Similar consolidation trends are visible in other foreign countries. The Korean and Israeli aerospace industrial bases, for example, are undergoing extensive consolidation and are expanding their links with third-country firms.

- **European and other foreign firms seek U.S. market access but resent barriers.** With an overall smaller market and smaller R&D funding base even when all the EU nations are included, the newly emerging pan-European firms and other foreign companies strongly desire greater access both to the U.S. market and to U.S. technology. However, European and other foreign firms are insisting with increasing aggressiveness on more equal business relationships with U.S. firms as well as on less restrictive U.S. policies regarding access to the U.S. market, technology transfer, and third-party sales of technology and products. Concerns over these issues, in addition to a variety of other economic and political factors, are also encouraging the new pan-European firms to offer European solutions for European and third-country system requirements in direct competition with U.S. firms and products.

- **European and other foreign firms view the acquisition of U.S. firms that primarily service DoD as the most effective means of penetrating the U.S. market.** The most successful recent penetrations of the U.S. market by European firms, especially those headquartered in the UK, have been through the acquisition of existing U.S. firms rather than through joint ventures or programs. To date, however, newly acquired foreign subsidiaries primarily service the U.S. DoD and are often restricted with regard to technology flow back to Europe. Thus, such market penetration does not necessarily promote equipment standardization or interoperability or help close the capability gap with Europe. In addition, while DoD officials believe that the CFIUS process has been significantly liberalized over the past decade, European industry still views U.S. regulation of foreign direct investment to be onerous.

- **Non-European foreign firms are forming strategic relationships with European and U.S. firms, potentially enhancing competition but complicating standardization and interoperability objectives.** The defense industries of some other important non-NATO allies have been aggressively seeking U.S. and European market access through the formation of new business relationships based on strategic alliances. Israeli industry has been particularly active in this area, forging important business alliances with both U.S. and European companies. In many cases, these alliances have clearly increased competition in key niche product sectors within both the U.S. and European markets in a manner that appears to be beneficial to the Air Force. In some cases, however, these relationships seem to have undermined U.S. attempts to promote equipment standardization if not interoperability. In addition, based on the open literature, the efficacy of the controls on technology security and third-party transfer remains unclear.

- **The findings above suggest that European and other foreign industry consolidation presents U.S. government and industry with unprecedented opportunities as well as risks.** If new cross-border collaborative business relationships that are mutually beneficial take hold, the consolidation of European and other foreign industries greatly increases the prospects for allied procurement of standardized or interoperable systems, thus enhancing the cohesion of U.S. alliances and the ability to conduct combined operations while potentially reducing system costs. On the other hand, the persistence of frictions over technology transfer and security issues and over foreign direct investment, combined with the increased capabilities and competitiveness of European and other multinational defense industries, means that the Europeans and other allies may be tempted to move increasingly toward indigenous solutions and more widespread global competition with U.S. firms. This could reduce alliance cohesion and equipment standardization and interoperability. Thus far the evidence is mixed, but there appears to be an emerging trend toward more nonstandardized indigenous solutions to European weapon system requirements, at least on the platform and major system and subsystem levels.[2]

DIRECTIONS FOR FUTURE RESEARCH

The findings of this initial study point to the need for greater understanding of the opportunities and problems associated with an increasingly globalized and consolidated aerospace industrial base. Three issues in particular stand out.

First, the tension between the goal of enhanced competition and that of allied equipment standardization may be indicative of a potentially much greater tension inherent in the three primary Air Force objectives regarding defense industry globalization, particularly when the national security objective is balanced against the other two. Put another way, to what extent are greater competition and allied equipment standardization possible given the United States' need to safeguard its defense technology in the interests of national security? This question needs to be explored in depth.

The outlook for increased competition and interoperability depends in large part on the U.S. regulatory environment, which leads to a second key issue in need of further research. As discussed in Chapter Four, critics of the existing regulatory regime—which is designed to provide technology security and to protect domestic capabilities—have alleged that the regime impedes U.S. industry–initiated attempts to gain the benefits of greater globalization. In response to such concerns, a large-scale effort was launched under the Clinton administration to reduce these impediments by reforming the U.S. export regime. In Europe, the six leading defense producers have initiated export control harmonization through the Letter of Intent (LOI) and Framework Agreement process. Significant questions remain, however, with regard to the impact of these reforms. What is the effect of these measures in enhancing globalization while also protecting U.S. national security objectives such as technology se-

---

[2]A dramatic case in point is the Hungarian decision, finalized in late 2000, to acquire the JAS 39 Gripen fighter, marketed by a BAE Systems/Saab joint venture, instead of the Lockheed Martin F-16. This decision was closely followed by a similar decision by the Czech Republic. U.S. government and industry officials fear a similar decision by Poland.

curity and maintaining critical national capabilities? What do key government players consider to be potential problems with the reforms? The follow-up study will address these questions in detail.

The third issue concerns the need for a deeper understanding of the industrial, political, and military environments in Europe. The consolidation of the European aerospace industry, as well as that of other important foreign industrial bases, is resulting in a changed landscape for global collaboration and competition in the aerospace industry. But to what extent and in what specific ways will the changes taking place in Europe affect the prospects for global reform and greater transatlantic collaboration? And how will political and military factors in Europe affect prospects for the expansion of the U.S. defense industry into overseas markets? The new study will take a closer look at the opportunities and problems involved in pursuing new cross-border collaborative business relationships.

Further analysis of these broad questions, together with additional in-depth case study analysis of the type described in the previous chapter, will help fill the gaps in our understanding and provide guidance to the Air Force in developing new strategies and policies regarding the globalization of the industrial base.

AIR FORCE GUIDANCE: A STATUTORY AND REGULATORY FRAMEWORK

FEDERAL LAWS, EXECUTIVE ORDERS, AND REGULATIONS

Article 1, Section 8 of the U.S. Constitution gives Congress the authority to support armies and maintain a navy. Thus, at the highest level, Congress authorizes and appropriates funds for, and passes laws governing, the U.S. military. These laws can be enacted as stand-alone pieces of legislation or as amendments to other related or unrelated bills. However, because it would quickly have become extremely difficult for citizens, attorneys, judges, and legislators to understand the laws and their interrelationships in a given area if these laws had been left to stand individually or as originally grouped, Congress established the United States Code,[1] a classification structure for U.S. law.

The USC helps prevent the U.S. legal system from developing intractable redundancies, inconsistencies, and obsolescence. Fifty titles constitute the first level of indenture in the USC structure, which is further subdivided into parts, chapters, and sections. Frequently, laws are passed that do not fit neatly into a single title. In these cases, unrelated elements of the act are separated and then codified in the appropriate titles, parts, chapters, and sections. Several titles in the U.S. Code include laws that are relevant to globalization, military weapon system acquisition, and the defense industrial base.

---

[1]The entire U.S. Code can be accessed and searched at http://uscode.house.gov/title_50.htm.

Many are captured in Title 10, "Armed Forces."[2] Other titles that also contain relevant laws include Title 15, "Commerce and Trade," which contains the original Sherman Antitrust Act, and Title 22 "Foreign Relations and Intercourse," which contains the Arms Export Control Act.

Executive orders are not laws but are directives signed by the President of the United States in order to manage the operations of the federal government. As the Chief Executive, the President uses these decrees to manage the operations of the executive branch and to fulfill responsibilities conferred by the Constitution or by federal law.

Executive departments and agencies of the federal government publish regulations that comply with federal laws and executive orders and that regulate the functions and processes they perform and oversee. These regulations also document procedures developed to comply with all of the relevant laws, thereby saving the individual federal employee or citizen from personally having to understand all these laws. The National Archives and Records Administration's Office of the Federal Register publishes executive orders and federal regulations and codifies these documents in the Code of Federal Regulations (CFR).[3] The CFR, like the U.S. Code, is divided into several titles and is further divided into chapters, parts, and sections. For example, Title 3 of the CFR, "The President," contains copies of recent executive orders.

An example of a body of federal regulations with keen relevance to the globalization of the defense industrial base is the Federal Acquisition Regulations System, which is codified at Title 48 of the CFR. This system of regulations prescribes uniform procedures for all executive agencies' acquisition of goods and services. The Federal Acquisition Regulations System includes the Federal Acquisition Regulations (FAR) as well as the agency acquisition regulations that

---

[2] Chapters 137 through 148 of Title 10—which deals with acquisition, international cooperation, research, procurement of commercial items, standardization of weapon systems with our allies, and the defense technology and industry base—bear direct relevance to this study.

[3] The CFR can be viewed at http://www.access.gpo.gov/nara/cfr/cfr-table-search.html.

implement or supplement the FAR. The Defense Federal Acquisition Regulation Supplement (DFARS), the Air Force Federal Acquisition Regulation Supplement (AFFARS), and command supplements such as the Air Force Materiel Command FAR Supplement (AFMCFARS) are elements of the system that directly guide the Air Force. For example, FAR Part 25, DFARS Part 225, and AFFARS Part 5325 are all entitled "Foreign Acquisition" and provide guidance for purchasing goods and services from foreign-owned companies within the bounds of the Buy American Act and related laws and regulations.[4]

DOD AND AIR FORCE GUIDANCE

While the Constitution, federal laws, and the FAR are certainly relevant to the services' acquisition corps and other professionals who work with the globalizing defense industrial base, they are not the first reference documents to which DoD's military and civil servants normally turn for guidance in navigating the intricacies of international programs. Rather, DoD has drawn the applicable elements from federal statutes and regulations and combined them with additional guidance tailored to military missions. DoD Directives (DoDDs) establish DoD policies and assign responsibilities in conformance with U.S. law and other federal regulations (DoDD 5025.1). The DoD-unique policies that feed these directives often take the form of Directive Memoranda, which are issued at the Secretary, Deputy Secretary, or Assistant Secretary level. DoD Instructions (DoDIs) are the primary means of implementing these policies. When further instructions are necessary to ensure uniform implementation processes or to disseminate administrative information, DoD issues DoD Publications in the form of regulations, manuals, handbooks, and the like. DoD manuals and handbooks are often a compendium of numerous directives and instructions that apply to a given activity and that save the interested parties the effort and time required to collect and digest all the relevant DoD Directives and Instructions.

---

[4]Other relevant FAR parts include (with parallel parts in some of the various supplements): Part 6—Competition; Part 7—Acquisition Planning; Part 12—Acquisition of Commercial Items; Part 34—Major System Acquisition; and Part 44—Subcontracting Policies and Procedures.

The "5000 series" is a trio of DoD publications that forms the DoD acquisition manager's front-line authoritative guidance for planning and conducting a weapon system acquisition program.[5] The first two documents in the series are DoDD 5000.1, "The Defense Acquisition System," and its implementing instruction, DoDI 5000.2, "Operation of the Defense Acquisition System." Each received a major revision in October 2000 and was reissued with slight changes in January 2001. The third publication in the 5000 series is DoD Regulation 5000.2-R, "Mandatory Procedures for Major Defense Acquisition Programs (MDAPs) and Major Automated Information System (MAIS) Acquisition Programs," issued in June 2001. All three of these publications incorporate DoD's latest acquisition reform policies, which emphasize competition and thus have direct relevance to globalization of the defense industrial base.

Finally, the Air Force uses Air Force Policy Directives (AFPDs) and Air Force Instructions (AFIs) to implement laws or higher-level directives or to establish uniform procedures and processes. Nondirective Air Force publications, including handbooks and pamphlets, provide consolidated information and recommended guidance (AFI 33-360). Because DoD's and the services' interests in national security and the defense industrial base are inseparably linked, Air Force documents tend to focus on Air Force-unique implementation issues rather than on higher-level policies.

---

[5]See USD(AT&L), June 2001.

SEVENTEEN AGREED PROPOSALS OF THE DEFENSE TRADE SECURITY INITIATIVE

Fact Sheet Released by the Bureau of Political-Military Affairs, U.S. Department of State, May 26, 2000

1. **Major Program License:** A single, comprehensive license (including hardware, technical data, defense services) issued at the beginning of a project where the U.S. firm is the prime contractor. The license, initially available via a pilot project, will permit a consistent line of supply from one end user to another or to identified subcontractors. A major program license can cover a wide range of ventures, including projects for the commercial development of defense articles. Licenses can be valid for up to eight years (vice the current maximum of four years). The U.S. firm will need additional licenses only when activities or transactions extend beyond the initially approved license parameters.

2. **Major Project License:** A single comprehensive license for a major commercial sale of defense articles to NATO, Japan, or Australia. This license would permit the U.S. prime contractor to define the parameters of an export license that would cover all or some of the exports associated with the sale. Once these parameters were defined with the U.S. government, the contractor (either at the prime or subtier level) would have smooth and expedited processing of its export license request for something within the project, as long as the export is within the parameters of the Major Project License.

3. **Global Project License:** A single, comprehensive license to cover all exports planned to occur under a government-to-government international agreement for a cooperative project. The Department of Defense will define a standard set of terms and conditions that will apply to all phases and activities identified in the international agreement. Once a firm receives an initial license permitting it to participate in some aspect of the project covered by the international agreement, it would need additional licenses only for activities that exceed the standard terms and conditions and/or exceed congressional notification thresholds, to add new end users or participants, and/or to expand the participation of existing end users or participants. Exports and reexports to and among the approved end users would require no additional licenses.

4. **Technical Data Exports for Acquisitions, Teaming Arrangements, Mergers, Joint Ventures, and Similar Arrangements:** A single, comprehensive export authorization to permit qualified U.S. defense companies to exchange a broad set of technical data necessary for teaming arrangements, joint ventures, mergers, acquisitions, or similar arrangements with qualified foreign firms from NATO, Japan, or Australia. Unlike export authorizations for marketing, this authorization would cover the much broader range of technical data needed to assess with some degree of depth and transparency opportunities for such undertakings.

5. **Enhance the Use of Multiple Destination Licenses:** Try to increase use of multiple destination licenses that permit U.S. firms to market specific products to specified end users for specified end uses. Using this license establishes a *de facto* sales territory, since there is a presumption of approval for sales to those end users that were approved for marketing.

6. **Enhance the Use of Overseas Warehousing Agreements:** Try to increase the use of overseas warehousing agreements that permit U.S. firms to export large numbers of items (such as spare parts) to a foreign company (including U.S. subsidiaries incorporated overseas). The warehousing agreement authorizes the foreign company to reexport the parts to a list of preapproved end users for specified end uses.

7. **Expedited License Review for NATO:** Expedite U.S. government review of export licenses for Defense Capabilities Initiative (DCI) projects or programs.

8. **Special Embassy Licensing Program:** Expedite U.S. government review of licenses submitted by the governments of NATO countries, Japan, and Australia via their embassies in Washington, D.C., for end use by the requesting government.

9. **Interagency Export License Electronic Control Process:** The Departments of State and Defense will enhance computer connectivity between the Department of Defense and the State Department's Office of Defense Trade Controls to permit greater and more timely exchange of data on license applications.

10. **Extension of ITAR Exemption to Qualified Countries:** An ITAR exemption would be extended to countries that share with the United States congruent and reciprocal policies in export controls, industrial security, intelligence, law enforcement, and reciprocity in market access. This exemption would be limited to unclassified exports to the foreign government and to companies that are identified as reliable by the U.S. government in consultation with the foreign government. This exemption would be contingent upon establishment of appropriate international agreements on end use and retransfer of defense items, services, and technical data and on close conformity to essential export control principles. It is envisioned that the UK and Australia are the two countries most ready to take advantage of this exemption.

11. **Defense Services Exemptions for Maintenance and Maintenance Training:** Create a new ITAR exemption for increased levels of maintenance services and maintenance training for NATO countries, Japan, and Australia, if such repairs provide no upgrade to the equipment's original capability and do not include the transfer of manufacturing designs, information, or know-how.

12. **Exemption for Department of Defense Bid Proposals:** This proposal will permit U.S. firms to export certain technical data and services in support of Department of Defense bid proposals without a license.

13. **More Effective Use of Existing ITAR Exemptions by the Department of Defense:** The Department of Defense will clarify how DoD components should use existing ITAR exemptions that are available to them.

14. **Streamlined Licensing for COMSAT Components/Technical Data:** This proposal will streamline the licensing process for parts and minor components and limited technical data needed to bid on projects and respond to insurance requests on COMSATs. This process will minimize the number of licenses needed to support COMSAT programs where all the parties to the programs are NATO countries. The proposal has been developed by the Departments of State and Defense in consultation with U.S. industry and is intended also to fulfill the requirements of Section 1309(a) of the FY 2000–2001 Foreign Relations Authorization Act.

15. **ITAR Exemption for Foreign Military Sales Defense Services:** This proposal will permit the license-free export of technical data and defense services if they are expressly authorized in a Letter of Offer and Acceptance (LOA) and the underlying contract with a U.S. company. License-free exports will be permitted for the duration of the LOA and the underlying contract.

16. **Advance Retransfer Consent for Items Sold or Granted by the U.S. Government:** This proposal will permit the retransfer of defense articles previously sold or granted by the U.S. government if (1) the articles are to be retransferred only between the governments of NATO countries, Japan, or Australia, which have already signed blanket end-use and retransfer assurances; (2) the retransfer involves only unclassified items that the recipient already possesses; and (3) the retransfer involves articles with acquisition values of no greater than $7 million.

17. **Review/Revise the U.S. Munitions List:** The process would involve a four-year review cycle, where one-quarter of the U.S. Munitions List (USML) would be reviewed each year. The objective would be to comport what is controlled by the USML more directly with the Military Critical Technologies List.

REFERENCES

Aerospace Daily, "Gripen International Gets a Surprise Win in Hungarian Fighter Selection," September 11, 2001.

Aerospace Industries Association (AIA), *Aerospace Facts and Figures 2000/2001*, Washington, D.C., 2000.

Aerospace Industries Association (AIA), "AIA Announces New Reform Initiatives for Export Controls," Press Release 2001-15, March 7, 2001, available at http://www.aia-aerospace.org/aianews/press/2001/rel_03_07_01.cfm.

Aerotech News and Review, "BAE Systems Announces U.S. Supplier Base for the XM777 Lightweight Towed 155mm Howitzer," September 26, 2000.

Aerotech News and Review, "BAE Systems Reaches Definitive Agreement to Acquire Lockheed Martin Aerospace Electronics Systems," July 18, 2000.

Aerotech News and Review, "Raytheon, Thales Launch Global Joint Venture Focused on Air Defense Command, Control and Ground-Based Radar," June 22, 2001.

Aerotech News and Review, "Raytheon, Thales to Form Global Joint Venture Focused on Air Defense Command, Control and Ground-Based Radar," December 19, 2000.

Air Force Federal Acquisition Regulation Supplement, available at http://web2.deskbook.osd.mil/htmlfiles/DBY_farsupp-4-department.asp.

Air Force Instructions (AFI) and Policy Directives (AFPD), available at http://web2.deskbook.osd.mil/htmlfiles/DBY_af-4-department. asp.

Albright, Madeleine K., Secretary of State, "America and the World in the Twenty-first Century," written testimony for the Senate Foreign Relations Committee, February 8, 2000.

American Institute of Aeronautics and Astronautics (AIAA), *A Blueprint for Action*, final report published in conjunction with the AIAA Defense Reform Conference, Washington, D.C., February 14–15, 2001.

Andrews Space and Technology, *Space and Tech Digest*, May 1, 2000, available at http://www.spaceandtech.com/digest/sd2000-08/sd2000-08-003.shtml.

Aponovich, David, "Industry Pros Give Thumbs Up to BAE," *The Telegraph*, July 16, 2000.

Assistant Secretary of Defense for Command, Control, Communications, and Intelligence (ASD [C³I], *National Industrial Security Program Operating Manual (NISPOM)*, DoD 5220.22-M, January 1995 (Change 2, May 1, 2000).

Assistant Secretary of Defense for Public Affairs, "DoD Is Satisfied That Deal Between Allison Engine Co. and Rolls Royce Does Not Endanger National Security," news release, March 27, 1995.

Associated Press, "New Israeli Missile Targets Potential American Market," *Jerusalem Post*, May 3, 2001.

Barrie, Douglas, and Christina Mackenzie, "Mergers Create Two Major European Players," *Defense News*, August 7, 2000.

Barrie, Douglas, and Frank Tiboni, "TRACER/Future Scout Program Terminated," *Defense News*, October 22–28, 2001.

Berger, Sharon, "Elbit Finalizes Acquisition of El Op for $178m," *Jerusalem Post*, July 9, 2000.

Bialos, Jeffrey, "Re-Inventing Defense Export Controls: A National Security Imperative," speech delivered to the Practising Law Institute, Washington, D.C., December 7, 2000.

Bitzinger, Richard A., "Globalization in the Post–Cold War Defense Industry: Challenges and Opportunities," in Ann R. Markusen and Sean S. Costigan (eds.), *Arming the Future: A Defense Industry for the 21st Century*, New York: Council on Foreign Relations Press, 1999.

Boeing Company, "Boeing Signs Agreement with Meteor Missile Team," news release, October 20. 1999.

Brzoska, Michael, Peter Wilke, and Herbert Wulf, "The Changing Civil-Military Mix in Western Europe's Defense Industry," in Ann R. Markusen and Sean S. Costigan (eds.), *Arming the Future: A Defense Industry for the 21st Century*, New York: Council on Foreign Relations, 1999, pp. 374–375.

Bureau of Economic Analysis (BEA), U.S. Department of Commerce, "Direct Investment Position for 1999: Country and Industry Detail," prepared by Sylvia E. Bargas, in *Survey of Current Business*, July 2000a.

Bureau of Economic Analysis (BEA), U.S. Department of Commerce, "U.S. Multinational Companies Operations in 1998," prepared by Raymond J. Mataloni, Jr., in *Survey of Current Business*, July 2000b.

Bureau of Economic Analysis (BEA), U.S. Department of Commerce, "Foreign Investment in the United States: New Investment in 2000," Ned G. Howenstine (ed.), in *Survey of Current Business*, June 2001.

Bureau of Economic Analysis (BEA), U.S. Department of Commerce, "The Net International Investment Position of the United States at Yearend 2000," Harlan W. King (ed.), in *Survey of Current Business*, July 2001.

Bureau of Economic Analysis (BEA), U.S. Department of Commerce, "U.S. Affiliates of Foreign Companies: Operations in 1999," William J. Zeile (ed.), in *Survey of Current Business*, August 2001.

Bureau of Export Administration (BXA), U.S. Department of Commerce, "Implementation of Presidential Announcement of January 10, 2001: Revisions to License Exception CTP," *Federal Register*, Vol. 66, No. 13, January 19, 2001.

Bureau of Export Administration (BXA), U.S. Department of Commerce, "Fact Sheet: How Do I Know If I Need to Get a License from the Department of Commerce?" undated a, available at http://www.bxa.doc.gove/factsheets/facts1.htm.

Bureau of Export Administration (BXA), (Office of Chemical and Biological Controls and Treaty Compliance), U.S. Department of Commerce, "Guidelines for Preparing Export License Applications Involving Foreign Nationals," undated b, available at http://www.bxa.doc.gov/deemedexports/foreignationals.pdf.

Bureau of the Census, U.S. Department of Commerce, Population Division, *Current Population Survey*, March 2000.

Bureau of the Census, U.S. Department of Commerce, *Annual Survey of Manufacturers*, March 5, 2001.

Center for Security Studies, "Center Welcomes CFIUS Decision on Thomson/LTV Purchase," Press Release No. 92-P 75, July 9, 1992.

Ciardello, Victor F., "The Defense Industrial Base: Past, Present and Future?", presented at Global Air and Space 2001, International Business Forum and Exhibition, American Institute of Aeronautics and Astronautics, May 7–9, 2001.

Clarke, Patrick E., "LITENING Strikes," *Citizen Airman*, February 1999.

Code of Federal Regulations (CFR), available at http://www.acess.gpo.gov/nara/cfr/cfr-table-search.html.

Codner, Michael, "Hanging Together: Interoperability Within the Alliance and with Coalition Partners in an Era of Technological Innovation," NATO Research Fellowship Final Report, June 1999, available at http://www.nato.int.

Cohen, William S., "DoD International Armaments Cooperation Policy," memorandum from the Secretary of Defense, March 23, 1997.

Cohen, William, "Shaping NATO To Meet the Challenges of the 21st Century," remarks to the NATO Defense Planning Committee,

Brussels, Belgium, June 11, 1998, available at http://www.nato.int/usa/dod.

Council of Economic Advisers (CEA), *Economic Report of the President*, Washington, D.C.: U.S. Government Printing Office, February 1998.

Council of Economic Advisers (CEA), *Economic Report of the President*, Washington, D.C.: U.S. Government Printing Office, February 2000.

Council of Economic Advisers (CEA), *Economic Report of the President*, Washington, D.C.: U.S. Government Printing Office, January 2001.

Defense Contract Management Command, Defense Logistics Agency, *Industrial Base Forecast* (1997–2010), DCM Agency West Commanders' Conference, April 1, 1997.

Defense Daily Network Special Reports, "Battlespace Technologies: ASTOR Countdown to Contract," November 1998.

Defense Federal Acquisition Regulation Supplement, available at http://web2.deskbook.osd.mil/htmlfiles.DBY_dfars.asp.

Defense Institute of Security Assistance Management (DISAM), *The Management of Security Assistance*, 20th ed., Wright-Patterson Air Force Base, OH, June 2000.

Defense Science Board (DSB), *Final Report of the Defense Science Board Task Force on International Armaments Cooperation: International Armaments Cooperation in an Era of Coalition Security*, Washington, D.C., August 1996.

Defense Science Board (DSB), *Report of the Defense Science Board Task Force on Vertical Integration and Supplier Decisions*, May 1997.

Defense Science Board (DSB), *Report of the Defense Science Board Task Force on Globalization and Security*, December 1999.

Defense Science Board (DSB), "Defense Science Board Task Force on Preserving a Healthy and Competitive U.S. Defense Industry to Ensure our Future National Security," presentation to the Under

Secretary of Defense for Acquisition and Technology, November 2000.

Defense Security Cooperation Agency (DSCA), "Defense Trade Security Initiatives," available at http://www.dsca.osd.mil/dtsi/dtsi_links.htm.

Defence Systems Daily, "Raytheon Suggests U.S. BVRAAM Export Approval," June 14, 1999.

Deloitte & Touche and Deloitte Consulting, *1998 Vision in Manufacturing: Aerospace and Defense Industry Report,* New York: Deloitte & Touche, 1998.

Denoon, David B.H., *The New International Economic Order: A U.S. Response,* New York: New York University Press, 1979.

Deputy Under Secretary of Defense for Industrial Affairs (DUSD[IA], *Annual Industrial Capabilities Report to Congress,* January 2001.

Deputy Under Secretary of Defense for International and Commercial Programs, *International Armaments Cooperation Handbook,* June 1996.

Deputy Under Secretary of Defense for Policy Support, *International Programs Security Handbook,* June 2000.

DoD Directives and Instructions (DoDD), available at http://web2-deskbook.osd.mil/htmlfiles/DBY_dod.asp.

Dunning, John, *The Globalization of Firms and Competitiveness of Countries: Some Implications for the Theory of International Production,* Lund, Sweden: Institute of Economic Research, Lund University, 1990.

Dworkin, Andy, "F-16 Sale to Israel Bolsters Lockheed Plant in FW," *Dallas Morning News,* July 17, 1999.

"Elbit to Formalize El Op Merger," *Eurosatory 2000 Daily News,* June 21, 2000.

Erwin, Sandra, "Air Force to Select Advanced Targeting Pod," *National Defense,* July 2001.

Federal Acquisition Regulations (FAR), available at http://web1. deskbook.osd.mil/htmlfiles/DBY_far.asp.

Fernald, John G., and Victoria Greenfield, "The Fall and Rise of the Global Economy," *Chicago Fed Letter* No. 164, Federal Reserve Bank of Chicago, April 2001.

Foss, Christopher, "United Defense Buys Bofors Weapons Systems," *Jane's Defence Weekly,* June 21, 2000.

Frankenstein, John, "China: Defense Industry Trends," *NBR Executive Insight No. 6,* Seattle, WA: National Bureau of Asian Research, August 1996.

Fulghum, David A., "Pentagon Demands Radar Upgrade Accord," *Aviation Week & Space Technology,* August 7, 2000.

Hamre, John, "Testimony of Deputy Secretary of Defense John Hamre before the Senate Armed Services Committee," February 28, 2000.

Hebert, Adam J., "The Small Diameter Bomb Is Emerging as One of the Air Force's Top Weapon Priorities: Smaller Bombs for Stealthy Aircraft," *Air Force Magazine,* July 2001.

Hill, Luke, "Alliance Selects TMD Study Contract Winners," *Jane's Defence Weekly,* May 25, 2001.

Hill, Luke, "NATO Considers Merging AGS," *Jane's Defence Weekly,* June 8, 2001.

Hoyle, Craig, "AMS and Boeing Sign JDAM Agreement," *Jane's Defence Weekly,* July 20, 2001.

Hummels, David, Jun Ishii, and Kei-Mu Yi, "The Nature and Growth of Vertical Specialization in World Trade," *Journal of International Economics,* Vol. 54, No. 1, June 2001, pp. 75–96.

Hura, Myron, Gary McLeod, Eric Larson, James Schneider, Daniel Gonzales, Dan Norton, Jody Jacobs, Kevin O'Connell, William Little, Richard Mesic, and Lewis Jamison, *Interoperability: A Continuing Challenge in Coalition Air Operations,* MR-1235-AF, Santa Monica: RAND, 2000.

Inside the Pentagon, "Quickly Fielded Small Diameter Bomb Among Top USAF Weapon Priorities," March 29, 2001.

International Institute for Strategic Studies (IISS), *The Military Balance: 2000/2001,* London: Oxford University Press, October 2000.

International Trade Administration (ITA), U.S. Department of Commerce, *U.S. Industry and Trade Outlook 2000,* New York: McGraw-Hill, 2000.

Jane's International Defense Review, "European Partners Give SOSTAR-X the Go-Ahead," March 22, 2001.

Kim, Kwant-Ta, "Competition Heats Up at Seoul Air Show over F-X Project," *Korea Times,* October 17, 2001.

Kovacic, William E., "Competition Policy in the Postconsolidation Defense Industry," *Antitrust Bulletin,* Summer 1999.

KPMG, *KPMG Corporate Finance Survey, 2001,* press releases, 2001.

Kresa, Kent, presentation before the France-U.S. Defense Industry Business Forum II, Baltimore, MD, December 10, 2001.

Kutner, Joshua, "State Department Defends Stance on Export Policy; Former Deputy Defense Chief Says Regulations Undermine Coalition Partners," *National Defense,* June 2000.

Lake, Darren, "Raytheon Thales Venture Clears Regulatory Hurdles," *Jane's Defence Weekly,* June 22, 2001.

Lewis, J.A.C., "A400M Nations Agree on How to Share Work," *Jane's Defence Weekly,* October 12, 2001.

Lockheed Martin Missiles and Fire Control, "U.S. Air Force Selects Lockheed Martin for $843 Million Advanced Targeting Pod Contract," press release, August 20, 2001.

Loeb, Vernon, "Up In Arms," *Washington Post,* January 11, 2002.

Lorell, Mark, and Julia Lowell, *Pros and Cons of International Weapons Procurement Collaboration,* MR-565-OSD, Santa Monica: RAND, 1995.

Lorell, Mark, Julia Lowell, Michael Kennedy, and Hugh Levaux, *Cheaper, Faster, Better? Commercial Approaches to Weapons Acquisitions*, MR-1147-AF, Santa Monica: RAND, 2000.

Los Angeles Times, "Raytheon, France's Thales Plan Joint Venture," December 16, 2000.

Mancuso, Donald, "The National Security Implications of Export Controls and the Export Administration Act of 1999," statement by Donald Mancuso, Deputy Inspector General of the Department of Defense before the Senate Committee on Armed Services, Washington, D.C., February 28, 2000.

Meth, Martin, Thomas Frazier, Jim Woolsey, and Andouiin Touw, *Defense Aircraft Manufacturing Capacity Study: Findings*, presentation to the 34th Annual DoD Cost Analysis Symposium, February 1, 2001.

Moran, Theodore H., *American Economic Policy and National Security*, New York: Council on Foreign Relations Press, 1993.

Morrocco, John D., "Looming Missile Decision to Shape Transatlantic Ties," *Aviation Week & Space Technology*, February 7, 2000.

Morrocco, John D., "Europe Nears Contracts for A400M Transport Meteor," *Aviation Week & Space Technology*, July 25, 2001.

Morrocco, John D., and Michael A. Taverna, "DASA Trainer Link Leads German Push in UAE," *Aviation Week & Space Technology*, November 22, 1999.

Mulholland, David, "EADS, Northrop Trumpet Co-operation," *Jane's Defence Weekly*, June 22, 2001.

Muradian, Vago, "Pentagon Considers Shifting TSD from Acquisition to Policy, May Help Exports," Defense Daily, July 30, 2001, p. 5.

National Research Council, *Recent Trends in U.S. Aeronautics Research and Technology*, National Academy Press, Washington, D.C., 1999.

National Science Foundation, Division of Science Resource Statistics, *Science and Engineering Doctorate Awards: 1999*, Susan T. Hill (ed.), NSF 01-314, Arlington, VA, 2001.

Neu, C.R., and Charles Wolf, Jr., *The Economic Dimensions of National Security*, MR-466-OSD, Santa Monica: RAND, 1994.

North Atlantic Treaty Organization (NATO), "NATO's Defence Capabilities Initiative—Preparing for Future Challenges," *NATO Review* (Web edition), Vol. 47, No. 2, pp. 26–28, Summer 1999, available at http://www.nato.int/docu/review/1999/9902-06.htm.

North Atlantic Treaty Organization (NATO), "NATO's Defence Capabilities Initiative," NATO Fact Sheet, August 9, 2000, available at http://www.nato.int/docu/facts/2000/nato-dci.htm.

North Atlantic Treaty Organization (NATO), "Financial and Economic Data Relating to NATO Defence," Press Release M-DPC-2 (2000) 107, December 5, 2000b, available at http://www.nato.int/docu/pr/2000/p00-107e.htm.

North Atlantic Treaty Organization (NATO), "Statement on the Defence Capabilities Initiative Issued at the Meeting of the North Atlantic Council in Defence Ministers Session held in Brussels," press release M-NAC-D-1 (2001) 89, June 7, 2001, available at http://www.nato.int/docu/pr/2001/p01-089e.htm.

Northrop Grumman Corporation, "Northrop Grumman Team Awarded $303 Million Contract for Multi-Platform Radar Technology Insertion Program," press release, December 11, 2000.

Pasztor, Andy, and Daniel Michaels, "Satellite Makers Seek Out Trans-Atlantic Partnerships," *Wall Street Journal*, June 18, 2001.

Peck, Merton J., and Frederic M. Scherer, *The Weapons Acquisition Process: An Economic Analysis*, Boston, MA: Division of Research, Graduate School of Business Administration, Harvard University, 1962.

Perry, William J., "Policy on Letters Encouraging Foreign Governments to Procure From American Sources," Department of Defense memorandum, July 21, 1995.

Presidential Commission on Offsets in International Trade, *Status Report of the Presidential Commission on Offsets in International Trade*, Washington, D.C., January 18, 2001.

Principal Deputy Under Secretary of Defense for Acquisition and Technology, "Subcontractor Competition," directive memorandum, May 5, 1999.

Reuters, "U.S. Eases High-Performance Computer Export Controls," January 10, 2001, available at http://www.infoworld.com.

Robertson, George, "NATO in the New Millennium," NATO Review (Web edition), Vol. 47, No. 4, Winter 1999, pp. 3–7.

Rosenberg, Barry, "UAVs Step Up to Paris Plate," Paris Air Show 2001 News Online, *Aviation Week & Space Technology*, June 17, 2001.

Secretary of the Air Force for Acquisition, "Using Specifications and Standards," memorandum, June 7, 1999.

Simpson, Glenn R., "U.S. Delays in ASML–Silicon Valley Deal Threaten to Strain Diplomatic Relations," *Wall Street Journal*, April 26, 2001.

Sirak, Michael, "BAE Systems North America Emerges as Major U.S. Player," *Jane's Defence Weekly*, January 19, 2001.

Sirak, Michael, "Raytheon, Rafael Market Missile," *Jane's Defence Weekly*, June 1, 2001.

Stockholm International Peace Research Institute (SIPRI), *SIPRI Yearbook 2000: Armaments, Disarmament, and International Security*, London and New York: Oxford University Press, 2000.

Stockholm International Peace Research Institute (SIPRI), "Sources and Methods for Arms Transfers Data," October 21, 2001, available at http://projects.sipri.se/armstrade/atmethods.html.

Study Group on Enhancing Multilateral Export Controls for U.S. National Security, *Final Report*, Washington, D.C.: Henry L. Stimson Center, April 2001, available at http://cox.house.gov/press/releases/2001/sgmecfinalreport.pdf.

Tarbell, David, "Testimony of Mr. Dave Tarbell, Deputy Under Secretary of Defense for Technology Security Policy and Director, Technology Security, Defense Threat Reduction Agency, before the House Committee on International Relations," July 22, 2001.

Taverna, Michael, "New Missile Giant to Expand," *Aviation Week & Space Technology*, May 7, 2001.

Taylor, Alan, "Air Force Programs and Plans for Defense Industrial Base Planning and Analysis," IBP Program, Air Force Research Laboratory, briefing presented February 21, 2001.

Under Secretary of Defense for Acquisition and Technology (USD[A&T], "Improving Acquisition Processes to Address Industry Vertical Integration," directive memorandum, May 6, 1997.

Under Secretary of Defense for Acquisition and Technology (USD[A&T], "Anticompetitive Teaming," memorandum, January 5, 1999.

Under Secretary of Defense for Acquisition, Technology, and Logistics (USD[AT&L], "Future Competition for Defense Products," memorandum, July 7, 2000.

Under Secretary of Defense for Acquisition, Technology, and Logistics (USD[AT&L], "The New DoD Regulation 5000.2-R," memorandum, June 10, 2001.

Under Secretary of Defense for Acquisition, Technology, and Logistics (USD[AT&L], with ASD(C^3I) and Director, OT&E, "Mandatory Procedures for Major Defense Acquisition Programs (MDAPs) and Major Automated Information System (MAIS) Acquisition Programs," foreword to DoD 5000.2-R, Washington, D.C., June 2001.

Under Secretary of Defense for Acquisition, Technology, and Logistics (USD[AT&L], *Study on Impact of Foreign Sourcing of Systems*, October 2001.

Under Secretary of Defense for Acquisition and Technology (USD[A&T]) and Under Secretary of Defense for Policy (USD[P]), *DoD Policy for Relations with U.S. Industry in Sales of Defense Articles and Services to Foreign Governments*, May 5, 1999.

U.S. Air Force, "International Affairs and Security Assistance Management," Air Force Manual 16-101, September 1, 1995.

U.S. Air Force, *America's Air Force Vision 2020*, 2000, available at http://www.af.mil/vision/vision.pdf.

U.S. Air Force Air Combat Command, *Litening II*, Air Combat Command Fact Sheet, Langley Air Force Base, VA, no date.

U.S. Department of Defense (DoD), *Study on Impact of Foreign Sourcing of Systems*, required by Section 831 of the National Defense Authorization Act for Fiscal Year 2001, October 2001.

U.S. Department of State (DoS), "New Export Exemption for Closest Allies to Promote Defense Security," news brief, May 26, 2000, available at http://www.state.gov/www/global/arms/bureau_pm/dtc/nb_000526_export.html.

U.S. Department of State (DoS), Bureau of Political-Military Affairs, "Seventeen Agreed Proposals of the Defense Trade Security Initiative," Fact Sheet, May 26, 2000.

U.S. Department of State (DoS), Bureau of Verification and Compliance, *World Military Expenditures and Arms Transfers 1998*, April 2000.

U.S. Department of State (DoS), Office of the Spokesman, "Defense Export Controls," press statement, June 19, 2000, available at http://secretary.state.gov/www/briefings/statements/2000/.

U.S. Department of State (DoS), Office of the Spokesman, "U.S.-UK Joint Statement on Defense Export Controls," January 17, 2001, available at http://secretary.state.gov/www/briefings/statements/2001/ps010117g.html.

U.S. Department of State and Under Secretary of Defense for Acquisition, Technology, and Logistics (USD[AT&L]), "Defense Trade Security Initiative: Background on Expedited License Review Process for Defense Capabilities Initiatives," Washington, D.C., May 24, 2000.

U.S. Department of the Treasury, Office of International Affairs, Office of International Investment, "Exon-Florio Provisions," undated, available at http://www.treas.gov/offices/international-affairs/exon-florio/index.html.

U.S. Federal Trade Commission, "Promoting Competition, Protecting Consumers: A Plain English Guide to Antitrust Laws," undated, available at http://www.ftc.gov/bc/compguide/index.htm.

U.S. General Accounting Office (GAO), *Defense Industry: Trends in DoD Spending, Industrial Productivity, and Competition*, GAO/PEMD-97-3, Washington, D.C., January 1997.

U.S. General Accounting Office (GAO), *Defense Acquisition: Rationale for Imposing Domestic Source Restrictions*, GAO/NSIAD-98-191, Washington, D.C.: GAO, July 1998.

U.S. General Accounting Office (GAO), *Defense Trade: Identifying Foreign Acquisitions Affecting National Security Can Be Improved*, GAO/NSIAD-00-144, June 2000.

U.S. General Accounting Office (GAO), *Defense Trade: Analysis of Support for Recent Initiatives*, GAO/NSIAD-00-191, August 2000.

U.S. General Accounting Office (GAO), *Defense Trade: Contractors Engage in Varied International Alliances*, GAO/NSIAD-00-213, September 2000.

U.S. Senate, Committee on Banking, Housing, and Urban Affairs, "Major Provisions: The Export Administration Act of 2001," Committee Documents Online—107th Congress, January 23, 2001a, available at www.senate/gov/-banking/docs/eaa/eaa 0123.htm.

U.S. Senate, Committee on Banking, Housing, and Urban Affairs, "Export Administration Act of 2001: Additional Views," *Senate Report 107-10*, Washington, D.C.: Government Printing Office, April 2, 2001.

Washington Post, "General Dynamics Moves into Europe," August 7, 2001.

White House Office of the Press Secretary, *Fact Sheet: Export Controls on Computers*, July 1, 1999.

White House Office of the Press Secretary, *Fact Sheet: Defense Trade Security Initiative Extended to Sweden,* June 14, 2001.

World Trade Organization (WTO), *International Trade Statistics 2000,* 2000.

Worthen, Drew, "Northrop Grumman Takes ASTOR Demonstration to London," *Aerotech News and Review,* August 21, 1998.

Zakheim, Dov S., *Toward a Fortress Europe?* Washington, D.C.: Center for Strategic and International Studies, November 2000.